KAY FANNING'S
Alaska Story

KAY FANNING'S
Alaska Story

Memoir of a Pulitzer Prize-Winning
Newspaper Publisher
on America's Northern Frontier

~

KAY FANNING
with
KATHERINE FIELD STEPHEN

EPICENTER PRESS

Epicenter Press is a regional press publishing nonfiction books about the arts, history, environment, and diverse cultures and lifestyles of Alaska and the Pacific Northwest.

Publisher: Kent Sturgis
Acquisitions Editor: Lael Morgan
Editor: Katherine Field Stephen
Copyeditor: Ellen Wheat
Designer: Elizabeth Watson, Watson Graphics
Proofreader: Susan Ohrberg
Indexer: Sherrill Carlson
Mapmaker: Robert Cronan, Lucidity Information Design, LLC
Printer: Transcontinental Printing

Library of Congress Control Number: 2006932053
ISBN 10: 0-9745014-6-8
ISBN 13: 978-0-9745014-6-8

First Edition
First printing, October 2006
10 9 8 7 6 5 4 3 2 1

Printed in Canada

To order single copies of this edition of KAY FANNING'S ALASKA STORY, mail $24.95 plus $6.00 for shipping (WA residents add $2.70 sales tax) to Epicenter Press, PO Box 82368, Kenmore, WA 98028.

The text pages for this printing of 5,500 copies of KAY FANNING'S ALASKA STORY were printed on 6,021 pounds of recycled, acid-free paper with 100% post-consumer content. According to the Green Press Initiative and www.environmentaldefense.org, use of this recycled paper made it possible to conserve 73 trees (a mix of hard and softwoods averaging 40 feet tall and 6-8" in diameter), 26,776 gallons of water, 51 million BTUs of energy, and 6,451 pounds of greenhouse gases (CO_2 equivalents). These calculations are based on information supplied by the University of Maine. For more information about GPI, visit www.GreenPressInitiative.org.

Contents

PART 2

Kay as We Remember Her   177

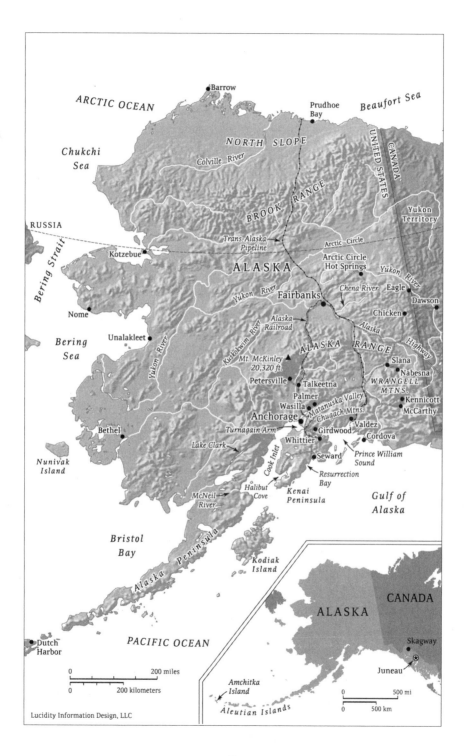

Foreword

Jill Ker Conway

I first met Kay Fanning when she returned to her alma mater, Smith, in 1980, to accept a Smith College Medal, an honor awarded by Smith alumnae to graduates whose lives best exemplified the values of a liberal education. Medalists came to the campus to receive the award in person at a special convocation, after which they met with students and faculty to talk about the relationship between their college education and their achievements.

The *Anchorage Daily News* and its publisher had captured headlines across the country for fearless editorial and news coverage of corruption in Alaska centering on the Teamsters Union. In 1976 this led to the paper's receiving the award of the Pulitzer Prize for Public Service "for its disclosures of the impact and influence of the Teamsters Union on Alaska's economy and politics." So of course I expected to meet a tough, crusading journalist. She didn't fit the stereotype. There was no doubt about her courage and commitment to great journalism. But she was a charming, gentle, and fun-loving woman, grieving the loss of a beloved husband, and continuing the mission to carry out the journalistic standards they had developed together.

We met again in the mid-1980s when we'd both moved to Boston, she to become editor of the *Christian Science Monitor*, and I (following a decade as Smith's president) to take up writing and teaching at MIT. We both belonged to a dining club for women, where I had a chance to learn about the range of her interests, and her growing sense of the economic and cultural issues that would bedevil print media in the 1990s and beyond. We also talked privately about the challenges of memoir writing, because she was considering writing a book that would capture her love for the life and people of Alaska and would convey what she had learned about journalism in her years there.

I strongly urged her to write her memoir. Hers was a story of a woman who was a natural risk-taker, who craved adventure, and cared deeply about social justice and political integrity. During her Alaska years, she also dealt with crippling grief at the loss of her husband. It was a story that needed telling, because she didn't fit any of the stereotypes then popular in the psychology of women, which emphasized women's supposed aversion to risk and their reliance on networks rather than serving as crusading leaders.

When I learned of Kay Fanning's death in 2000, I knew she would not have had time to finish the memoir. So I was doubly delighted when her daughter, Katherine Field Stephen, got in touch with me for advice about how to deal with the unfinished manuscript.

When I read the manuscript, it was clear to me that Kay's first-person voice came through powerfully. The draft was lively and highly personal, although incomplete. It would be a disappointing anticlimax for even the most accomplished writer to finish the story. Kay had talked with me about how intensely she valued the friendships she had made in Alaska, a lively circle she kept in touch with even though she had left the state. So it seemed likely that those same friends might want to help complete the narrative, and could do so by adding their own first-person accounts of events, people, motivations, and challenges.

And this proved to be the case. The reader of this book will have the rare privilege of coming to know a remarkable woman leader, and of hearing about her from an equally remarkable set of friends and associates. It's a compelling story, and Katherine Field Stephen has done a masterly job in assembling it.

Introduction

KATHERINE FIELD STEPHEN

Kay Fanning was working on the manuscript that forms part 1 of this book for four years before her passing in October 2000. As a journalist and editor, Kay had brought many Alaska stories to light. Her own story had never been told in her own words. So Kay was striving to piece together for the record an account of her life at the *Anchorage Daily News*.

Initially Kay called the book "Survival." That one-word title captured the essence of her story: her struggle to purchase and keep the *Daily News* afloat against incredible odds. For the *Daily News* to compete with what was then the entrenched, almighty *Anchorage Times*, as well as survive and eventually become the dominant paper in Alaska, is a story of the triumph of the underdog. For Kay to achieve this victory as a woman in such a male-dominated frontier state elevates her tale into the realm of newspaper legend.

In publishing Kay's manuscript as a book, my foremost motive has been for the book to remain Kay Fanning's own story—to be as close in spirit to her words as possible, and reflective of the time in which it was written. With that as my goal, I was fortunate to connect with people who gave me guidance in completing the story of this remarkable woman, my mother.

It was apparent to most people who knew Kay Fanning that she was an extraordinary person. I leave it to others to attempt to describe the qualities that made Kay such a unique individual, but vivacity and persistence were certainly among them. Kay was in love with Alaska, drawn to the state in 1965 by her love of adventure and an attraction to the magnificence and freedom of the North. Her fascination with the state probably began when she was a child and was given a sled dog puppy her father brought back from a hunting trip to Alaska. And as a teenager, she was fond of the poetry about the North by the Canadian poet Robert Service. Perhaps these aspects of her early life were indications that someday she would reach Alaska.

While she was working on the book, Kay kept the project confidential. But after her death, Kay's husband (my stepfather), Mo Mathews, brought Kay's computer to my home in Washington, D.C. Upon reading the manuscript, I learned that it ended abruptly with the passing of Kay's second husband, Larry Fanning, in 1971. Kay's telling of the *Daily News* story ended just when she was about to take the helm of the paper following Larry's death, though Kay's story was far from finished.

How could the book be completed by someone else and still remain Kay's story? I finally found the answer, with the help of Jill Ker Conway. A former president of Smith College, Jill had been head of the college when I attended. Jill Ker Conway is a preeminent author of three autobiographical books: *The Road from Coorain, True North: A Memoir,* and *A Woman's Education.*

After reading the manuscript, Jill recommended that I find an Alaska publisher for the book, and that I finish it by using reminiscences from other Alaskans in Kay's life. By getting Kay's friends and colleagues to write about her, the personal immediacy of her story would be maintained. Those chosen to write could do so with authority because they had been witnesses to the events they were describing. Jill Ker Conway's wisdom was a godsend.

Soon after, the task of finding an Alaska publisher fell into place. I contacted Kent Sturgis, publisher of Epicenter Press, and he expressed immediate enthusiasm for the book. One crucial aspect of the project was that Kent and I agreed that the book would be a nonprofit venture: my royalties from its sales would go to a selected Alaska charity in memory of Kay Fanning.

I was surprised and grateful that the book project proceeded smoothly. Almost everyone I approached to write a remembrance of Kay for the book responded enthusiastically. And their memories of Kay Fanning offer a perfect supplement to her manuscript, making her Alaska story complete.

PART I
North to Alaska

1

Our 1963 Buick station wagon had just plunged deep into the mire alongside the Alaska Highway. It was August 1965, and my three children and I were moving to Alaska. The moving van had preceded us before our teary farewell in Chicago and would be in Anchorage to meet us the next day. But here we were, stuck in the slimy Yukon mud.

"Oh, dear, now we're going to have to *walk* to Alaska," sobbed eight-year-old Barbara, while her eleven-year-old sister, Kathy, shivered, and thirteen-year-old brother, Ted, struggled to be manly.

I started to laugh and grabbed the movie camera to record the unlikely scene. Here we were, thousands of miles from our Chicago home, heading for a new life in Alaska, and already we were in trouble. I wondered if it was a metaphor for this bizarre idea of starting anew on America's "Last Frontier." And perhaps it was. We quickly learned that people were always helping you in the North. Before long, a senior couple in a camper stopped. So did another car, and another. They helped pull us out, and shortly we were bumping our way north again through the heavy gravel and around the Alaska Highway's twisting turns, which yielded breathtaking glimpses of massive mountains and glaciers visible through the heavy forest.

~

The early 1960s had been a time of deep personal struggle for me. My husband, Marshall Field, was facing his own personal challenges. By 1963 I came to the reluctant conclusion that a divorce was my only option.

After a six-week summer residency in Lake Tahoe, Nevada, I obtained a divorce in Reno while the children were with their father in Hawaii. Marshall had agreed to the divorce very reluctantly. At the end of the summer, the children and I moved into a town house in Chicago's

Sandburg Village. It was located on LaSalle Street on the city's north side near Old Town, several blocks from Lakeview Avenue on Chicago's Gold Coast, where we had lived with Marshall. I quit the Junior League and joined the Urban League, perhaps a mini-statement of the change of lifestyle I sought. The children spent weekends with their father at his country place in nearby Libertyville.

The next two years were very difficult. One Saturday afternoon, Eppie Lederer, better known as Ann Landers, came to visit. I offered her a glass of sherry and took one or two myself. Eppie looked me straight in the eye and said, "You know, Kay, you could be an alcoholic." I was stunned. I always thought of myself as one who didn't drink—well, not usually hard liquor, anyway. After she left, I headed outside and walked Chicago's streets and thought and thought. I knew she was right. My life felt out of control, like a San Francisco cable car headed down a steep hill for a crash landing.

As I walked the streets through Old Town and Lincoln Park and down LaSalle Street, it became clear that for me there was one solution that could put my life back on track: Christian Science. I had been intro-duced to it by my mother when I was ten or eleven years old. She had briefly sought Christian Science treatment for her health problems and she urged me to read its textbook, *Science and Health with Key to the Scriptures*, by Mary Baker Eddy. I was deeply impressed by the book because it taught a lot about divine love, and, for me, it explained in a deeply satisfying way what "being" was all about. My mother never became a Christian Scientist, nor did I until many years later. But from that time on, I carried the Bible and the Christian Science textbook with me to boarding school and college, but did not join the church or live in accord with its teachings. As I searched for answers wandering Chicago's streets that evening, I prayed intently and I knew, *Now is the time, if ever.*

Christian Science teaches its adherents to take seriously the First Commandment, "Thou shalt have no other gods before me." One of the things that meant was not leaning on material props such as alcohol, ciga-rettes, or drugs. I was drinking wine, smoking two or three packs of cigarettes a day, and taking tranquilizers and sleeping pills. At the end of my walk, I returned to the Sandburg Village house, threw out all my bottles of wine and all my pills—for good. The cigarettes took a few months longer. I was on a new path. I began seriously studying Christian Science, sought help from a Christian Science practitioner, and prayed for guidance over what to do next. It was evident to me that our family needed a change, a new beginning. That meant moving away from Chicago, but where? Washington? New York? I wanted to go to a new location, but somewhere that I would know someone.

While the children and I were visiting my mother in Hobe Sound, Florida, during the 1964 Christmas holidays, Tay and Lowell Thomas Jr., good friends from college days, and their children were visiting Tay's family there. Lowell lectured in the local theater on living in Alaska. He showed slides of Anchorage, including some dramatic ones taken after the Good Friday earthquake that year. I was transfixed by the beauty of the scenery but I remember thinking, *Anchorage is really an ugly city. I wonder why I'm going to move there.*

But I felt by intuition that I was being guided, urged, in that direction—that Alaska would provide the new life I was hoping for.

I quickly devised a plan to encourage the children's enthusiasm for the adventure of moving north. First we went on a ski trip with a friend from Montreal, Canada, during the winter school break. None of us had ever skied before, but by the end of the week, Ted, Kathy, and Barb were swishing down the slopes at a pretty good clip, with mom somewhat behind.

During the spring vacation we flew to Anchorage and stayed at the Travelers Inn, then one of the four or five hotels in town. March is "breakup" month in Anchorage, which means the ice and snow are melting and it is sloppy underfoot. The skies were gray, too, but the beauty took our breath away. The children and I took a quick arctic tour by plane to Nome and Kotzebue, exotic places where dog teams were still the primary form of transportation, Eskimos fished through holes in the ice along the waterfront, dilapidated trucks picked up the "honeybuckets"— large buckets with attached seats that served as indoor plumbing and were dumped at a disposal site. Snow and fog prevented our plane from leaving Nome for most of one day and we found ourselves stranded, touring the Nome jail for lack of anything else to do, accompanied by the president of Greenland, who also happened to be visiting Nome and who was similarly weathered in. On the way back to Anchorage we stopped in Fairbanks and stayed overnight with another Smith College classmate, Penny Teal, and her husband in their log house on the banks of the Chena River.

Back in Anchorage for the last three days of our trip, the three children and I drove the winding road along Turnagain Arm, so named because eighteenth-century explorer Captain James Cook had turned into the long, deep fjord in his search for the Northwest Passage and had to "turn again" when he came to its end. The road led to the village of Girdwood and the Alyeska Ski Resort, where the Thomases and Peggy and George Wichman, more school friends from back east, had taken us skiing several times during our visit. The narrow road clings to the slope of the snow-covered mountains that rise directly from the sea. The view is so breathtaking we stopped constantly to take pictures. While we drove and absorbed the beauty, seven-year-old Barbie exclaimed from the backseat, "Oh, Mommie, why don't we move to Alaska?" I skipped a beat before replying, took a deep breath, and said, "Okay." All three kids burst out, "Do you really mean it?!" And I said, "Yes." It was as simple as that. From that moment we had decided we were going to be Alaskans, at least for a year or so.

Finding a place to live in Anchorage wasn't simple, though, due to the shortage of housing after the earthquake. But in the few remaining days, and with help from Tay and Lowell, we bought the house on Madison Way, arranged a mortgage, investigated the schools, and made our plans to move north in August.

I knew our plans would cause shock waves among our friends and relatives back home. When the kids returned to the Latin School in Chicago and announced we were moving to Alaska, word traveled quickly. It was difficult for Marshall, who dearly loved his children and wanted them nearby. But we promised to return often on vacations and I hoped he wouldn't take it too hard. Marshall's own personal life was in upheaval, and perhaps it would be easier for him to straighten it out without the children coming every weekend, I rationalized. Marshall had married Lynne Templeton, a woman the age of his oldest daughter, Joanne. They were expecting a baby, and they were also in the process of splitting up.

Within that year, 1965, I had finally successfully quit smoking for good and become a member of the Christian Science Church. I had taken a two-week course of serious Christian Science study during the summer while the children attended camp in Colorado. While they spent time with their father in Bermuda, I packed for the driving trip to Alaska.

My cousins, the Ingram family, and a small group of friends were there to wave us off in the heavily loaded Buick station wagon we called "Bui." Nearly everyone we knew heartily disapproved of our plan to relocate to Alaska. Heading away from everything and nearly everyone we knew was frightening. My new faith and one particular hymn sustained me. It began, "In heavenly love abiding, no change my heart shall fear. . . ."

～

Two days after being pulled out of the mud along a Yukon stretch of the Alaska Highway, we drove up to our small white house with blue shutters on Madison Way in Anchorage. All the houses in the development called College Village (with street names such as "Princeton" and "Stanford") were new since the Good Friday earthquake the previous year had devastated much of the city's neighborhoods. There hadn't been a wide choice in houses when we had made an exploratory trip a few months earlier.

You couldn't rent anything at all, and the developer of College Village wasn't interested in selling to some unknown woman from Chicago. I had to shed tears before he relented. Most of the local streets were not yet paved, and there would be no telephone service for at least six weeks. Moose prowled in the back yard. But there were advantages: the house was cozy and warm and it was built on stable ground, not the mushy slide area of the bluff, where so many houses had slipped into Cook Inlet during the earthquake.

Tay and Lowell were on hand to greet us. They had lost their house and barely preserved their family's lives in the earthquake. Their house had been sliced in two, and one half had slid down the bluff into Cook Inlet. Now they were living in a tiny house while the bedroom wing of their home was being renovated and attached to a new living room and kitchen being built on a more stable piece of ground. But their welcome was warm and their help indispensable.

The Wichmans helped a lot, too. Peggy English Wichman, a distant cousin of my father's, had been a classmate at Westover School in Connecticut during my high school years. She married George Wichman, a doctor who had emigrated from Germany and acquired a degree in orthopedic surgery at Northwestern University in Evanston, Illinois. An avid outdoorsman and mountain climber, George had set up a practice in orthopedic surgery in Anchorage. Peggy and George met in Alaska after Peggy, seeking adventure, had signed on as a stewardess on Reeve Aleutian Airlines, one of Alaska's pioneer aviation companies, flying in some of the world's worst weather out to the Aleutian chain of desolate islands.

The Wichmans' house was unique. Hardly more than a tiny shack in some beautiful woods in the university section of Anchorage, the bedroom opened onto the kitchen. When the Wichmans had guests for dinner, you sat on the bed holding your plate in your lap while Peggy cooked dinner a couple of feet away. But a full basement had been installed under the house to display a splendid array of silver and china wedding presents the Wichmans had received at their fashionable East Coast wedding.

Another East Coast friend in Anchorage was Daphne Milbank White. Daphne was a year ahead of me at Smith College and had lived across the hall on the fourth floor of Hubbard House. She was dating Barry White, a senior at Harvard. I thought she was quite daft when I heard their plans to marry and move to Alaska. But by the time I reached Alaska, they had been in Anchorage more than fifteen years, had four children, established several businesses, and had recently split up.

These three old friends were indispensable to us. While we were back in Chicago preparing for the Alaska move, Tay, Peggy, and Daphne oversaw the completion of the house on Madison Way that I had hastily bought unfinished. They sent samples of tile and wall coverings to me in Chicago so I could make choices. And after we arrived they helped us learn the unique ways of Alaska.

The Alaskan way was displayed on many cars' rear bumpers: WE DON'T GIVE A DAMN HOW THEY DO IT OUTSIDE. From Alaskans' smug perch on top of the world, they referred disdainfully to the rest of the country as "the Lower 48." And the popular excuse when things didn't get done the right way was, "Oh well, this is Alaska."

Eighteen days after our arrival in Anchorage, and just as the children were well installed in the public schools that were an easy walk from Madison Way, we got a devastating phone call from Chicago. Marshall had died of a heart attack in his sleep. The message came through the Thomases because we still had no phone. We were numb. We felt so disconnected from the world we had left five weeks earlier in Chicago. Lowell attempted to console Ted by taking him for a sightseeing ride over the mountains in his single-engine airplane. I made plans to return to Chicago for the funeral.

~

Soon things were picking up. Just as the first big snowfall arrived, so did the paving equipment, great black steaming machines creeping down Madison Way. Huge snowflakes sizzled as they fell on the hot asphalt. Soon, too, the telephone man came to install our telephone line. I was so happy to have a phone, I invited him and his wife and kids to dinner a couple nights later.

And I went to work on a newspaper. Having taken writing courses at Smith College, worked on a college newspaper, and been married to a newspaper publisher for thirteen years, I loved newspapers. When my former husband would bring his publishing problems home to talk over with me, I had found myself thinking, "I could do that job." So now I was eager to get started in the newspaper business, but apprehensive about the leap into my first job.

There were two newspapers in Anchorage at that time: the *Anchorage Times*, a hefty, established afternoon paper owned by Bob and Evangeline Atwood, and a thin, feisty morning paper, the *Anchorage Daily News*, started by a former managing editor of the *Times*, Norman Brown, and his wife, Blanche. The *Times* had more than three times the circulation of the *Daily News* and about five times the advertising. But it never really occurred to me to apply for a job at the *Times*. The *News*, with its vitality and its underdog status, appealed to me much more.

So I went down to the dingy warehouse in the industrial section of town that housed the *Daily News* to see Joe Rothstein, news managing editor. When I said I wanted a job, he asked what experience I had. "Well, a college newspaper," I said. But he hired me anyway for part-time work at $2 an hour. Years later I asked Joe why he hired me. "You had been around a lot of newspaper people," he said. "I couldn't resist hiring you. I just created a job. I always figured if you didn't work out you would have been a good story." I shudder to think what kind of good story he meant. But a good story was what we pursued at the *Daily News*. It was always a top priority.

The job Joe created was a clip-and-paste affair. The *Daily News* had no "morgue," as newspaper libraries and photo archives were called. I was to cut out and file stories and photos—an ideal way to learn about the issues and personalities of my adopted state. My "office" was an expanded closet shared with the clattering Associated Press wire machine.

"I could do that," I thought, as I read the stories written by *Daily News* reporters. So, without anyone asking me to, I wrote one. It was about the notorious Dr. Ivy, then on trial in an Illinois court for promoting Krebiozen, a fake cancer drug. My contact for the story came through Ivy's granddaughter, who lived in Anchorage, the daughter of an Anchorage doctor. She was a school friend of my daughter Kathy's. I interviewed the Anchorage Dr. Ivy and wrote about the case from the local angle, a son's perspective on his criminally indicted father in a case that had become a national story. My story was accepted, and it appeared on the front page of the *Daily News*! And bingo, I was a reporter. At least that was what it said in the byline: Kay Field, Daily News Staff Writer.

Joe Rothstein, my boss, was an ardent editor. He pursued local stories relentlessly, and he knew how he wanted them to come out. One of the active volcanoes on the Alaska Peninsula erupted one day. From the top of the Captain Cook Hotel in downtown Anchorage, you could see it spewing smoke. There was a small earthquake the same day, so Joe assigned me to call some experts and write a story about how the volcano caused the earthquake. After calling half a dozen geologists, I came back to Joe.

"The experts say volcanoes don't cause earthquakes."

"Keep calling until you find one that says they do," he said.

Finally I found one—Don Richter at the State Division of Mines—who said earthquakes and volcanic eruptions are occasionally related, but not in this case. I wrote it that way, and Rothstein didn't fire me. In fact, I went on to cover a wide variety of stories, many of them without byline credit. I loved general assignment reporting. When you got up in the morning, you never knew what you'd be into that day.

During the World Championship Sled Dog Race held each February during Anchorage's Fur Rondezvous winter carnival, I hung in a cherry-picker bucket over the Fourth Avenue start-finish line. Joe Rychetnik, a flamboyant photographer for the *Daily News,* had hired the crane truck for photographing the races. He was a stringer for *TIME* magazine, whose dollars had rented the rig. That was the way a lot of things got done at the *Daily News,* with its minuscule news budget. Many of the reporters moonlighted as correspondents for publications Outside (outside Alaska). When a big Alaska story broke, these well-financed organizations footed the bill for airplanes, helicopters, whatever was necessary, and the *Daily News* got the story, too. In a state with very few roads, it took ingenuity to cover breaking news in remote places.

The view from the bucket above the street was of teams of twelve to sixteen of Alaska's fastest racing dogs hitched to sleds. The musher would usually stand on the back of the sled, shouting commands. The teams started at two-minute intervals down snow-packed Fourth Avenue in the middle of town. In the morning, snowplows had picked up all the snow on the avenue for the Fur Rondy Parade, a homeblown affair with floats and marching bands. By early afternoon the plows and trucks had put the snow down again for the sled dog race.

The teams ran twenty-five miles each of three days on trails around the Anchorage bowl. The whole town viewed the race, either on television or from crossing points around town. Planes and helicopters zoomed overhead following the mushers' progress. When they looped around toward downtown, you knew the leaders were approaching the finish line because aircraft began converging on the Cordova Street hill, and then there would be shouts of "*dogs on the street.*" Excitement mounted when the two leading mushers, George Attla, an Alaska Native, and "Doc"

Roland Lombard, a Massachusetts veterinarian, fought it out coming down the final stretch of Fourth Avenue. Sometimes one of the racers would have "a dog in the basket." The contestants were required to bring back all the dogs they started with, even if one was tired or hurt. So the dog would be in the sled while the musher stood at the back of the sled.

Most of the assignments I got were modest at first. Many were about Fur Rondezvous events such as the Miners and Trappers Ball, the ice sculpture event, the outdoor fair, where kids and their parents, bundled against the 10- to 20-degree cold, screeched on the Ferris wheel and dug their faces into cotton candy. I wrote a story about an injured sky diver, about some mentally disabled kids bowling, about an ice show, about a new Japanese restaurant in town (how each stone in its garden had been lovingly carried from Japan), about the new tax forms and how people hate to pay taxes.

Then there was my first tragedy. Two Alaska Methodist University students on a class field trip died of exposure on Eklutna Glacier, a few miles from Anchorage. The group of eight students and teachers had encountered a sudden storm on that May day and, due to high winds and whiteout conditions, had bivouacked on a six-foot ledge on the glacier. During the night the students had fallen out of their sleeping bags and dropped thirty feet down the slope. Efforts to revive them had failed. I had to talk to the tearful teachers who had led the expedition and write a minute-by-minute account of what happened. I'd had no training for a story like that so I decided to just let the story tell itself.

My biggest investigation was a seven-part series on birth control in Alaska. Joe Rothstein had assigned me to interview Alaska Senator Ernest Gruening about his advocacy of birth control. Birth control was then as controversial in Alaska as abortion became later. The exceptionally high birth and infant mortality rates in Native villages and the influence of Christian missionaries in various regions of the state made the issue so complex and intriguing I had proposed a major project.

The only problem was time. I had vowed to be always available when the children were home from school. That meant piling the research and writing into other hours. The only way I could fit it all in was to do my writing from 3:00 a.m. to 7:00 a.m.

The series debuted at the top of page one on a Sunday in May. The timing was interesting. It was the same day Alaska's first Catholic archbishop arrived in town, an event receiving much attention from the *Anchorage Times*. Joe Rothstein mischievously displayed a large photo of a hand holding an intrauterine device to introduce the series. A few months later, the birth control series and my coverage of the two AMU students' glacier deaths each won Alaska Press Club awards for the *Daily News*. In retrospect, I doubt there were many entries competing, but I was thrilled and on a high about journalism, Alaska style!

About the time I was beginning work on the birth control series, a longtime friend from Chicago, Larry Fanning, came to Anchorage to visit. Larry had been deposed as editor of the *Chicago Daily News* earlier in the year in the wake of publisher Marshall Field's death. He was in the process of divorce and he was also looking for a new job. At one time he had told me that his fondest dream would be to own his own newspaper. It was rumored that the Browns might be interested in selling the *Daily News*, so I introduced Larry to Joe Rothstein and the Browns. As my friendship with Larry blossomed, we began to examine the possibility of buying the *Daily News* together.

Newspapers were Larry's love and passion. He had begun as a copyboy on the *San Francisco Chronicle* in high school to help support himself and his widowed mother. He quit the University of San Francisco after a couple of years because he disagreed so vehemently with the Catholic church's pro-Franco position in the Spanish Civil War—a hot-button topic in those years. Briefly, he transferred to San Francisco State University, but soon withdrew to work full time at the paper, where he rose quickly to become managing editor at age twenty-six. His were the glory days at the *Chronicle* under close friend, colleague, and boss Paul Smith. But things began to go amiss for Larry when a change of editors in the early 1950s caused the *Chronicle* to veer sharply from Larry's brand of substantive, courageous journalism. So he moved to Chicago, hired by Marshall. When Field Enterprises purchased the *Chicago Daily News* from John S. Knight in 1959, Marshall made Larry its editor.

I had known Larry Fanning as one of Marshall's closest colleagues, who shared with him a deep love for newspapers and politics. Marshall had made me his liaison with four members of the management team at Field Enterprises during periods when he was unable to come to the office or attend meetings. Larry, as editor of the *Daily News,* was one of them. He was a beloved mentor to countless journalists and an outstanding developer of talent. He had recruited and taught Ann Landers to write her column and had been her editor for years. Joe Kraft, Mike Royko, and Nicholas von Hoffman were among Larry's discoveries. But in a power struggle after Marshall's death, Larry had been ousted, and he had accepted a job as head of the Field Newspaper Syndicate on a temporary basis while he scouted for new opportunities.

So when Larry visited us in Anchorage in the spring of 1966, he was excited by Alaska and curious about the opportunities the *Daily News* might offer. After he returned to Chicago he contacted his old friend, Bob Chandler, owner, editor, and publisher of the *Bend Bulletin* in Oregon. Bob did newspaper consulting in his spare time and agreed to come to Anchorage to look over the newspaper situation and to examine the financial feasibility of the *Daily News.* His report was discouraging. Dated May 6, 1966, his conclusion was, "I cannot recommend the purchase of the *Anchorage News* by a buyer with limited capital resources" unless the purchase price was less than $750,000 and the printing plant was merged with the *Anchorage Times.*

Chandler's report summarized the Anchorage of 1966: "As the most vigorous city in Alaska, Anchorage has about 100,000 residents that are 'young and filled with a sense of Manifest Destiny.' " He reflected on the city's rapid growth and many municipal problems, its current economic boom, and the probability that it could double in size in the next decade. "There is little doubt Anchorage is the most competitive media town of any size in the United States." He pointed out that it had four AM and two FM radio stations, two TV stations with a third about to debut, and two daily newspapers, separately owned. It was the smallest city in the United States to have two competing newspapers published in separate plants. "There are few cities of this size that approach Anchorage for competitive media factors, and all the others are surrounded by a populous hinterland, something Anchorage does not have."

That was the good news. On the other hand, Chandler also noted that the *News,* which had been founded in 1946 as a weekly, became an evening daily in 1948, shifted to a morning paper in April 1954, and added a Sunday paper in June 1965, had made a total net profit of less than $150,000. Most of the profit came from the job printing shop, which the Browns did not wish to sell. The production equipment was old and terribly outmoded (it had a seventy-five-year-old press) and it had a $200,000 debt, a Small Business Administration (SBA) loan the Browns negotiated after the earthquake damaged the paper's building. In short, the financial prospects for the *Daily News* were not bright. Nevertheless, the report simply whetted our appetite to own a newspaper in this dazzling new land.

~

But there were other things to be addressed first. The children and I headed back to Chicago for a month's summer vacation. Ted, now fourteen, worked as a volunteer in Chuck Percy's senatorial campaign in Chicago, while we all stayed in the Percys' guesthouse. A longtime friend of our family's, Percy, then president of Bell & Howell, had been narrowly defeated in his race for governor of Illinois two years earlier. Each morning Ted drove to Chicago with Valerie Percy, one of the Percys' twin daughters.

At the end of the summer, 1966, Larry Fanning and I were married in a simple ceremony in the Presbyterian church in Bensonville, Illinois. My cousin, the Reverend Gordon Ingram, officiated. The three children knelt with us as Gordon pronounced the benediction. We caught the California Zephyr for Disneyland with the children right after the ceremony, and we were ecstatically happy. We felt like a whole family once more, and the future, still undefined, looked bright.

It might seem unusual to spend your honeymoon with three children at Disneyland, but Larry felt he had neglected his own two children, now grown. When they were small he had spent so many hours, day and late into the night, in the *San Francisco Chronicle* newsroom. He longed to do a better job the second time around.

Just as our new family unit was getting to know each other midst the Disney fantasyland, Ted heard tragic news on the radio. Young Valerie

Percy had been murdered in the middle of the night in her bedroom at the Percys' house. Larry and I flew back immediately to try to help the Percys, while the kids stayed on at Disneyland with a former nanny who had retired to California.

By the beginning of the school year we were back in our house on Madison Way in Anchorage. Larry was restive, without a job for the first time since he was sixteen. Following Bob Chandler's recommendation, Larry approached *Anchorage Times* owner Bob Atwood about the possibility of a joint printing arrangement if we were to acquire the *Daily News*. Over lunch at the Chart Room in the Anchorage Westward Hotel, Atwood, handsome, graying, courtly, and always polite, said, "Why don't you buy the *Times*?" Startled, and stalling while doing some math in his head about the possible price, Larry said that would be an interesting idea. But, typically, Atwood was just toying with Larry. He wasn't serious about selling the *Times* and he had no intention of facilitating a couple of outlanders in their acquisition of the competition.

For the next several months we all enjoyed Alaska together. Thinking the *Daily News* out of reach, Larry began wondering if it wouldn't be best to get us all "back to civilization," which would involve selling the Madison Way house and leaving Anchorage. But, in spite of himself, he was falling in love with Alaska.

One day we drove the three hours to Seward, a small town south of Anchorage on Resurrection Bay, one of the world's most spectacular glacier-bedecked harbors. We were swept away by the majesty of its beauty. When we returned I dug out a diary of my father's dated 1936, the day he had sailed into Resurrection Bay headed for a hunting expedition on Kodiak Island. He, who from our home base in Joliet, Illinois, had traveled the world, commented in his diary that this was the most glorious harbor he had ever seen, including Hong Kong and Rio de Janeiro. I noted a remarkable coincidence: the diary entry was dated October 15, 1936, exactly thirty years earlier to the day. Just one more proof of destiny, I thought: Alaska is where we belong.

To the friends we left behind in the Lower 48, we had disappeared to the end of the world. But, in fact, during those years, nearly everyone who flew from the Lower 48 to Asia had to stop in Anchorage. The *Anchorage*

Times labeled Anchorage "the Air Crossroads of the World." Government leaders and dignitaries stopped at Elmendorf Air Force Base just outside of Anchorage for refueling on the Great Circle Route to and from Asia.

In early November 1966, when President Johnson was returning from a trip to Vietnam, Korea, Australia, and New Zealand, he landed at Elmendorf Air Force Base just before midnight. News junkies that we were, without any newspaper to report for, Larry and I headed out to the base to witness the arrival. Johnson stepped off the plane in the light rain without an overcoat, beaming benignly at the crowd of some 6,000 greeters. The *Daily News* wrote that "his reaction to the big crowd was more enthusiastic than even the most optimistic of planners could have hoped." He plunged into the crowd shaking hands and beaming.

At one point he "surged away from the Secret Service and climbed onto an elevated platform" (that was not intended for him). He seemed to be in a state of ecstasy. The paper reported that the president emerged from the crowd on the platform, holding hands with the persons nearest him. Then he jumped into an open-topped convertible and rode in a motorcade to downtown Anchorage, where thousands lined the streets, cheering, and where an enormous bonfire greeted him. Repeatedly he jumped into the crowd, clearly taking great comfort in close contact with so many people. To the consternation of the Secret Service, Johnson seemed oblivious of the cold and to any possible danger to himself. It was as though the adulation wiped away the scars of criticism over the Vietnam War he was enduring back home and abroad.

That night Larry and I had a party at 3023 Madison Way. Several of Larry's good friends, Pete Lisagor of the *Chicago Daily News* and Hugh Sidey of *TIME* magazine among them, came by our house. They had all been traveling in Asia with Johnson on Air Force One, and for them, flying in from Japan, it was mid-day and not midnight. Larry plied them with welcoming drinks and they regaled us with hilarious tales about the bizarre doings of the president on this trip, among them Johnson's telling the troops in Korea how his father was a hero at the Alamo (a tale that he later admitted was untrue), and how Johnson would lean across several guests at a dinner party and spear something with his fork off someone's plate. The national press analysts, informally gathered in our living room in front of the fire, agreed that there were clear signals that LBJ was feeling the heat of the controversy over Vietnam.

The next day we attended President Johnson's speech at the Anchorage Westward Hotel, where he spoke of his Asian trip and the goals of the United States in Asia. He departed from his text to say that he had made his first visit to Alaska soon after the Japanese attack on Dutch Harbor during World War II, and how the United States had "kicked the s - - - out of the Japanese in the Aleutians. So you people know why it is so important to stop a would-be conqueror in his tracks." This comment was an affront to many in the audience, because Japanese investment money was flowing heavily into Alaska at that time, and a number of the investors were present.

~

The first ever winter climb of Mount McKinley was one diversion in the winter of 1967. Our good friend George Wichman was one of eight men to attempt the climb. An international group of seven mountaineers had been planning and laying up provisions for the expedition for months. We had been enthusiastic kibitzers. When the designated February day came, Larry and I drove the gravel road north to Talkeetna, a remote hamlet near the base of McKinley that serves as the launching pad for McKinley climbs. We wanted to be on hand with George's wife, Peggy. Don Sheldon, an Alaska bush pilot famous for his incredible aviation and rescue achievements, flew the two-seat bush plane that ferried the climbers to base camp in shifts. For each shuttle, the plane was crammed to the roof with equipment. As George strapped himself into his seat, he mentioned that he was hungry. Larry and I handed through the window the hamburgers we were about to munch—the last hamburgers those climbers would see for many weeks.

Both Anchorage newspapers followed the progress of the ascent avidly. The third day out, the expedition almost ended tragically. Jacques "Farine" Batkin, a French member of the team, fell into a crevasse and was killed. After an agonizing debate, the remaining seven climbers decided to continue. Several weeks later, three of the group, Ray Genet,

Dave Johnston, and Art Davidson, were spotted on the summit. But a paralyzing storm with windchill temperatures to −148 degrees set in. The expedition's radios were inoperative, and there was no word or sightings of the climbers.

A massive rescue operation was launched. Planes and helicopters and the national press from Seattle and beyond descended on Talkeetna. Larry and I, with Peggy, anxiously awaited word of George at the Talkeetna airstrip. An air force rescue team erected a communications tent. A bevy of helicopters kicked up dust from the nearby military airstrip and roared overhead. Journalists were arriving in force for what had become an international story. Whoops and hollers went up when the air force radio reported that the three successful summiteers had been spotted alive by a circling high-altitude plane. Endless hours later, two helicopters circled the landing strip and landed amidst a mob of reporters, rescuers, and friends. They carried five climbers including the three who made it to the top: Art Davidson, who later wrote a harrowing book about the climb, *Minus 148 Degrees: The First Winter Ascent of Mount McKinley*, Dave Johnston, the six-foot-seven forest ranger, and jaunty Swiss climber Ray "Pirate" Genet.

But there was still no sign of George and Shiro Nishimae, the Japanese member of the group. We huddled with Peggy in the communications tent, praying and holding our breath. Finally, a barely audible radio report described a helicopter crew's daring attempt to land at 14,000 feet on Mount McKinley. The elevation was higher than helicopters could ordinarily fly. The pilot entered an ice shelter that had been constructed earlier in the climb. Finding the huddled forms of George and Shiro, he announced, "You're rescued." "From what?" asked the startled George, who had no idea that they were supposed to be lost. They had simply dug themselves into the shelter to wait out the storm. Shiro had proved to be an excellent cook, George said later. They were warm and safe but entirely isolated. The seven climbers survived, mostly intact except for Dave Johnston, who lost some toes from his frostbitten feet.

Being so close to such a big story and having no newspaper to cover it for made Larry increasingly restless. Nothing much was happening about the purchase of the *Daily News*. Norman and Blanche Brown hadn't decided whether they really wanted to sell or for how much. A couple of other prospective buyers were sniffing around, most notably one of the biggest advertisers in town, Larry Carr, owner of the Carrs grocery chain, and his partner, Barney Gottstein.

Rather than wait idly for the Browns to come to a decision, we decided to look into other newspaper prospects Outside. Bob Chandler, who, after his investigation of its prospects, was never high on the idea of our buying the *Anchorage Daily News*, flew us in his plane over the rolling green hills of Oregon. He introduced us to the owners of the *Corvallis Gazette*. The publisher and the editor each owned 50 percent of the paper and the editor wanted out. He would sell us 49 percent and the publisher 1 percent so the publisher would retain control. Larry would have full responsibility for the news side of the business. The paper was profitable. Corvallis was a lovely, peaceful college town. It seemed like an ideal setup. We thought we had a deal as we headed east to investigate some other job prospects that Larry had lined up. But in the pit of my stomach, I wondered if Corvallis was really the right place for us.

During the course of our trip—to Livonia, Michigan, where Larry's friend, Phil Powers, offered him a job as editor of his string of small Michigan newspapers, on to New York and Washington—we pondered. And we thought about Alaska. In the midst of the trip we discovered by phone that daughter Kathy was about to be named to the National Honor Society at East Anchorage High School. Larry said, "Let's go back." So we did, flying some twelve hours for the event to honor Kathy and then returning another twelve hours back to the East Coast to continue the job quest.

We were actually relieved when we finally returned to Anchorage and got word that the Corvallis editor had changed his mind: he didn't want to sell his stock in the paper after all. By that time, we knew what we really did want: to stay in Alaska and buy the *Anchorage Daily News*.

2

The *Anchorage Daily News* was born as a weekly paper to Norman and Blanche Brown on January 13, 1946. At sixteen pages, it weighed three ounces—hardly a match for the hefty *Anchorage Daily Times*.

Norm Brown had come from a newspaper family in Brooklyn, New York. They first traveled north to Alaska in 1906, and left again for Snohomish, Washington, where Norm's father ran a weekly paper called the *Advance*. Young Norman headed early toward journalism. He would go to his father's paper to light the fire under the lead pot on Sunday evenings so the lead would be hot for setting type the next morning. Then he went on to two years at the University of Washington School of Journalism. His parents returned to Alaska, where Norm Sr. started a newspaper in Valdez. Young Norm worked various jobs, but landed his first real newspaper job in the tiny Prince William Sound town of Cordova.

Blanche Sutherland, meanwhile, had headed north to teach school after graduating from college with a degree in Spanish from the University of Washington. She and Norman met and married in Valdez. Soon after their first child, Susan, was born in 1936, publisher Bob Atwood offered Norm a job as managing editor of the *Anchorage Times*. So the Browns packed up baby Susan and flew in a little plane in the middle of December to Anchorage from Cordova. During the next years, Susan remembers going to visit her dad, "wearing his green eyeshade that they wore in those days," in the *Times* office on Fourth Avenue.

Norman became frustrated at the *Times*. Publisher Bob Atwood "was notoriously penny-pinching" and didn't give him much of a salary—$100 a month, while the family's monthly rent was $50—according to Susan (now Susan Cappon). And Blanche resented Atwood's treatment of her husband after his nine years with the paper.

Although political conservatives themselves, the Browns thought the town needed another journalistic voice besides that of Bob Atwood, who by the 1960s had become a super-conservative. So Brown and two partners, Alvin DeJulio and E. E. Brambell, a printer and a businessman, each put up $5,000, bought some used printing equipment, and installed it in a ramshackle Alaska railroad building at Third and F streets. The plant consisted of a 410 Babcock press, a couple of ancient linotypes, and a Ludlowe for headlines.

Susan spoke of the early days when she was ten and her brother, Cole, was seven. The two spent all their spare time outside school at the paper. They would help get the paper out on Friday nights, sometimes all night because the press would often break down. The Babcock sheet-fed press would print four pages at a time, each page fed by hand and turned over to be put through again to print the other side. They were all hand folded, too, and the wives of all the five staff members would come down to help, along with the Brown children, who were paid five cents a stack for folding and collating the papers with the comics folded on the outside. Sometimes there were babies there. Susan remembers the wife of one staff member washing her baby in the newspaper sink when she was at the paper with the other wives to fold, cut, and collate.

"Friday night was the big social night," said John Bigelow, in an interview some fifty-two years later. It was a night of bonding among the tiny staff, which had burgeoned to ten by the paper's first anniversary in 1947. Bigelow, described as the "advertising man," and his wife, Madeline, had come from Princeton and Smith respectively, to try their hand in the Last Frontier. Bigelow had wanted to be a reporter, but the two news-side slots had already been filled by Edna Foster, city editor, and Wally Graves, reporter and sports editor. He had to sell ads, and considered himself a failure because he had great trouble selling ads at $1 per inch versus the *Times* price of 50 cents per inch for three times the circulation.

Bigelow remembers mechanical department superintendent Al DeJulio staring at crates of parts to a used press that he had just had shipped from the Lower 48. With it the paper would graduate from the hand-fed flatbed press to an automatic rotary press. But the Goss Printing Press Company wanted $1,500 to assemble the press. For that, the mechanically talented DeJulio thought he could figure out how to do it. "And it worked," said Bigelow.

By the time Bigelow left in late 1947 to work for *Forbes* magazine in the Lower 48, the total staff, including printers and pressmen, had doubled from five to ten. After school and on Saturdays, Susan and her brother would run around town selling subscriptions. But the Browns weren't making money from the paper. They took no salary. "I don't know how they put food on the table. There was no money coming in," Susan remembers.

Blanche Brown was the business head of the operation. She did the accounts and a lot of the worrying. She was the prime mover, who stayed in the background while Norman was out front. He wrote the editorials and directed the news coverage. "My father never said a bad word about anybody," Susan says. "Whatever he wrote in his editorials, he wrote them from the heart. He didn't attack very much. My mother was very protective of him. . . . He was not aggressive, and she went overboard the other way. Whatever slight she felt someone might do to him, she felt she had to jump in and protect him, and she did."

Blanche also guarded the financial resources of the paper fiercely. She would count the pencils at the end of the day. She bitterly resented the Atwoods because of the *Times,* domination of advertising. "They sewed up the advertising and never gave the *News* a chance," Susan says. The Browns thought what would have "put the paper on a nice black road" would have been to get some grocery ads. But Bob Atwood had the grocery ads locked up. "My mother was convinced that there was something going on with some kind of big business . . . that was keeping those ads in a . . . situation so only the *Times* would get them." Her words may have been an exaggeration, but *Times* domination of advertising was a state of affairs that would persist until the "great newspaper war" nearly fifty years later.

Despite the hardships, the Browns converted the *News* to a daily afternoon paper on May 1, 1948, going head-to-head with the entrenched *Times.* No doubt they were persuaded that advertising would be easier to acquire for a daily paper. In a folksy front-page editorial in the first issue of the daily paper, Brown spelled out what the new paper would include: "The Saturday paper will also have funnies. Of course this is all still in the planning stage, but we think we can do it. We will earnestly try."

The editorial goes on to spell out some of the basic positions the *News* would continue to advocate: It would plug for "renewing the Alaska and Seattle friendship that has bogged down in a fog of misunderstandings"; it would oppose the city manager form of government; and "the *News* has continually urged that statehood is premature for Alaska." All of these issues were the favorite causes of *Anchorage Times* publisher Bob Atwood. Brown's editorial concludes, "We have gone into things as we see them and that will be our policy in the daily, and we plan to stick to what we say and believe until we find out we are awfully wrong." It was an honest and humble approach to the publishing of a daily newspaper.

Unquestionably, the driving force behind the conversion to daily was the sharp division between the *Times* and *News* on the controversy over Alaska statehood. Atwood had made immediate statehood his primary crusade with persistent editorials. And the most determined opposition to statehood came from wealthy empire builder Captain "Cap" A. E. Lathrop. As owner of most of the movie houses in Alaska, and of coal mining and transportation interests, Lathrop also owned a daily newspaper, the *Fairbanks Daily News-Miner*, the largest newspaper in the territory outside of Anchorage. He had built his empire through association with Seattle financial interests. Atwood wanted Alaska to shed its dependence on Seattle and the federal government. Both men were Republicans, but they represented opposing wings of the Alaska Republican Party. Not long after Bob Atwood had bought the *Anchorage Times* in 1935, Cap Lathrop told him, "Either you sell me the paper or I'll run you out of town." The two talked price but, as so often happened with Atwood's offers to sell the *Times*, it came to naught. After that, Lathrop would pointedly refer to a lot he owned on Anchorage's Fourth Avenue as the site for the newspaper he would someday start in opposition to Atwood.

The titanic struggle between the newspapers over statehood had begun as soon as the Browns launched the weekly *News* on January 13, 1946. It didn't take Bob Atwood long to strike back. Less than a month later, on February 10, he started a weekly paper of his own, *The Forty-Ninth Star*, with a mission to promote statehood for Alaska and the growth of Anchorage. The *Star* lasted until June 1951, when it quietly folded. By that time the *Times* had adopted the *Star*'s booster agenda. The intense newspaper rivalry for the hearts and votes of Alaskans was well under way.

Exactly how the Browns obtained the financing to convert the *News* to daily publication and move it into larger quarters on Post Road in the industrial section of town is a mystery. Susan says a contract to print the Anchorage telephone book combined with revenue from Northern Publishing Company's job print shop may have resulted in sufficient profit to finance the expanded daily. There were persistent rumors, encouraged by Atwood in the *Times*, that Atwood's rival, Cap Lathrop, had bankrolled the Browns. In an angry refutation of that rumor, Norman Brown responded to a 1949 *Times* innuendo in an editorial, "If there was a kernel somewhere in the *Times* comment last night, it must have been the old chestnut implying Cap Lathrop's ownership of the *News*. We are weary of answering this jibe, but, again, tersely and concisely, NO!"

In any case, Cap Lathrop and his opposition to statehood probably contributed to the decision to make the *News* a daily. According to Al Swalling, venerable Anchorage contractor and banker, "Harry Hill was the godfather of the *Daily News*. He got Norman to start the paper" and put up some of the money. Hill managed Lathrop's theaters and other interests in Anchorage. Clear evidence of a representative of the Lathrop Company's financial involvement with the *News* is a Northern Publishing Company (the parent company of the *Daily News*) stock transfer book dating back to the beginning of the incorporation of the *News*. It records that the Browns sold Hill $25,000 worth of stock two months before the paper converted to daily publication. Hill's wife, Elsie Hill, purchased 100 shares. In a 1999 interview, Elsie Hill, then a widow, didn't remember her $100 investment. Nor did she know if Cap Lathrop had invested any funds. But she confirmed, "There were such bad feelings between Cap and the Atwoods, even before statehood was dreamed of."

Whether Hill made the investment individually or Lathrop was the angel in the background may never be known. Elsie Hill says her husband made the investment out of friendship for Norman Brown. As for Lathrop, Elsie says, "If he did it I have no knowledge of it at all. I don't think he did." Susan Cappon says her parents always hoped Lathrop would put up some money, but she also doesn't think he ever did. The Browns' son, Cole, owner and proprietor of a successful printing business in Anchorage, agrees emphatically. He remembers an occasion when he was very young: He and his sister were told by their parents that a very important man, Cap Lathrop, was coming for dinner. He remembers the preparations and that the children were told they must be on their best behavior and must not sit on the couch because after dinner Mr. Lathrop likes to lie down. When all was in readiness the family breathlessly awaited the great man's arrival. But he never came.

Cole Brown is sure that if Lathrop had been backing the *News*, things would have been easier. He remembers his mother often in tears over the struggle for money, trying to make ends meet. "They had a horrible life. They talked in front of us. Maybe they thought we were too young to listen."

Despite all the pain, Brown says his father was so proud of the paper that, years later, Cole found a silver cigarette box topped with a brass replica of the *Daily News* masthead listing Norman Brown as publisher in Norman's hospital room the day he died. Larry Fanning had given it to him years before.

Nevertheless, on the first day of publication of the newly daily *News* (coincidentally the same day Lathrop started his Anchorage radio station), the Lathrop-owned *Fairbanks News-Miner* ran a front-page story that pointedly identified Harry Hill as president of Northern Publishing Company, the parent company of the *Daily News*. Even if Lathrop never did put up cash to help launch the daily, the paper's agenda was parallel to his—to counter the influence of the powerful *Times*. In a 1979 interview published in the *Daily News*, Brown confirmed that intent: "Our policy was to be opposite in thinking to the *Times*. The *Times* was promoting Anchorage, and rightly so. But we were impressed with the thought that it could cause divisiveness in the state to put all the emphasis on Anchorage." Tiny as it was, the *News* always thought of itself as the territorywide paper.

Hard times didn't end when the *News* became a daily paper. Hiring good people was always a problem, especially on the business side. "*Editor & Publisher* magazine was my parents' bible," says Susan Cappon. "They would pore over these ads and finally decide to hire somebody and then pay his way up here from wherever he was. First he would come up and they would decide he was OK. They would decide he would work out and they'd pay for the whole family to come up. A few months later he'd turn out to be a drunk or a deadbeat." Advertising continued to be elusive after the *News* became daily, and Blanche continued to believe that Bob Atwood was behind a conspiracy to deprive the *News* of grocery ads.

Conspiracy or no, Bob Atwood was generally viewed in the community as an authoritarian but benevolent community booster. Born in Chicago in 1907, growing up on Chicago's north shore, he seemed destined from boyhood for a role in Alaska. Two of his uncles had spent substantial portions of their careers there. Atwood's paternal uncle, Wallace W. Atwood, a professor of geology at the University of Chicago, had made a scientific discovery useful in prospecting for gold and had headed for Alaska in 1903. He spent the next five summers working for the U.S. Geological Survey, testing his theories on the Alaska Peninsula. And in 1908 he did a survey of the Matanuska and Bering coalfields for a group of potential investors from Chicago.

On the other side of Bob Atwood's family, a maternal uncle, Andrew Stevenson, established the first branch banking system in Alaska in 1916. Headquartered in Skagway, it was called Bank of Alaska. Later it became Alaska's largest and most powerful financial institution, the National Bank of Alaska. Atwood would eventually marry the daughter of Edward A. Rasmuson, who succeeded his uncle, Andrew Stevenson, as head of NBA.

Bob Atwood seemed to follow his uncles around. He trailed uncle Wallace Atwood, then president of Clark University in Worcester, Massachusetts, to that institution, where he graduated with a major in geography in 1929. Then, foreshadowing his newspaper career, he was managing editor of the *Clark News* and on weekends reported for the *Worcester Telegram*. Returning to Illinois, Bob reported on courts for the *Illinois State Journal* in Springfield, where he met and married social worker Evangeline Rasmuson from Skagway. Soon after their marriage, the Atwoods bounced back again to Worcester and a court reporting job for Bob at the *Telegram*.

But it wasn't long before the call of the North prevailed. Atwood's banker father-in-law, E. A. Rasmuson, had himself been one of several early investors in the tiny *Anchorage Times*, now for sale. Two other prominent Alaska names had been among the stockholders: media and transportation baron Captain A. E. Lathrop and J. B. Gottstein, who, with his son, Barney, were to become major forces in Alaska commerce and politics. From the time of its acquisition in 1924 by Rasmuson for $10,000, representing a group headed by Gottstein, ownership of the *Times* had shifted from one group of local businessmen to another with Rasmuson's bank extending loans as needed.

The banker saw the fledgling newspaper, in the small but growing town of Anchorage, as an opportunity for his journalist son-in-law. Bob and Evangeline Atwood didn't hesitate. They jumped on an Alaska-bound steamer and sailed through the Panama Canal to Seattle, where they boarded the SS *Aleutian* for Anchorage. On June 15, 1935, Bob Atwood arrived in Anchorage and took the reins of the eight-page tabloid *Anchorage Times* with its four employees and circulation of 650. He later described the Anchorage of 1935 as "a tiny island of people surrounded by a sea of wilderness called Alaska." From that time on, Atwood made it his life's work to promote the growth and welfare of the "tiny island" of about 2000 souls.

Atwood didn't invent a booster role for the *Times*, though. Before he came, in the early 1930s, the front-page slogan of the *Anchorage Times* was "Anchor with Anchorage—Your Ship of Hope Will Never Strike Shoal Water." When hotel man Frank Reed borrowed half a million dollars for a power plant at Lake Eklutna, the *Times* had published a special edition to congratulate him. Soon after Atwood took over, the *Times* began publishing special editions it called "progress editions." During the summer of 1937, a fifty-four-page progress edition forecast Anchorage as the future "Chicago of Alaska."

Bob Atwood fashioned the *Times* around a series of crusades. Even before he assumed control, the paper had promoted moving the state capital from Juneau, in southeastern Alaska, to southcentral Alaska, a cause he advocated for the rest of his life. In a 1962 vote on the issue, the capital move lost 32,000 to 26,000, despite Atwood's all-out support.

The last day of the campaign the *Times* published a poster three feet long, saying ERNIE GO HOME, because Senator Ernest Gruening was campaigning to keep the capital in Juneau.

At another time, Atwood's editorial firepower supported the city manager form of government for Anchorage. Alaska's military and its oil industry were always top Atwood priorities. But his greatest campaign was Alaska statehood. From his first editorial advocating immediate statehood in 1943 until Alaska became a state in 1959, Atwood wrote over 250 editorials on the topic. He was appointed chairman of the Alaska Statehood Committee, financed by the territorial legislature in 1949, and spent months testifying before Congressional committees in Washington, D.C., and traveling the country advocating statehood. He even ran for the provisional U.S. Senate seat before statehood, and was roundly defeated. When the Congress voted for Alaska to become the forty-ninth state on June 30, 1958, the *Times* sported a seven-inch headline: "WE'RE IN." Another *Times* story proclaimed, "ANCHORAGE BLOWS ITS LID." As President Eisenhower signed the statehood bill on January 3, 1959, Bob Atwood stood beside him, receiving one of the six pens Ike used for the signing. Bob Atwood was deservedly celebrated as one of the fathers of Alaska statehood.

In July 1957 Atwood struck it rich with the Richfield oil strike on the Kenai Peninsula. He and a group of cronies used to have lunch regularly at the Elks Club on Third Avenue in downtown Anchorage. The group included his brother-in-law, Elmer Rasmuson, who had succeeded his father as head of the state's biggest bank, and several other bankers and storeowners. Although Atwood denied ever hearing the term, the group was known in some quarters as the "Spit and Argue Club." When news of oil strikes on the Kenai Peninsula ignited a rush of oil people to Alaska from the Lower 48, the group pooled their funds and filed for oil leases based on whatever intelligence they could assemble. In July 1957 a huge headline in the *Anchorage Times* announced, "Richfield Hits Oil." The oil rush was on and Bob Atwood became a participant and cheerleader, although he always claimed he became involved more to promote the development of Alaska than to enrich himself.

With the advent of oil, the pace of business in Alaska accelerated. But, ironically, the dawn of a new era of growth and success for Alaska was ushered in by a disaster. On March 27, 1964, at 5:36 p.m., there was a terrible roar, and for a terrifying four minutes North America's most powerful earthquake devastated downtown Anchorage and many other parts of the state. It was then measured at 8.4 on the Richter scale. Loss of life was mercifully low, 115 statewide, but damage was huge, estimated up to $500 million. Both newspaper publishers, Atwood and Brown, were hard hit. Brown's newspaper plant was temporarily incapacitated, so he had to rely on Bob Atwood's *Times* to print the *News* for one day. Although Brown was grateful, it was a blow to his pride to be forced to rely on Atwood, even for a day.

Bob Atwood lost his house, and almost his life. The Atwood's log house, perched on the cliff overlooking Cook Inlet, was vulnerable. Atwood was at home that Good Friday afternoon, practicing his trumpet. He was fond of telling the story of how, as his house broke apart and was tumbling down the bluff, he was trapped. He couldn't pull his arm free until he reluctantly let go of his trumpet, which had been buried in the sand.

Norman Brown's son-in-law, Jack Cappon, then editor of the *News*, was at the paper on that Good Friday afternoon. "We were just putting on our coats to have our little martini at the Highland Fling when this came. We generally paid no attention to tremors; we had them all the time. Except this one kept going and going and I saw all the old-fashioned "turtles" [that held the lead type] begin to slide all over the floor, and I said we'd better get out of here. I went across the street and it was still going. I remember standing watching our building. It was like a ship on a stormy ocean. The telephone poles were going up and down. . . . I watched part of our wall ripped off. It was slightly snowing. Then there was a moment of silence, and all the hydrants exploded. I ran all the way to our apartment on K Street. There was a fissure that ran down the alley. I ran upstairs and there was my wife, Susan, with our daughter on her lap coloring Easter eggs. Then we put up a tent on my father-in-law's lawn for a newsroom." The plant had no power and the back wall was caved in.

Despite the loss of Atwood's house and the damaged *News* building, both newspapers made a quick recovery. The *Times* urged people to rebuild Anchorage immediately, bigger and better. Bob Atwood took his own advice and built a white-pillared mansion on what had been

Anchorage's only nine-hole golf course. The *Daily News* was back in its own building two days after the quake. In three weeks the *News* had proceeded with its pre-earthquake plan to convert to morning publication. Soon, because massive amounts of federal dollars were flooding into Alaska, bringing with it lawyers, bankers, architects, developers, builders, investors, and adventurers, Anchorage was booming.

But news editor Jack Cappon had had enough of Alaska. He had come to Anchorage from the Associated Press in New York to take over as editor while Norman Brown was recovering from a heart attack. He had weathered the earthquake and converted the paper from an afternoon to a morning publication. With Brown now recovered, Jack and Susan went back to New York, where Cappon rejoined the Associated Press, becoming its news editor.

On the first anniversary of the earthquake, a *Daily News* editorial encapsulated the experience: "One year ago, the *Anchorage Daily News* was a pretty grim sight. Beyond the twisted machinery and incredible stacks of debris was the evening sky, clearly visible through the collapsed back wall of the plant. There was only one thing to do—get a broom and shovel and whatever else was necessary to clean up the mess. We had a paper to publish. By Monday the *Daily News* was back on the stands and at the subscribers' doorsteps. We had big plans that day. . . . Within two weeks the *Daily News* was scheduled to begin publication of Alaska's first morning newspaper. We went ahead with those plans. The result was one of the most dramatic success stories in newspaper publishing history."

But more changes were in the works. On June 13, the scrappy little paper started a Sunday edition, the first Sunday paper in the state. Publisher Norman Brown wrote, "People of Anchorage have been asking for a Sunday publication for many years. We believe there is a need for a quality Sunday newspaper, and that is what we will offer our readers." The paper had also been adding to its news resources. It became a member of the Associated Press, and by September 1966 it added the *Los Angeles Times–Washington Post* News Service. An editorial boasted that the paper offered "*Daily News* readers the most complete range of national and world news available in any publication in Alaska."

But still no grocery ads.

Jack Cappon's replacement as managing editor of the *News* was Joe Rothstein, who was then an intense young journalist and recent graduate of UCLA. Talented, liberal, idealistic, and cocky, Rothstein had been editor of his high school and college yearbooks, finished the UCLA journalism program, and decided he didn't want to live in Los Angeles anymore. Alaska had just become a state that year and was in the news a lot. It seemed like an exciting place to go. Like so many young journalists attracted to Alaska, he expected to get some experience on a small newspaper where he "could actually do a lot of reporting and writing instead of carrying out sandwiches as a novice at the *L. A. Times.*" So Joe, with his pregnant wife, Adele, arrived in Anchorage the summer of 1959 and went to work as a reporter for Norman Brown that fall.

At the same time Jude Wanniski, an ambitious young classmate of Joe's at UCLA, began working at the *News* as an unpaid intern. He would become the first of many *Daily News* staffers to ultimately make himself a big reputation in the Lower 48. "He was even more liberal than I was, then," says Rothstein. He wrote some pieces that were too liberal for the Browns, and they sent a telegram telling him he was fired. Jude went on to Las Vegas, where he became a well-known columnist and personality. His whole outlook, especially on economics, changed. He became a prominent conservative, a reporter for the *Wall Street Journal,* and wrote a book about supply-side economics. As a missionary for the concept, along with Congressman Jack Kemp and other conservatives, he became known as the father of supply-side economics.

Meanwhile, after a year as a reporter covering everything at the *Daily News,* Joe Rothstein caught the eye of Governor Bill Egan, Alaska's first elected governor. Joe had covered the governor for the *Daily News* every time he came to Anchorage. Everything in the state was getting organized in those early days of statehood: the brand new court system, all the different administrative departments, the civil service. One day in late 1960, Governor Egan asked Rothstein to come to Juneau and work with him on his staff. "I wasn't sure what that meant, but I knew it was more money and I thought it would look good on my resume."

Just as Joe was returning to Anchorage after nearly four years with the governor in Juneau, the Browns were looking for a replacement for Jack

Cappon. They tapped the energetic Rothstein to become editor even though he was far more liberal than Norman Brown. "Yes, I had a liberal bias," admits Rothstein. Norm Brown told him he could have a free hand to write editorials. "As it turned out I was writing editorials he didn't agree with and, even worse, his friends didn't agree with them. They thought he was writing them, so one day he suggested we sign our editorials, put our initials there. . . . That way his friends would know it was that radical" and not Norm.

One thing Rothstein and the Browns did *not* disagree on was their opposition to Bob Atwood and the *Times*. Joe's liberalism tilted the paper more and more toward coverage of topics left untouched by the *Times*—the rights of Natives, issues regarding minorities, the economically disadvantaged—while the *Times* focused on stories about downtown business, oil, politics, and the military. Comparing the two papers any given day, it might be difficult to discern that they were reporting on the same town. In 1965 Rothstein assigned the entire *News* reporting staff (then about six people) to do a groundbreaking series of articles on Alaska's Natives entitled "The Village People."

"We sure did despise the *Times*," Rothstein confessed many years later. "It's a natural feeling for the underdog to feel that way, but we just felt their whole paper was slanted toward downtown economic interests. The older I've become, the more I realize there's an inherent young journalist bias against people with money. If you had money, you must have done something wrong." What Rothstein said he really resented was that the *Times* was successful enough and had sufficient money to do a really good job in journalism, but it never really tried. The *News* couldn't afford it, yet it was the first paper to send its own reporter to cover the legislature in Juneau. "Atwood was not a journalist; he was a community builder," Rothstein charged. "He had no problem using his newspaper for it and not reporting on things that were negatives." The *Daily News* became a haven for young, idealistic journalists and had no problem attracting good reporters away from the *Times*, often for less money.

But Rothstein, in hindsight, was critical of himself as well. "I look back at a lot of the things I did, the decisions I made, and I'm sort of humiliated. I was very young, inexperienced. There was a lot I didn't know. I needed a wiser hand up there straightening me out. But overall we were covering the things that were important. People appreciated it. We didn't have a large audience but it was certainly a passionate audience."

By the summer of 1965, the Browns could look back on a tumultuous year. There had been the earthquake with its damage to their building. The paper had been converted from evening publication to morning. A Sunday paper, complete with comics and a locally produced magazine, *Alaska Living*, had been created. And a new editor had been hired. As they were reaching retirement age, the Browns were starting to think about life outside the business. But there was still that pesky problem of the absence of grocery ads. Susan Cappon admits that their family lived on the proceeds of the commercial printing operation. There still wasn't enough advertising to really support the paper or the family.

Barney Gottstein and Larry Carr, owners of the Carrs grocery chain, became close friends of Joe Rothstein's. They and their wives, along with a young state legislator, Mike Gravel, and his wife, Rita, used to have dinner together at one of their houses nearly every Saturday night. Larry Carr had come from California in 1947 and established his first grocery store in a Quonset hut on Anchorage's Gambell Street in 1952. Barney Gottstein's father, J. B. (Jake) Gottstein, had arrived in Anchorage even earlier, in 1915 when it was just a tent city. He set up a business supplying construction workers and miners, often delivering goods by dogsled to outlying areas. The business had developed into a wholesale grocery company run by Barney, the junior Gottstein.

In the early 1950s, Barney Gottstein and Larry Carr began to collaborate to start a grocery store in Fairbanks. The partnership grew over the years to include stores that sold liquor, pharmaceutical drugs, hardware, convenience items, and processed foods. They worked together to develop Anchorage's first modern, enclosed shopping center, the Sears Mall, in 1968, and branched out to include residential and commercial real estate developments. In short, they commanded great financial power and a lot of advertising.

Joe Rothstein had taken on more than the tasks of the newsroom. He was branching out into general management, so he was well aware of what the grocery ads could mean to the paper. For some time he had been quietly coveting the idea of owning the *News*, knowing the Browns were getting close to retirement. "I went to Barney and Larry early on, after I got back from Juneau, and said, 'one of these days it's going to happen, be an opportunity. I can't guarantee it will be a money-maker but you don't like Atwood any more than I do. You'd hate to think you live in a state where the only opinions are the ones he has.' They were one step ahead of me. They said, 'If we owned the *News*, we would advertise in the *News*.' " Gottstein and Carr explained that it wouldn't be just a matter of selling groceries; they thought they'd make money on the *News* because other businesses would have to advertise if the Carrs grocery stores did.

Joe Rothstein began to quietly promote the idea of getting the Browns to sell the *Daily News* to Larry Carr and Barney Gottstein. Atwood didn't need the *Daily News*, but he was in the mix to acquire it if anybody did. And about the same time, Larry Fanning and I came on the scene and thought *we* might like to buy the *Daily News*.

3

Why were we so attracted to the *Daily News*? Why did Larry Fanning, a sophisticated newspaper editor from San Francisco and Chicago, consider investing his life savings in a tiny, struggling paper so far outside the range of big-time newspapering? We asked ourselves this question as we put the wheels in motion to make it happen.

Larry was a hands-on editor who knew intimately the vagaries of the news operations. But he had no experience with the business side of newspapers. My practical experience was limited to a half year working as librarian and reporter on the *Daily News*. But we both had a strong sense of the role of a newspaper as a public servant, of an opportunity to make a difference. We felt that my children—Ted, Kathy, and Barb, then 15, 13, and 10, who Larry had taken on as his own—could be an integral part of the newspaper project in our adopted state, which we had all come to love. The paper would be a family project and the kids were enthusiastic. Alaska needed an alternative voice to the often strident big-business-building polemics of the *Anchorage Times*. Alaska was on the march to development. A newspaper could influence the direction that development took. Professional people had surged into the state after the earthquake—people with a wide range of motives. There were those who just wanted to make a fast buck, but on the other end of the spectrum there were idealists who, on this new frontier, wanted to make decisions in accord with those ideals in a way that didn't seem possible in the Lower 48. News stories seemed to be hanging on every tree. We itched to be part of it.

So we plunged. Ted Stevens was our Anchorage lawyer. In June 1967, it would be eighteen months before he was named U.S. senator. When we approached Stevens to take on the task of negotiating with the Browns for the *News*, he put all his cards on the table. He was close friend and personal attorney to Bill Snedden, owner-publisher of the *Fairbanks Daily*

News-Miner, he had done legal work for Bob Atwood, and for the *Daily News* under the Browns. But Ted was a forceful advocate and forthright about these prior connections. He would represent us with vigor and obtain the paper for us, if it could be done, at a price that would be reasonable for us and for the Browns. The Browns trusted Ted Stevens, too. At one point on the path to purchase the *News*, Stevens was representing the paper itself, his fees split by the Browns and Fannings.

Chicagoan Newton Minow, the man who as Chairman of the FCC under President Kennedy had dared to dub television as a "vast wasteland," was lawyer and financial advisor to us and to my children. Newt kept in touch with Ted Stevens and made a couple of trips to Alaska during the process of negotiations. But Newt warned us of the hazards. He thought the *Daily News* would be a risky undertaking since it was the weaker paper in Anchorage, the smallest city in the United States with two separately owned competing newspapers. Instead, he wanted us to buy KTVA-TV, Channel 11, in Anchorage, from owner Augie Hiebert. We had some discussions with Augie, but Larry and I were committed to newspapers. To us, television, however powerful and lucrative, could never be the influence for good in a community that a newspaper could.

We were taken aback when newspaper broker Marion R. Krehbiel of Norton, Kansas, hired by the Browns to make an appraisal of Northern Publishing Company, came up with a figure of $813,470. That sounded way beyond our pocketbook. Larry wrote our ongoing consultant, Bob Chandler, in Bend, Oregon, to update him: "I suspect you will think we are crazy, Bob, but we are anxious to proceed here, even if it appears to be a fairly lousy economic gamble." Plaintively he asked if it was Chandler's unwavering judgment that the *Daily News* could not be turned into a viable, competing newspaper unless Atwood agreed to jointly printing the *News* with the *Times*. The answer was "yes," it was Chandler's unwavering opinion.

So Larry proceeded to have several lunches with Bob Atwood to discuss the possibility of a joint printing plant, maintaining separate editorial entities. He also offered to buy the *Times*. After letting a few days slip by, Atwood again advised Larry that he would not sell the *Times*. "Mrs. Atwood and I wouldn't know what to do with ourselves if we didn't have the newspaper," Atwood said. He expressed no particular enthusiasm for a third company that would handle production, circulation, and advertising, but he left the door slightly ajar in the event we decided to go ahead on a deal with the Browns. He did tell Larry that he wanted us to know that he had decided to make a pitch to buy the *Daily News* himself, with some confidence of prevailing since he could afford to bid a higher price, already holding a stake in the market. That apparently was a bluff. There is no evidence that Atwood ever did make a specific offer for the *News*.

In *Bob Atwood's Alaska: The Memoirs of a Legendary Newspaper Man*, the book about his life drafted by Bob Atwood just before his death in 1997 and published in 1999, Bob described his various lunches with Larry over a period of several years. "Larry was a member of a breed that drowned themselves with martinis at lunch. We had several luncheon talks, but he would end up too drunk to follow up on specifics." By the time Bob wrote this, his memory must have been cloudy. Larry never drank martinis. It was his habit to have one or possibly two Bloody Marys at lunch, but he never showed them.

By spring 1967, Larry and I were traveling in the Lower 48, looking for partners. We stopped in Hastings, Nebraska, to talk to Fred Seaton, owner of several small Midwestern newspapers, and try to interest him in a partnership. Seaton had more than a passing interest in Alaska. It was during his incumbency as Eisenhower's Secretary of the Interior that the territory became a state. We approached Seaton about a joint venture that would add Anchorage to his newspaper chain. Seaton sounded positive. He would own 51 percent, we would own 33⅓ percent, and the rest would be split among the publishers and editors of his other papers. Seaton assured us that in his newspaper group the local man always had complete editorial autonomy, and that was what meant the most to Larry. Seaton told us he would decide within a couple of days whether he was interested enough to make a trip to Anchorage. He would also want to talk to Bob Atwood about a common production plant.

We heard the same story at our next stop at Lee Newspapers in Davenport, Iowa: the absolute necessity of a joint production plant with the *Anchorage Times*. David Gottlieb, president of Lee, indicated he would be interested in pursuing the idea of a joint venture with us if Seaton backed out. Not long after our visit, Seaton called Ted Stevens and asked him to contact Bob Atwood about whether he would consider a third company to handle printing, advertising, and circulation for both papers if Seaton formed a joint venture with us. Stevens made the call and relayed Atwood's answer: a flat "no." That response chilled the Seaton enthusiasm and had the same effect on Lee Gottlieb. It looked as though we would have to go it alone.

There was one more intriguing option that had wormed its way onto our agenda. Larry had been talking with Pierre Salinger, his longtime friend and colleague from the *San Francisco Chronicle*, who had more recently been press secretary to President Kennedy. Pierre was promoting the idea that we might acquire the *Bangkok World*, a feisty English-language paper in Thailand. Jimmy Greenfield (later of the *New York Times*) had reported in a cable that "an Italian national had bought 60 percent of the paper with the intention of selling off a large chunk of his interest." According to Greenfield, the *Washington Post* was also bidding for the *World*, but "for perhaps obscure reasons, strategically placed people hoped Fanning would get it," wrote Larry in a letter to Newt Minow; "God knows what he meant by that last part of his cable. . . ."

Greenfield suggested a call from Pierre Salinger to the U.S. Ambassador to Thailand, William Martin, to find out what was going on. The deal seemed to have more to do with politics, and perhaps espionage, than journalism. "If it turns out to be Bangkok, friend, I am damned if I know what I will do with that handsome parka," Larry wrote to Newt Minow. Enticing as the idea of owning a paper in Bangkok was, Larry and I were uneasy about some of the implications. Apparently the CIA was quite interested in this transaction, a potential conflict of interest that made us very uncomfortable. Besides, Anchorage seemed like a better place to raise kids than Bangkok with its obscure undercurrents.

The price tag of $813,470 that the newspaper broker, Marion Krehbiel, had put on the *Daily News* appeared prohibitive to us. A preliminary negotiating session had taken place in late February 1967, with Krehbiel present and with First National Bank of Anchorage president Dan Cuddy representing the Browns. Our lawyer, Ted Stevens, was unable to be present because the Alaska Legislature was in session in Juneau and Ted was then majority leader of the House of Representatives. Cuddy strongly recommended that the Browns accept only an all-cash deal for a sale of the assets of the *Daily News.*

A contentious point was whether a contract to print the Anchorage telephone book would go with the sale of the paper. Krehbiel acted as an intermediary because, as he put it, we had approached the Browns and hence he was getting no "finder's fee." He felt free to talk to each side privately. He persuaded the Browns that they would have to cut the purchase price approximately in half if they decided to withhold the phone book, since any profit from the operation was being generated by the phone book printing contract, not the newspaper. At that early session we agreed that if we acquired the paper we would operate it as an independent newspaper (independent from Bob Atwood) and the Browns would agree to a noncompete clause. They also gave us an oral first refusal.

In his report to Ted Stevens on the meeting, Larry wrote, "they are anxious to turn the paper over to us and they are not interested in the Gottstein group. They are even less interested in Atwood." While Krehbiel was in town, he and the Browns had lunch with Bob Atwood and apparently, in an effort to smoke him out, told him that the Browns had awarded a first refusal on the paper to someone else. He didn't counter with any specific offer to buy it himself.

Larry wrote Stevens that the *Daily News* "bookkeeping procedures are so primitive . . . it is impossible to tell whether the newspaper itself is in the black today or in the red."

Nevertheless, Bill Scott, of the local office of accounting firm Peat, Marwick, Mitchell & Co., examined the Northern Publishing Company's financial statements and established that for the preceding four years, the newspaper itself had lost money each year, from $111,000 in 1963 down to $40,000 in 1966. The "job shop" (printing operation) had roughly broken even, and the big winner was the telephone book, which made a profit each year, up to $179,000 in 1966. Before going back to the Lower 48 in February, Krehbiel had roughed out a preliminary agreement for Ted Stevens to formalize. The price began to look somewhat more attainable. Although still listed at $850,000, $213,000 had been subtracted as the approximate balance of an SBA loan we would be assuming on purchase. That brought the cash outlay down to $637,000. But, having exhausted the prospects for partners, after having been turned down by Fred Seaton and Lee Enterprises, it still seemed a formidable sum.

Then, in June, a new sparkplug entered the picture. The Browns retained Edgar Paul Boyko, the flamboyant lawyer from Los Angeles who had been Governor Wally Hickel's attorney general. Since Boyko divided his time between his Los Angeles and Anchorage offices and he was shortly leaving town, he applied pressure to get the job done. In a letter to Ted Stevens dated June 1, 1967, Boyko wrote of his clients' concern about the "considerable notoriety which has attached to the negotiations, which in turn led to rumors." Boyko announced that the Browns would entertain an offer from the Fannings up to the close of business June 5, 1967, and that if this did not occur they would announce that the paper was not for sale.

And we took the bait. By this time we saw our whole future wrapped up in this small newspaper in Anchorage, Alaska, and we didn't want to lose it. Newt Minow flew into town. As the Eight-Day War broke out in the Middle East, making headlines, we pounded out our deal. Our team of Newt Minow and Ted Stevens negotiated with the Browns' Dan Cuddy and Ed Boyko. By June 6 we had a "Memorandum of Intent and Understanding." The price would be $8 a share for 57,632 shares of Northern Publishing Company, majority control of the *Daily News*. We were buying all the stock owned by the Browns, their son, Cole Brown, and daughter, Susan Cappon. We would not be buying out the three minority stockholders. We would have to deal with them later. The total purchase price came to $461,056: $100,000 would be the down payment, and the balance of $361,056 would be paid over a ten-year period at 6 percent interest. In addition we agreed to pay the Browns, Susan Cappon, and Cole Brown a total of $12,000 per year for ten years for their agreement not to compete with the *Daily News*. After the closing, designated for September 5, the Browns agreed to repurchase the job-printing shop for their son, Cole Brown, at a price of $50,000. So for all practical purposes this brought the total outlay to $531,056.

A note here about Fanning finances, which became a crucial element of this story. Larry Fanning, as one of Marshall Field's top circle of executives at the *Chicago Sun-Times* and *Daily News*, owned a substantial chunk of Field Enterprises stock. It had been issued to the key executives of the company when it was "underwater"; that is, the stock had negative worth. As Field Enterprises grew and prospered under Marshall's leadership, the stock had become valuable indeed. So when Larry departed from Field Enterprises, there was a requirement that his stock be sold back to the company for approximately $400,000. After payment of the taxes and using some of this money for us to live on the past year, Larry had something like $200,000 remaining.

My financial bracket was similar. When I was divorced from Marshall Field in 1963, my one concern was the three children and having them with me. I told my lawyer that I didn't want to take any of Marshall's money or the houses that we owned jointly. The lawyer positively insisted I couldn't take *nothing*. He finally persuaded me to accept $100,000 outright and $400,000 in trust for the children, but I would receive the income from the trust during my lifetime. In addition, my banker father had also left me some money, mostly in trust so that I would have the income but couldn't use the principal for such enterprises as buying newspapers. From him I did have about $100,000 worth of First National Bank of Joliet stock that formed the collateral, along with the shares of Northern Publishing itself, to enable us to buy the *Daily News*. In essence, Larry and I each put up $100,000 cash and planned to pay off the Browns from the newspaper's profits at the rate of $4,008.40 per month. Of course, we knew that if there were no profits we would be in a tight spot. But the euphoria over completing the deal was so great, such a thought didn't cross our minds until much later.

But it did cross the mind of Dan Cuddy, the tough-talking banker who was sitting across the table to advise the Browns as their personal friend. On the advice of Newt Minow, we had set up Fanning Communications Corporation to buy the paper and take on the debt. That way we wouldn't be personally liable, Newt told us. But Cuddy wasn't about to buy that. As we sat in Cuddy's lavish office completing the negotiation, he insisted that Larry and I personally guarantee the note.

Unfamiliar with the ways of business then, I burst into tears. "You don't trust us," I said. Cuddy told us that if we were to be trusted there was no reason not to sign a personal guarantee. And so, of course, we did.

On June 16, 1967, we signed the documents that would give us controlling interest in Alaska's only morning paper on the date of closing, September 5. A terse announcement appeared in the upper left-hand column of the *Anchorage Daily News* on Sunday, June 18: "Purchase of the controlling interest of the *Anchorage Daily News* by Lawrence S. (Larry) Fanning, former San Francisco and Chicago newspaperman, was announced last night by Norman C. Brown, the paper's publisher for the past twenty-one years." No mention of Blanche Brown or Kay Fanning, except to say near the bottom of the piece that Larry, the children, and I lived in College Village. After the signing, the Browns had a reception for us at their home on Fifteenth Avenue, to introduce us to some of the longtime Anchorage residents and politicians who were their friends.

After the signing, Larry sent out a flurry of telegrams to friends, family, and his prodigious network of media contacts. To our surprise there was considerable national media attention given to this acquisition of a small newspaper in far-off Alaska. While the *Anchorage Times* played the story in a slim four-paragraph item on page two, *TIME* magazine jumped on it. Accompanied by a picture of Larry and me, both beaming, on the deck of our Madison Way house, *TIME* ran a piece in its "Press" section in the June 30 issue. Under the headline, "A Cheechako Takes Over," it began, "In the gold rush days, Alaska's Indians referred to intruders from the U.S. as *cheechakos*—a corruption of the word "Chicago." Last week Larry Fanning, 53, a latter-day *cheechako*, who arrived in Alaska nine months ago after an illustrious twelve years in the competitive world of Windy City journalism, became the owner of the state's only morning newspaper, the *Anchorage Daily News* (circulation 18,000)." The article went on to describe "Republican Larry Fanning. . . ." Larry, of course, was a passionate, undisguised liberal Democrat. So much for the accuracy of *TIME*'s "Press" section, which was then the space most coveted by news people for coverage of their publications.

In a longer piece filed for *TIME* by Joe Rychetnik but not published, Joe described my role as he saw it. Larry's "wife, Kay, who worked for the

Daily News for six months in 1966 (the only paid job she ever had and for an amount, undisclosed, that didn't exceed the amount she paid her cleaning woman back home), has no comment about the new venture. She plans to stay home and raise the Field children. When asked if she is going to share in the management of the paper, Kay Fanning retorted 'I haven't been invited.' She is letting Larry run the show and has no plans to join him unless needed." I have no particular recollection of saying those words, but I'll trust Joe that I did.

Larry wrote to his brother, Geof, in California: "As you may guess, Kay and I are immensely excited at the prospect of operating a daily newspaper on this pulsating frontier, surrounded as we are by young, energetic, creative, contentious, and involved people. Let those who regard America's society as soft, self-indulgent, supine, and conformist take the time and trouble to visit Alaska. Here you'll find a new breed of Americans living hard, fulfilled lives in a geographical setting that is unmatched anywhere else in the U.S."

One of the "new breed of Americans" that we had become close to since moving to Alaska was its senior senator, Ernest Gruening. Larry was intensely opposed to the war in Vietnam. Gruening was one of the only two senators to vote against the expansion of the war represented by the Tonkin Gulf Resolution (the other was Senator Wayne Morse of Oregon). While our family lawyer from Chicago, Newt Minow, was in Anchorage, he, Larry, and I had breakfast one morning at the Captain Cook Hotel with Ernest Gruening and discovered we were all equally passionate in opposition to the way President Johnson was conducting the war. So we sent a telegram to the president: "Dear Mr. President: Mindful of your dedicated pursuit of peace and that the United States seeks only a stable, unfettered government in South Vietnam, we respectfully propose a tri-partite program for your consideration at this moment in history. Immediately following Sunday's free election in South Vietnam, we suggest that you electrify the world. . . . "

The telegram proposed that Johnson announce (1) immediate cessation of the bombing of North Vietnam and the withdrawal of U.S. combat forces from South Vietnam; (2) the U.S. intention to place the Vietnam question before the United Nations; and (3) that "the massive national resources mobilized for the war in Vietnam" be re-deployed for the war at home, the war on poverty, crime, and pollution. It was signed "Ernest Gruening, Senator from Alaska; Newton Minow, former Chairman of the Federal Communications Commission; Larry Fanning, editor and publisher, the *Anchorage Daily News* (effective September 5)." Larry, who had met LBJ on several occasions when he was editor of the *Chicago Daily News*, clearly intended to participate in the national scene, even from his new perch at a small newspaper in Alaska.

The period between the June document signing and the assumption of ownership on September 5 was one of soul searching and struggle for Larry. He had planned to spend all summer on the redesign of the paper. But confronted with the reality of his dream of newspaper ownership, he seemed emotionally paralyzed. He couldn't get it done. He consulted some of his friends who were expert in typography and layout, retained John Wallace, a typography expert, considered adding more news resources, equivocated over naming department heads. He simply had no experience with the business side of a newspaper to fall back on. And the freedom to actually design and construct his own newspaper was overwhelming.

There were plenty of distractions, too. In early July we departed with the three children for the Lower 48 to visit family in Chicago and to attend Expo '67, the Montreal World's Fair. Then the plan was to ride the train from Montreal to Vancouver, Canada, before flying back to Anchorage. Larry loved trains, and he thought that three days of total peace traveling across Canada would enable him to gather his thoughts and lay out a comprehensive plan for the *Daily News*. Instead, he was crippled by a migraine headache for the entire trip, a trip that had begun in chaos in Montreal.

Larry, by his own admission, was a champion procrastinator. He was always devoted to whatever he was doing at the moment, with little thought for what he needed to do next. This applied to catching planes and trains. The morning we were to leave our Montreal hotel for the train after a wondrous two days at the fair, Larry discovered his laundry had not been returned. It was a Sunday, and the hotel said there was no way he could have it back before Monday. "That won't do," said Larry. So he pried out of the person on the desk where the missing laundry could be found, took a taxi to retrieve it half done from some befuddled laundress's house, and returned with it to the hotel. By that time we were on the verge of missing the train. I still have a clear vision of a bellman from the hotel wheeling a cart down the street piled with our luggage and Larry's still unfolded laundry flowing from it, the five of us running behind. We lunged onto the train at the very last minute, baggage and laundry thrown on after us, as the train moved out of the station.

We arrived back in Anchorage in early August 1967 with the planning barely started. Larry had just begun tackling the project again when a catastrophic flood hit Fairbanks. After many days of rain, the Chena River, which flows through the center of the town, hit a crest of eighteen feet, six and a half feet above flood stage, and overflowed its banks. Hundreds of Fairbanks homes and downtown buildings were inundated, thousands of people stranded. All the roads into Fairbanks were underwater, the railroad was inoperable, only a single telephone line was working at the Alaska Communications System building, and one runway at Fairbanks Airport remained in service. Just three and a half years after the calamitous Good Friday earthquake, Alaska faced another major tragedy.

The *Daily News* did what it could. Larry, still not in charge, brainstormed with editor Joe Rothstein, who directed the flood coverage, and sent several reporters and photographers to Fairbanks. He published a special edition of the paper each day for five days after the flood crested. This edition carried a double nameplate of the *Anchorage Daily News* and the flooded-out *Fairbanks Daily News-Miner*. The papers were flown to Fairbanks by air force and national guard planes and distributed free to Fairbanks residents. Many of those who had lost their homes were evacuated to Anchorage, where a refugee center was set up in one of the hangars at Anchorage International Airport. Like many others in Anchorage, I volunteered at the center, checking in passengers who came down from Fairbanks and helping them find a place to go. Anchorage residents opened their hearts and their homes to some 4,000 people escaping Fairbanks.

Among the refugees were our good friends John and Penny Teal, with whom we had stayed in their beautiful log house perched on the bank of the Chena River on two visits to Fairbanks. John Teal was well known in Alaska as "the musk ox man" and Penny had been my college classmate.

John had devoted much of his life outside Fairbanks to raising musk oxen and teaching Native women in villages in several arctic regions of the world to weave beautiful items—scarves, hats, and other garments—out of their warm underlayer of hair, *qiviut,* which is softer than cashmere. John believed arctic poverty could be alleviated by this industry. The musk oxen are gentle creatures, contrary to their reputation, that naturally shed their wool.

To establish his musk oxen herds, John took an expedition to Nunivak Island in the Bering Sea (near the delta of the Yukon and Kuskokwim Rivers) where he, with several associates, wrestled the wild musk oxen into nets and onto airplanes. He was nurturing his first herd outside Fairbanks when the flood struck. John, a huge hulk of a man who looked a little like a musk ox himself, had just left Fairbanks on a trip to Vermont where he hoped to start another musk oxen herd. Penny and the four children were home alone.

In a letter written a week later, Penny described their experience to us: "With the return of daylight at 4:30, the spectacle of that great gray stream 300 feet wide out the living room windows was awesome. Now it was up to the base of the birch tree ten feet from the house and had cut a fast flowing channel around the north side that was eating away the sand rapidly. Debris of all kinds was racing by in the main current—and our watch was enlivened by the irrepressible Binkley boys (neighbors) out chasing tires and bundles of shingles and oil drums in the raging flood." By 8:00 a.m. the river was rising so fast it was clear they were being flooded out, so she sent the kids off with a neighbor to higher ground. "It's heart stopping to send off that three-year old imp (her youngest son) in his little red hood and orange life belt into the unknown through the water-filled woods." The friend returned with a boat and evacuated Penny and others to the university on high ground, where she was reunited with her children. We got word to Penny offering the family quarters in our house in Anchorage, but she was determined to stay in Fairbanks to salvage what she could. She sent the four children to the East Coast, where John was on business. The log house on the banks of the Chena was ruined, but the musk oxen and the people had survived. In fact, incredibly, there were no deaths from the flood.

The foreword to a special book on the flood published by the *Daily News* described this major event in Alaska history this way: "The Chena River occupied Fairbanks while most of the city was asleep. There was little warning. No roaring wave signaled the onset of disaster. The Chena, around which Fairbanks winds, quietly surmounted its banks and rose six feet higher than anyone would have believed possible. Beneath the water was Alaska's second largest city—its streets, businesses, homes and autos. From August 14, 1967, to August 21, when the water returned to its banks, Fairbanks belonged to the Chena River."

Easily distracted as he was by a major news event, Larry was at his best under deadline pressure. By the time the waters subsided in Fairbanks and things returned to normal in Anchorage, he had just two weeks until we were due to begin operating the *Daily News*. What he accomplished during that flurry of last-minute activity was extraordinary. He established a new Bodoni typeface for the headlines. He converted page one to a six-column format, soon to be followed by other pages converted to the new format. A new nameplate or logotype was designed. The top of the page carried a bright red line that outlined two "ears" on each side, one framing the words "Alaska's Only Morning Newspaper," the other containing the weather forecast. Between the words *Daily* and *News* was a small globe viewed from a polar perspective. It looked attractive, tidy, and very readable. The arrangement of the paper's content was being reorganized, concentrating news, sports, editorial, and business pages in the first section, and women's features, comics, classified ads, and entertainment in the second section. A second editorial cartoonist, Bill Mauldin, who was well-known nationally, was to be added, along with a new column on national and international affairs by Washington, D.C., journalists Rowland Evans and Robert Novak. Larry also managed to persuade the *New York Times* news wire to shift from the *Anchorage Times* to the *Daily News* through his connections at that organization. The persuasive argument: Although the *Anchorage Times* bought and paid for the news wire, it never used any *New York Times* copy.

The day of the actual takeover of the *Daily News* on September 5, 1967, was one of the most exciting of our lives. Barbara Andrews, longtime legal secretary and legislative assistant to Ted Stevens, tells me of her memory of the signing ceremony this way: She recalls my being all keyed up, which she considered unusual because she thought of me as usually so composed. "You came in [to the Stevens office] and said you were so nervous that you had mistakenly used your deodorant spray to spray your hair instead of hair spray." She and Stevens drove Larry and me over to Dan Cuddy's office at the First National Bank on Fourth Avenue. She vividly remembered that coffee was brought to us in "real china cups and saucers," as we sat around the table and signed the multitude of documents. "I recall Larry was such a gentleman, and you were all so happy. The Browns were happy, too."

When the legal formalities were completed later that afternoon, Larry and I and Ted, Kathy, and Barbie greeted some thirty-five well-wishers from the community at the *Daily News* office on Post Road. As we shook hands with Anchorage Mayor Elmer Rasmuson, Borough President John Asplund, and other local dignitaries, hopes were high. We were going to make a difference in this town. We were going to bring real journalism to Alaska. Euphoria bubbled from each of us. Pictures were taken of us and the kids, as we stood beside the ancient seventy-five-year-old press with its shiny brass rails. To us it was the most beautiful little press in the world. It symbolized all our dreams coming true.

The next morning's *Daily News,* with an entirely new look, carried a top-of-the-page headline, "Fanning Takes *Daily News* Helm." Alongside was a boxed editorial signed by Larry headlined simply "Good Morning" and saying "Today control of the *Anchorage Daily News* passes from the Norman C. Browns, founders of this newspaper, to my wife and myself. We are grateful to the Browns for selling their controlling interest to us and we are equally grateful to the Browns for having built well and gallantly, turning over to us a lively, vigorous newspaper that has persevered in the face of formidable odds."

In describing Norman Brown, Larry said, "To put it simply, and perhaps best, he is a good man." And tipping his hat to the competition, "Atwood is one of the country's best known and highly respected newspaper executives and we have no illusions about the caliber of the competition we can expect. The struggle will be rugged and we think it will be interesting. We are confident it will also be entirely honorable. And the city will benefit because its citizens will continue to have available two quite separate and often differing editorial viewpoints.

"The *Anchorage Daily News* will be a politically independent newspaper. We expect to be outspoken on issues and candidates. As a consequence, no political organization or power structure is likely to applaud our efforts consistently. Our purpose is to serve the interests of all the people and to provide a forum for dissent as well as consensus."

Larry concluded, "In sum, we intend to improve our service to the community—to readers and advertisers alike—and to that end we seek a meaningful dialogue with everyone who shares our interest in a better Anchorage, a better Alaska. We selected this community above any other in the United States as the place where we most want to live, work, and raise our children. Although relative newcomers to Alaska, our heart is here. And we have lived here long enough to discover how much we do not know and understand about Alaska. But we are eager to learn.

"Finally, we propose to work alongside our fellow Alaskans toward the development of a city and state where the quality of life, the strength and integrity of our social and economic structure, will match the beauty, the peace, the grandeur of our environment."

Only a day later, we began to discover just how rugged and how interesting the struggle would be.

4

As we surveyed our new acquisition the next morning, some realities began to set in. For one thing, we soon discovered that the nearly 18,000 circulation we thought we had was considerably inflated. We were only able to verify about 9,000 paid circulation while the *Times* claimed 22,000.

No Alaska paper had an officially audited statement of its circulation in those days. Larry had already determined to change that as soon as possible. He had arranged to bring in representatives of the Audit Bureau of Circulation (ABC) to begin setting up our circulation systems to be audited. But at the time we bought the paper, the only verification of circulation numbers was the sworn publisher's statement that the post office requires every newspaper to print on October 1 of each year. It claimed an average daily paid circulation for the year ending September 30, 1966, of 17,793 and Sunday average paid circulation of 20,104.

Before we actually took over the paper, there had been no way to check the figures. In fact, we discovered that the press run for the day preceding our takeover was 10,000, making it impossible to have 17,000, paid or unpaid, distribution. We believed that although the Browns may have recorded the high end of the circulation numbers on their books, they truly did not know how many papers had been paid for. This was a significant blow because what newspapers can charge for ads is directly determined by the size of their circulation. A year later, in conformance with ABC standards, we showed a paid circulation for the preceding year of 11,000 daily and 13,000 Sunday. That seemed like a backward march for the first year. But "the water had been squeezed out," as Larry described it.

We found we had major production problems, too. The linotype machines, those marvelous great black monsters that created strips of hot lead letters as the operator typed in the copy, were, to quote one of the typesetters, "held together with rubber bands and baling wire." The press, beautiful as it was, broke down incessantly. Or if it kept running, there would be "web breaks," meaning the newsprint had to be rethreaded through the press, causing constant delays. The Browns simply had not had the funds to maintain the equipment.

Then there was another wrinkle that came to light right after we took possession of the *News*. Before we signed the deal in June, the Browns had told us that three individuals owned about 20 percent, or 15,000 minority shares, of Northern Publishing Company. They were Joe Rothstein, executive editor of the *Daily News*, Owen Jones, a former accountant for the Browns, and Ted Schmidtke, formerly a *Daily News* employee, now mayor of Palmer. Soon after the announcement of our purchase in June, Larry and I met with each of our new partners, explaining that it was not our intention to buy out the minority stockholders. That seemed to be agreeable to them. We talked with Owen Jones at the *News* office and then drove the forty miles to Palmer, where we had a delightful lunch with Ted Schmidtke. He was all smiles and congratulations.

It was quite a shock when a stranger, a huge mountain of a man, walked into the *Daily News* office the day after we took over and announced himself as "Locke Jacobs, your new partner." Jacobs had owned the 9,703 shares all along, not Ted Schmidtke, he claimed. Schmidtke was just a front for Jacobs.

We had never heard of Locke Jacobs. Who was he and why had he put us through this charade? Naturally, we made it our business to find out in a hurry. Locke Jacobs, an improbable oil millionaire, had come to Alaska in 1947, young, penniless, inquisitive, energetic. His first job in Alaska was as a section hand on the Alaska Railroad at the Whittier railroad tunnel. There, with extra time on his hands, he began reading books on oil geology. His next boss, captain of the Yukon River sternwheeler *Nenana*, was a graduate of the Colorado School of Mines, and he helped Jacobs learn about mining and minerals. After various jobs around the state, including staking out mining claims for others, Locke went to work in Anchorage in 1952 as a shoe clerk at the Army-Navy Surplus Store owned by Glenn Miller and John McManamin. Between sorting shoes, he spent every spare minute learning about oil leasing and geology. He haunted U.S. Geological Survey offices and the Alaska Land Office, and he tried to persuade his fellow employees at the Army-Navy store to join him in filing for leases. Finally Jacobs' bosses, Miller and McManamin, asked him, "How much would it cost to have you shut up about oil and gas?" Jacobs snapped back, "One thousand dollars." Miller wrote him a check for that amount, and Jacobs filed oil and gas lease applications in the names of Miller and McManamin.

Jacobs' oil career took off from there. As Lower 48 oil companies began searching for oil on the Kenai Peninsula, Locke Jacobs was the man with all the information on leasing, geological maps, etc. A group of Anchorage businessmen who met for lunch each week at the Elks Club included McManamin and Miller. Also in the group were Bob Atwood of the *Anchorage Times* and his brother-in-law, Elmer Rasmuson, of the National Bank of Alaska. This was the group that had become known in some circles as the Spit and Argue Club. Locke Jacobs was a member by reason of his encyclopedic knowledge of the field. One of the group, contractor Kelly Foss, according to Jack Roderick in his book, *Crude Dreams: A Personal History of Oil and Politics in Alaska* (1997), turned to Jacobs at one of their lunches and said, "Do you really know what you're doing? Last year you were digging ditches for me. Today you're spending my money and my banker's money."

"You're right," Jacobs replied. " I might not know much about oil and gas, but what I know puts me way ahead of the rest of the crowd up here."

By strategic investments in oil leases, and with Bob Atwood's *Times* churning up oil excitement daily, the Spit and Argue Club helped fuel the Kenai oil boom, and the members of the group hit it big, all becoming oil millionaires.

Locke Jacobs' stock and trade was information. He had more of it on oil, gas, and minerals than anyone else in Alaska. He also loved secrecy, a key to out-maneuvering other oil investors. That may partially explain his clandestine investment in the *Anchorage Daily News*. Whether he was a spy for Bob Atwood, as some observers believed, or whether he was just trying to make mischief, as I came to believe, he owned about 10 percent of the *Daily News* stock, and Larry and I had to pay attention to him. One of my jobs, only half jokingly, became "vice president in charge of Locke Jacobs."

But Larry had a lot more things to cope with as he moved into the publisher's office just off the tiny newsroom. Our building was a squat, rectangular structure, slightly pinkish in color, located on Post Road, a commercial street that led to the big army post, Fort Richardson. When you entered the building, on the right was a walkup counter for classified ads. Then came the advertising and circulation departments, a three-person accounting department, the publisher's office, and a windowless (and virtually airless) newsroom with about nine desks. Some staffers had to share a desk or find a corner in some other portion of the building where they could work. Then you went through some heavy doors to the manufacturing section. First were four or five linotype machines, then the Scan-a-Graver, a machine for engraving plates for the photos to go on the press, the photo dark room, and behind that the four-decked rotary press with its shiny brass rails. The arrangement of the building's interior was awkward, at best, so Larry retained an architect to do some modest interior renovation.

In a letter to Dick Trezevant, a friend from San Francisco and Chicago days, Larry drew a picture of the situation those first few months: "The situation here continues to be interestingly wild, and we are a hell of a long way from solving the problems that cry out for solution. A couple of weeks ago we had to unload the circulation manager; and while the new guy has inherited an ungodly mess, he is moving ahead with reorganization. . . . A week after the bloodletting, I had to lower the boom on a gal who was handling the principal accounting job. In two short months she contributed to making a confusing situation out of our financial records. As you well know, high finance doesn't happen to be one of my strong points.

Alas, this would be the first of many "bloodlettings" in those same jobs. I remember going to the home of one new circulation manager (about two or three beyond the man described above). He and his family were just moving to Anchorage from the Lower 48. I noticed a large, empty cage in the living room and looked around to see what kind of dog it contained. Just then its inhabitant slithered around a corner from the bedroom: an enormous pet boa constrictor. I wondered how long *this* circulation guy would last.

The accounting department was the other continuing enigma. The woman in charge when we took over could not come up with accurate payroll information. "Her first effort . . . was so inaccurate, it was entirely without value," Larry said in an exasperated memo. After trying several accountants, he finally installed his daughter, Judith Hunt, who had moved to Anchorage to have her second son. Judy, a musician, was a quick study with a little accounting experience, and she brought some order to the chaos.

The newsroom staff consisted of ten full-time people, most of whom earned between $125 and $200 a week, when Larry took over. There was Joe Rothstein, John Ratterman, Ed Isenson, four reporters, a society editor, a magazine editor, and one photographer. There were two part-time sports writers and a weekend photographer. This small staff was producing a twenty-page newspaper seven days a week. To produce this newspaper, the "back shop," as we called it, consisted of seventeen printers over a day and a night shift, five pressmen, and a proofreader. The mechanical workers were unionized and made similar wages for "straight time," but overtime cost much more and there was a lot of it. Living in Alaska was expensive, and Larry was sympathetic to cries of need for better salaries. In the early years he would give raises that we couldn't afford, because the staff members needed them.

Joe Rothstein became executive editor, supposedly to handle day-to-day news operations, but Larry loved nothing more than to sit on the news desk and handle the copy himself. With his shirtsleeves rolled up, bowtie untied, unlit pipe hanging out of his mouth at a jaunty angle, he was in his element. When he probably should have been putting out fires on the business or production side, he was often immersed in handling wire copy, ordering up stories, working with the writers to improve their copy, and teaching the young, idealistic staffers how it's done in the big time.

Larry was a perfectionist. Sometimes one of the printers would be waiting impatiently by the window from the newsroom to the back shop where copy was shoved through while the boss microedited a story, thereby missing the copy deadline. This in turn was a huge problem in the battle to keep costs down. The chronic problem of missed copy deadlines cost money because it kept printers and pressmen, highly paid union employees, standing around. It caused overtime and it backed up the whole process of getting the paper delivered. Just after midnight, when the papers were supposed to roll off the press, there would be a long line of assorted cars and trucks waiting to receive papers at the pressroom door. The *Daily News* had no delivery trucks, and the delivery people were all contract employees using their own vehicles.

Among the many lessons Larry had to learn was that, even for the boss, deadlines needed to be absolutely sacrosanct. If news stories weren't as perfect as they should be, you had to shove them through on time, regardless. That involved a lot of teaching time on Larry's part. All the reporters and editors were young and green. To produce the excellent paper that Larry envisaged took a lot of training, something Larry was good at and loved to do, but it took valuable time. He saw the *Daily News* as a laboratory paper, a place where young, talented, ambitious reporters from the Lower 48 would work for a couple of years and revolve back to major newspapers Outside. Meanwhile we would make good use of the talent.

Soon I was one of his pupils, too. Writing for the paper made me feel part of the operation. I thought the paper needed a newsy, gossipy column, so I started to write one. It was called "The Scene," the term being popular vernacular at the time. The column appeared once a week in the Sunday paper and was supposed to be a repository for tidbits of news other staffers discovered during their reporting rounds. Larry was a tough taskmaster, critical of the column and the feature stories I would occasionally write. And I often resisted his criticisms—something I have regretted over the years because I should have taken advantage of the opportunity to learn everything I could from him. But he was my husband, too, and that made it complicated.

Before long Larry had me editing the Sunday paper's weekly magazine, *Alaska Living*. A neophyte journalist, now become editor, I had to learn how to use the pica pole to measure copy, how to lay out a page, how to write headlines that would fit, how to read copy mirror-fashion on the "chase." The chase was the frame into which the galley (strips of metal type arranged in columns) set by the linotypes was deposited. It sat on the turtle, sometimes called the stone, a wheeled cart that was then taken to the stereotyping room. The page was slid off the turtle onto a mat roller made of a cardboard-like substance, and hot lead was poured into it making a semicircular metal plate weighing over thirty-five pounds that was then bolted onto the press. The used plates were recycled into the flaming pit, melted down to become pages in the next day's paper.

It was a heavy industrial process, labor intensive and demanding. As magazine editor, I had to learn to interact with this process on deadline. On the day the magazine went to press, I would take all the copy, photos, and graphics for its twenty-four tabloid-size pages down to Karen Howitt's apartment on L street. Karen was a freelance page designer. Karen and I would lay out the pages on her apartment floor, then I would rush back to the paper and start turning in pages to the composing room.

One night, precariously close to deadline, George Wood, the composing room foreman, inadvertently tipped over the whole chase holding two pages of the type that had been set for my magazine. The lead type splattered all over the concrete floor. Poor George! Here he was nervously working with the boss's inexperienced wife, who had brought the copy in late, and in his rush to get it into the stereotype room, he had a chase of pied (disordered) type all over the floor. There is no way you can put pied type back together. You have to start all over, so the copy all had to be reset on the linotype, holding up the whole process a half hour or so. I'm not sure whose face was redder, George's or mine.

One reason I tended to be late for my deadlines was that Larry was trying to teach me to write good snappy headlines and to create innovative layout. He loved sidebars in boxes and rules between columns, but those things were time consuming for the typesetters. Since I usually wrote at least one of the feature stories in my magazine, he would also edit my copy heavily, often at the last minute, occasionally reducing me to tears of frustration. I could not accomplish all this on deadline nights without going back to the paper after cooking dinner for the kids and overseeing homework. Sometimes I brought Larry his dinner. Often we would both stay until 1:00 or 2:00 a.m. Then we would drive home side by side, he in his sporty red Volkswagen Beetle convertible, I in my Buick station wagon. We'd head down the deserted Seward Highway toward College Village. As we approached the turn at Northern Lights Boulevard near our house, I would always drop behind him and follow him to the house. We never talked about it, but to me it was symbolic of our relationship. We were equals most of the day but in the end I would usually defer to him.

The kids soon found their niches, too. Kathy ran the switchboard after school or on weekends. All three would go door to door after school, selling subscriptions to the *Daily News*. Ted wrote high school sports stories and learned how to work the Scan-a-Graver. It was the only backshop job a nonunion member was allowed to do. But what he enjoyed most at age fifteen was playing chess with the linotype operators. Later Kathy and Barb each did reporting stints, and Barb took classified ads over the phone. It was a full family affair, as we hoped it would be. The smell of printer's ink pervaded the place and so did excitement. It was hard to stay away.

The only immediate news source for national and international news we had was the Associated Press Radio Wire. Intended for use by radio stations, it consisted of short snippets of news. To make a real newspaper story out of it, you had to piece the snippets together and try to construct some sort of cohesive narrative. Our competition was way ahead of us on this. The *Times* subscribed to the main Associated Press A-wire, which included full-length stories. But we couldn't afford the A-wire. To make up for this deficiency, Larry arranged with his friends at the *Chicago Daily News* to send us a packet of national and international stories every day by air mail. At minimum cost to us we also received the *Christian Science Monitor* service by mail. Our AP wire photos weren't by wire either. They came in the mail packet, too.

Still, we had a pretty good roster of news sources, columns, and features for a little paper in the hinterlands, even if they weren't very timely. Alaskans were accustomed to this kind of time delay. Televised Sunday Outside football games were a week late, too. Football fans would ask friends not to tell them what happened in last week's game until they could watch it.

We also got air mailed news features from the *LA Times–Washington Post* news service: Herb Block political cartoons, Sylvia Porter's personal finance column from the *Chicago Sun-Times*, Ann Landers' column (which Larry continued to edit for a while until time pressures forced him to give it up), Washington columnist Drew Pearson, and the recently added *New York Times* service. We subscribed to many Sunday comics, too. The delivery of the funnies was a particular problem. They were printed Outside in New Jersey and trucked to Alaska via Canada and the Alaska Highway. Every once in a while, weather, truck breakdowns, or other calamities would prevent the comics from making it into the Sunday paper and our switchboard would be alight with complaints. The next Sunday the paper would contain two sets of funnies.

Larry's greatest strength (and greatest weakness) was his tremendous empathy with the staff. If someone had a financial problem, Larry would lend the person money or give him or her a raise. He was never too busy to hear people's problems. When he was at the *Chicago Daily News*, his secretary used to call the long line of people waiting to talk to Larry at the end of a day the "poor things." She would ask Larry if he really had time to talk to so-and-so, and he would say "oh, yes, I've got to see him (or her), 'the poor thing.'" It was an asset and a liability he brought with him to Anchorage and it often caused him to be hours late getting home for dinner, if he got there at all.

Writing editorials was the other activity that delayed Larry's home-coming in the evenings. With his tendency to do things just short of deadline, writing the next day's editorial often didn't happen until after he had talked to all the people waiting to see him, and I'd be on the phone saying that the kids and I were waiting dinner. On those days the editorial would be short.

But the editorials were passionate, well reasoned, and effective. Sometimes they were displayed in a box on the front page, if there was an especially important issue. Not many days after he moved into the editor's chair, Larry was back with a front-page editorial on the upcoming race for Anchorage mayor, endorsing George Sullivan from a field of four to succeed Elmer Rasmuson. But he deplored the lackluster campaign: "What about effective zoning and planning; what about the city's mass transportation needs . . . improved park and recreational facilities; the city's action in putting such ludicrous items as a snowplow on the ballot as a bond issue?" This was new in Anchorage—raising such public issues and endorsing a candidate. The *Anchorage Times* never endorsed candidates, although it was always evident where it stood from what it opposed. Just before the mayoral election, Larry had another long, rather ponder-ous front-page editorial headlined, "Where We Stand on the Issues."

He took the obligation to be up front with our opinions very seriously.

Larry believed in making the editorial page participatory long before such concepts as civic journalism were discovered. In an editorial during the first month of our ownership, under a headline "We'd Like to Hear from You!" he said "The point of this piece is . . . to underline the fact that we really are interested in what our readers think. . . . We look forward to a continuing dialogue with the people of Alaska—ex-governors and governors; senators and congressmen; lawyers, teachers, doctors, merchants, and housewives. Regular readers, occasional readers. Youngsters, oldsters, truck drivers and bankers, generals and GI's. We have some rather strongly held opinions, and we propose to continue lobbing them up in unmistakable terms. We hope to avoid pedantry and didactic rigidity, although we cannot promise never to sin in this, or other, respects." Readers responded. Under a headline "Our Readers Sound Off on Tuesday's Editorial," he printed a whole page of reader opinions—long before such features were common in newspapers.

But readers did think the new *Daily News* had sinned on several issues. A shrill editorial campaign favoring gun control was a dismal failure. In Alaska, people's guns were almost as precious as their children. Most pickup trucks would feature a gun hanging across the back window. Larry had to back away from persistent gun control editorials. He tended to take the environmental side on most conflicts of development versus environment, and he abhorred brutal animal hunting practices. In one of his shortest, angriest editorials, headlined "Exactly What is a Sportsman— A Gun in an Airplane?" he said, "Shooting wildlife from an airplane is an absurd—if not obscene—strain on the usage of the word 'sportsman.'"

Perhaps his most memorable campaign of that first year was his crusade against "the overhead sewer pipes." Downtown Anchorage is certainly not one of the world's beautiful cities. But its setting is spectacular. It is surrounded by the Chugach mountain range on three sides and by Cook Inlet to the west, with, on a good day, views of Mount Susitna and the Alaska Range with its magnificent Mount McKinley visible to the northwest across the inlet. If one were depressed by the mostly gray, often funky, buildings, one could lift his eyes to the majestic mountains visible at the end of the street. But the city's traffic engineer, one George Easley, had made a unilateral decision to erect heavy metal pipes bearing traffic signals to hang over the street at each downtown intersection, thereby obstructing the view of the mountains.

Deploring the lack of oversight or any process for citizen input, Larry launched a series of editorials against the overhead sewer pipes, many of which were already in place: "We're devoting what some readers may regard as a disproportionate amount of space today to an exhaustive inquiry into the latest aesthetic atrocity to be visited upon Anchorage. The atrocity: Those curious structures which have been installed on Third and Fourth Avenues to support new traffic signals. When the construction program is completed next year, forty-two intersections on seven major arteries will sport our newest eyesore." The editorial went on to complain that nearly everyone a *Daily News* reporter had talked to, including the newly elected mayor, the city manager, city councilmen, and private citizens, except Mr. Easley, was "unhappy with the appearance of these horrendous tubular structures." Now, Larry continued, "we're stuck with this brand new form of civic blight." Larry had a facetious idea: "Let's give the tubes a red and green striped paint job for the Christmas season . . . If we paint the structures in Christmas colors, perhaps we can still salvage something from the $672,000 investment."

This was pretty strong stuff for Anchorage. For days the onslaught continued. Letters from readers on both sides of the question rolled in. And then on November 15, this headline ran at the top of the editorial page: "A Last Word on an Issue That's Beginning to Bore Us, Too," followed by the editorial: "Today, gentle readers, is the moment of truth, and the *Anchorage Daily News* is tossing in the towel on the Great Traffic Signal Controversy. We . . . are accused of an attempt to deceive the public by publishing a 'before' drawing that omits any standards, either for lighting or traffic control. Con artists we are not. The omission pointed out by our sharp-eyed readers simply did not strike home to us. . . . The standards are there and they are obviously going to remain there. And we propose to shut up, after giving voice to one last devout hope: That out of this experience, the city fathers of Anchorage will now set about establishing a municipal art commission—a collection of citizens qualified to evaluate structures that will become a permanent and inescapable part of the landscape."

A few days later, new Mayor George Sullivan did create and appoint the Urban Beautification Commission—and appointed me as a member! Already the new management of the *Daily News* was making an impact. The *Anchorage Times* and the downtown business community regarded such a commission as left wing, unnecessary. As the *Daily News* took positions that favored the environment on issues that brought it into conflict with development, some downtown business leaders began referring to the paper as "*Pravda* North."

The other *Daily News* campaign that riled the Chamber of Commerce was its sympathy for the lot of Alaska Natives—the Eskimos, Indians, and Aleuts. At the bottom of the social and economic totem pole in Alaska, the Natives were beginning to stir and to plead for their aboriginal rights to land. Two years after an initial series on the lives of Alaska Natives, called "The Village People," the *Daily News* explored the topic again in another major series, "The Emerging Village People."

Reporters and the one photographer traveled to Native villages around the state, traveling on small bush planes and often sleeping on the floor in villagers' homes. Both series were entered into the Congressional Record and became an important element in the Natives' fight in Congress in Washington for their land claims—a fight that would become a major news story during the next several years. The *Daily News* became a persistent advocate for this Native cause. But it was a cause that did not have the support of most of the downtown business establishment, the people who controlled the advertising.

This was one of the reasons that advertising was hard to get. But more important was circulation. With the *News* having about one-third the readers of the *Anchorage Times*, advertisers didn't think they really needed the *News*, and efforts to increase circulation lagged. Many folks in Anchorage literally did not know the *Daily News* existed. To address that problem, Larry retained Jay Perry, a local public relations specialist. Perry suggested a *Daily News* television interview show modeled on the very successful NBC News program "Meet the Press." Working with Perry, Larry and Joe Rothstein came up with the concept of a program called "Target." Three or four *Daily News* people would question a politician or public official seated in front of the bull's-eye of a giant target.

The weekly program debuted on Anchorage's KTVA, Channel 11, on Sunday, April 28, 1968, at 5:00 p.m., with Governor Wally Hickel seated in front of the target. Questions were lobbed at him by Larry, as anchor of the program. The other panelists were all *Daily News* staffers, usually Joe Rothstein, Stan Abbott, managing editor of the *Daily News*, and Bob Zelnick, a new hire. Several other members of the news staff appeared on occasion, too. But the small, dedicated staff was stretched thin to accomplish all of Larry's goals. Stan Abbott remembers staying down at the paper one Saturday night until 2:00 a.m. to oversee the production of the Sunday paper, then climbing out of bed a few hours later to tape "Target" in the studio at 7:00 a.m. As he was waiting to go on the set, he discovered he had on one brown sock and one blue one. *Oh well*, he thought, *it's only black-and-white television.*

In succeeding weeks virtually all the political establishment appeared on the show: Ted Stevens, majority leader of the State House of Representatives, who was running in the Republican primary against Elmer Rasmuson for the U.S. Senate; Senator Ernest Gruening; Elmer Rasmuson; former governor Bill Egan; and Alaska's one U.S. congressman, Howard Pollock. Alaska Native leaders Willie Hensley and Emil Notti also took turns in front of the target. The exchanges were lively, the questions often hardball. Before the 1968 election, candidate debates were held on "Target" with Larry as moderator.

Bob Zelnick, the new hire, was an immediate success on TV. Trained as a lawyer, Bob had left the law to spend a year in Vietnam as a freelance writer working on a treatise against the war. When he returned to the Lower 48, he applied to several publications for a job as a journalist. At *Newsweek* he encountered Hal Bruno, the news editor, who was a friend of Larry's. Bruno told him that *Newsweek* couldn't hire him with so little experience, but he would put him in touch with several papers that, historically, had been good starting points for journalists. He mentioned such papers as the *Louisville Courier Journal*, the *Charlotte Observer*, the *Miami Herald*. But as Zelnick was walking out the door Bruno said, "There's one other place, but I don't think you'd be interested, the *Anchorage Daily News* in Alaska. It's a very small paper but it's run by a world-class publisher and editor . . . and I worked for him. His name is

Larry Fanning." Journalists who had worked for Larry in Chicago or San Francisco had landed in many high places, a factor that contributed enormously to what we were able to do in Anchorage.

Zelnick called his wife, Pam, that night and mentioned the various cities where they might go. When, as an afterthought, he mentioned Alaska, Pam shouted, "Yippee." It turned out that Pam had long had a fascination with Alaska, had even wanted to go to the University of Alaska to college. So Zelnick placed a long-distance call to Larry (which was an expensive proposition in those years) to apply for a job. Already strapped for working capital, Larry told him there were no openings. But Zelnick didn't give up; he just kept calling. Larry couldn't resist talent and finally gave in. If Bob would pay his own way to Alaska with his family, he could have a job. He didn't know where he would find the money to pay him, but the few writers we could afford had to be good. So Bob came, and immediately shook up the *Daily News* newsroom and all of Anchorage with his aggressive, in-depth reporting and his flair as a TV panelist.

Anchorage people were talking about "Target," according to plan. The only problem was they were talking about it more than about the *Daily News*. There was one adjustment to the program that had to be made after the assassinations of Martin Luther King and Bobby Kennedy. Although still called "Target," the bull's-eye disappeared from the set to satisfy viewers who thought it in bad taste. The program ran for two years, and was finally booted off the air in January 1970 by improved technology. KTVA had acquired new color tape machines and was able to acquire Sunday CBS network programming.

For a number of years, the tapes of the network evening news programs continued to be flown in from Seattle to appear about 10:00 p.m. on weeknights. Every so often, as one settled in the easy chair to watch the news, a bulletin would come up: "We regret that the CBS evening news missed the plane tonight. Please tune in tomorrow morning. . . ."

This problem of access to the news grew to major proportions during the incredible news year of 1968. It was a time of huge news stories, both in Alaska and in the nation. It was also a financially perilous year for the Fannings and the *Anchorage Daily News*.

5

When a big story broke, the only way the *Daily News* could publish a *big* headline was to roll out the wood type. Our headline-setting machine, the Ludlow, could only set heads up to 48-point type. Sometimes we needed to make a bigger impact. We had a limited number of large wooden letters that could be dropped into the chase to form a huge headline. When there was a big story, Larry believed in letting people know it. No year provoked as many wood-type headlines as 1968.

The biggest events of the year began relatively quietly. In February the U.S. Senate Interior and Insular Affairs Committee held three days of hearings in Anchorage to investigate the long-simmering issue of Alaska Natives' claims to millions of acres of federal lands in Alaska. Many of the speakers came in mukluks to plead with the three senators on the panel for their people's rights; they spoke eloquently, if in broken English, of their culture, their history, and their rights as Americans. It was the kickoff of a long campaign to secure justice for the Natives, a conflict that would ultimately put economic development on hold in Alaska for several years. And the Natives' cause was an issue Larry and I and the *Daily News* were to champion in the years ahead.

The wood type came out again on what began as a routine Sunday in late March. Larry was working in his office and I was in the newsroom laying out pages for *Alaska Living* magazine. Larry called several of us into his office to listen to the radio to a speech by President Johnson. It began with LBJ's announcement that he was taking dramatic steps to deescalate the war in Vietnam. This had been part of the president's advance text. But LBJ concluded his speech with something that was not: "With America's sons in the field far away, with America's future under challenge right here at home, with our hopes and the world's hopes for peace in the balance every day, I do not believe that I should devote an hour or a day of my time to any personal partisan causes or to any duties other than the awesome duties of this office, the presidency of your country." Larry and I looked at each other—what's coming? Johnson continued: "Accordingly, I shall not seek and I will not accept the nomination of my party for another term as your president."

Totally unexpected, the political landscape of the country was altered with one sentence. In an editorial, Larry described the reaction at the *Daily News*: "There's an electrifying quality about a newspaper office when a big story breaks. The atmosphere is supercharged . . . there was a shocked silence, mixed with disbelief, then a rapid-fire cross check to determine if we had all heard the same words, and if they meant the same thing to each of us." Then the phone began to ring. The executive editor, Joe Rothstein, said, "I'll be right down."

Fortunately we had made arrangements to tape the text of Johnson's speech because our Associated Press wire report was so limited, it would only carry excerpts. Larry was determined to print the entire text of so historic a speech. He and Joe found two excellent typists to transcribe it. One of them was Pam Zelnick, wife of Bob, who had come to us as a reporter a few months earlier. Another talented new staff member who wrote every single story on the front page that day was Tom Brown. Tom had been with United Press in Anchorage and Helsinki. We had hired him from Helsinki and he was to prove an indispensable member of the staff during the news-heavy year of 1968. Tom had a masterful facility for gathering news from many sources, including the frustrating AP radio wire, arranging it all into coherent order and in lightning-quick time, pouring out several major news stories.

For a tiny newspaper in the subarctic, we did pretty well with stories like this. Having come from big-time newspapers in San Francisco and Chicago, and being dedicated to the concept of the newspaper as a public service, Larry insisted on massive coverage of important national or international stories as well as of local happenings. That day the *Daily News* devoted several pages to national and international reaction to Johnson's surprise withdrawal and another page to the full text of the speech.

Larry liked to give credit—in the newspaper as well as out—to staff members who did well. In his editorial he included due praise: "Joe Rothstein was all over the lot, writing copy, writing headlines, helping with layout, supervising the rest of the people involved, making special arrangements with AP for special coverage in words . . . and pictures." And about Tom Brown: "A man who had joined the staff three days earlier wrote every story that appeared on Page One of Monday's *Daily News*." (The fact that "Page One" is treated with capital letters in Larry's editorial suggests the importance he attributed to that page.) He continued, "Bob Zelnick, a lawyer turned journalist, is another example. Sunday was his day off, but he (and his wife) just had to be here, doing whatever he could to help, because here is where it was Happening." Stan Abbott, a very young reporter, who would play a major role in the stormy story of the *Daily News* in years ahead, got credit from Larry, too: "Stan Abbott, who was presiding over the news desk, cleared the decks for an avalanche of copy triggered by the President's speech . . . and kept copy and layout dummies moving. Equally important, he kept his cool despite the chaos and confusion."

He concluded, "We are proud of them—immensely proud."

Alongside the editorial, Larry reran a column by Joe Rothstein that had appeared in the *Daily News* a month earlier. There had been virtually no national press speculation that LBJ might not run again. But in Anchorage our headline had asked, "What if LBJ Does Not Run Again?" The politically astute Joe Rothstein suggested that Johnson "would be inclined to bow out if advance signs pointed unmistakably to a political debacle." Larry put a tagline on the excerpt from the column: "We're reprinting a part of it [the column] today because it demonstrates either Joe is equipped with an exceptionally clear crystal ball or he is shot full of luck."

The dust from this blockbuster story had not even settled before, tragically, the wood type was needed again. Four days after the LBJ surprise, there was an even greater shocker. This time the black headline read, "A Sniper Kills King—And the Trouble Starts." Below it there was a subhead, "Disorder Hits Ten Cities." Again the *Daily News* was faced with inadequate news sources on the momentous event, the shooting of Martin Luther King, that occurred close to deadline. The indispensable Tom Brown put the story together from the sparse radio wire and from information gathered over the phone from the Memphis newspapers. Wanting to contribute to the story, I telephoned my Memphis friends,

Mimi and Alex Dann. They held their radio up to the phone while I took down some of the live radio coverage from Memphis, so the latest information could be incorporated into the stories Tom Brown was churning out.

Larry, always a passionate critic of racism, asked some questions and let his emotions flow in an editorial headlined, "Hate and an Assassin's Gun Strike at America."

"Raw, naked hate struck down a gentle, compassionate man of peace, Thursday. The assassin has more than the blood of Martin Luther King on his hands—he has left an ugly stain on the United States of America, a country justifiably proud of its tradition of freedom and—yes, of tolerance. Today every American, white and black, must look into his heart and conscience and ask himself these questions: What is the nature of the illness, the madness that is ripping our society into shreds? What bold steps—something a great deal better than pious, empty platitudes—is this country prepared to take to destroy the sources of malaise? Is there something in the American psyche that elevates and dignifies violence as the quick and brutal answer to social injustice? What answers do we have for the sinister phenomenon of extremism—both black and white—the extremism of mutual hate that results finally in silencing one of the most eloquent voices of moderation and justice the people of this nation have ever heard? How can we substitute the rot and decay of mind and spirit with those solid qualities of decency, compassion, and understanding that most Americans, most people everywhere, possess?"

Although hundreds of miles from the scenes of carnage that followed the King assassination, the *Anchorage Daily News* didn't allow their city to forget. The wood type made another appearance two days after the assassination. A huge black banner screamed "Cities in Siege. The Riots Erupt; 15 Die; Guard Called out; Snipers, Looting, Arson." Other front-page stories proclaimed, "In Chicago: Eight Dead, Mobs Running Wild," and "In Washington: LBJ Calls out Federal Troops." It seemed surreal that such things could be happening in a world we had only recently left behind. A small story beneath a photo of the King funeral reported that Bobby Kennedy had canceled his planned visit to Alaska that week, where he was to have been keynote speaker at the Democratic State Convention in

Sitka. At the last minute, Massachusetts Senator Ted Kennedy replaced him, no doubt to promote Bobby's campaign for the presidency, now much reinvigorated by LBJ's removal from the race. And in Anchorage, the *Daily News* reported, and supported, a silent march of 1,000 people in downtown Anchorage honoring Dr. King.

The country was still reeling from the King assassination when the next shocker hit, barely two months later. After winning the crucial California primary and making a joyous, triumphant appearance before 2,000 ecstatic supporters, Senator Bobby Kennedy was gunned down in the kitchens of Los Angeles's Ambassador Hotel by a "mysterious young Arab assassin," as the Associated Press dispatch described him. When the bells clanged on the AP wire machine announcing an urgent story, I was in the newsroom trying to get the copy out on deadline for my Sunday magazine. Once again, all the news staff who had left for the day came rushing back to man the horrific story. No one could believe such violence was happening again in the United States.

Incredibly, we had not one single picture of Bobby Kennedy that we could locate. Most newspapers in those days had a "morgue" where pictures and clips were filed in an orderly fashion. Although my first job on *The Daily News* had been to start one, I was soon sidetracked by the more exciting opportunity to cover news as it was happening. But since we received no photos by wire and the assassination occurred late in the evening, just before deadline, we were in a pickle. Although I was valiantly trying to focus on getting the magazine out by deadline in the midst of all the excitement, I remembered a good picture of Bobby Kennedy in a magazine we had at home. So I was glad when I could be part of the action by rushing home to bring back a cover photo of Bobby Kennedy from the current issue of *Look* magazine. My son, Ted, was manning the Scan-a-Graver that night. Ted knew his machine well and remained cool under pressure. He knew you couldn't push the maddeningly slow process of making the photo plate that went on the press.

Larry held the press run for the front-page picture, and we all— reporters, editors, printers, and pressmen—stood watching Ted's progress. When he was finished, the plate was quickly fastened in place and the press grunted slowly to a start. Then it gradually gathered speed until it was humming along at high pitch, and someone rushed forward to extract early copies as they came off the press. I always felt a thrill when I heard that old press grunting and groaning and then hitting its high-pitched stride. There was a ritual at the *Daily News* in those days. Whenever we had a big story, people wouldn't go home, even though it might be one o'clock in the morning, until they had seen the paper come off the press. That night, June 5, 1968, the front page rolled off with the huge wood-type headline, "RFK SHOT." A subhead declared, "Gunned Down In L. A. Hotel After California Victory Speech; His Wife Ethel: 'Dear God, Say it Isn't So.'" Occupying the center of the page was the beautiful photo of Bobby scanned by Ted, taken from our *Look* magazine.

For twenty-five hours, Bobby Kennedy held onto life while the nation prayed and held its breath. And then Bobby Kennedy died. Larry called for the largest wood-type letters we had, allowing space at the top of page one for only six letters. He fashioned the headline, "HE DIES." I asked him, "Isn't that a little jarring?" Larry said, "People need to be jarred," and he stuck with his big black headline.

It was only a few weeks later, on Friday, July 19, when the wood type came out again, this time for good news. "Alaska's Oil Bonanza," screamed the headline, announcing a whole new oil era for Alaska. "The world's most massive oil deposits lie below Alaska's North Slope," the story began, somewhat extravagantly. Atlantic Richfield's "electrifying news" of the discovery of oil reserves from five to ten billion barrels at Prudhoe Bay "produced shock waves in Alaska, in the petroleum industry, and in the New York and London financial markets." It touched off the great oil rush of the late 1960s and would change Alaska forever.

By coincidence, a different headline on the front page that day portended another great issue of the late sixties and early seventies, one that would collide with and delay the development of oil: "Congress Gets a New Native Land Claims Bill." Senator Ernest Gruening had introduced a bill recognizing Native title to 40 million acres of land in Alaska and providing $500 million in compensation for other lands. "The idea is to bring the whole region up to the last quarter of the twentieth century standards . . . and provide an economic base on a level with the rest of the country," Gruening said.

These parallel developments heralded momentous change for Alaska—and for the *Daily News*—because they would bring a major lift to the Alaska economy and touch off great conflicts. By this time, Larry and I recognized that if our newspaper were to survive, the Anchorage economy would have to improve enough to support two newspapers. The problems were legion: With about one-third the circulation of the *Anchorage Times* and much of that duplicated (that is, people subscribed to both papers), advertisers simply didn't need a second paper. And we were seen as *cheechakos,* naïve newcomers from Outside.

The long established *Times* completely dominated the downtown business community. Many of the editorial positions we had taken were not popular with that group: gun control, urban beautification, environmental conservation, and the cause of the Natives. Our paper was actually denounced from the podium of the Anchorage Chamber of Commerce. Furthermore, much of the power structure in Anchorage was literally afraid of our reporters. Larry had added several talented youngsters to the staff from the Lower 48. They saw Anchorage as a rich repository for more than oil. They soon discovered a mother lode of unreported news lurking just beneath the surface. The *Anchorage Times* didn't believe in rocking the economic development boat by reporting anything critical of business practices or anything that might set back potential boom times. So, as the oil story developed and plans were announced to build an 800-mile-long pipeline from Prudhoe Bay to Valdez, fear was rampant that something like Native land claims or environmental concerns might slow or halt the boom.

On the other hand, believing as we did, that the ultimate purpose of a daily newspaper was public service, not the generation of profits, we intended to report the news as we found it. As the oil boom gathered steam, the *Daily News* was the only voice in the state asking the hard questions such as, "What will be the effect of an 800-mile-long oil pipeline on the arctic tundra?" Reporter Tom Brown was soon to write a thirty-eight-part series of articles in the *Daily News* examining these questions about oil and the environment. It eventually became a book titled *Oil on Ice* and made a major contribution to the literature on that controversial subject.

Immersed as we were in the great issues bombarding our new state and the country at large, there was still the nagging knowledge that the *Daily News* was not a financial success. By the fall it would be clear that the loss for the year would be close to a quarter million dollars. In July, Larry was back in touch with Lee Newspapers' Lloyd Schermer, hoping that Lee would intervene with Bob Atwood on the subject of a joint printing plant. Atwood had ordered a new offset press, which would bring a substantial improvement in the quality of printing in the *Times* and would leave the *Daily News* far behind.

In a letter to Schermer, Larry said, "It is going to be difficult to move the *Daily News* into the black unless overhead can be substantially reduced through a joint printing arrangement with the *Anchorage Times.* Despite the obstacles . . . we have made significant progress in both circulation and advertising." Ad revenue had increased by 30 percent, daily circulation was up 22 percent and on Sunday 32 percent. But there was a catch to all this. These increases, while promising, were still far from satisfactory, because to do any building at all called for a considerable increase in overhead. " In terms of organization," Larry continued, "our most pressing weakness continues to be in the area of business management. We do not have the answer to this vulnerability, but we are still searching, still interviewing, still praying." That sentence carried a load of frustration and worry.

In the smallest city in the country with two competing papers under separate ownership, with a competitor that was entrenched and well financed, and with the difficulty of hiring competent business-side employees, the situation was becoming desperate. Journalists were intrigued by the idea of coming to Alaska and working for a paper on the exciting frontier. It appealed to their sense of adventure. Not so business staff—circulation, advertising, and accounting personnel were an entirely different problem. We soon discovered that many of the people available for such jobs in Alaska were either incompetent or were running away from something in the Lower 48.

That was why some corporate connection with a newspaper organization like Lee Enterprises, headquartered in Davenport, Iowa, had enormous appeal. Lee operated newspapers in Iowa and Montana. The

Montana connection was particularly close because Larry's older brother, Ward Fanning, was publisher of the Lee paper in Butte and Lloyd Schermer, the heir apparent of Lee Enterprises, was publisher in Missoula. The Lee people thought the Anchorage market promising, but they were cautious and didn't want to be involved unless there was a joint printing arrangement between the *Times* and the *Daily News.*

Nineteen sixty-eight was a year on the cusp of change for the newspaper industry. Offset printing was clearly superior in quality to letterpress, and computers were on the horizon for the news process. All this change portended labor troubles, and Bob Atwood was afraid he might have to take a strike. That would be a problem if he had a lively, if financially weak, competitor in the *Daily News.* Apparently that was one reason he indicated, through an intermediary, that he might be willing to talk to Lee about some sort of mutual arrangement. But then he backed off again. When Larry had a brief conversation with Atwood in early August, he was beginning to "wonder what on earth Lee newspapers could offer" him that would tempt him to abandon his own plans to operate his new offset plant. Larry replied, "Know-how and peace of mind." The idea had some appeal for Atwood, but not enough to move him to action.

Just as it was appearing that some sort of money-saving deal with Lee and the *Anchorage Times* might be possible, the legality of newspaper combinations was attacked by the federal government. Nationally, more than a dozen combinations of two newspapers under separate ownership in the same city shared printing and business operation while maintaining separate news staffs, a couple of them at Lee Newspapers. So when the Justice Department filed a federal antitrust lawsuit against the two Tucson papers, there was consternation in the newspaper industry. The Tucson antitrust suit would ultimately lead to passage by Congress of the Newspaper Preservation Act of 1970, a development that would eventually play a major role in the *Anchorage Daily News* story. But in 1968 Lee, understandably, pulled back from consideration of a joint operating agreement in Anchorage, and Bob Atwood went ahead successfully with his own conversion to offset printing.

That left us still holding a badly leaking financial bag. If we were to keep the *Daily News* in business, we had to find some way to stem the outflow of cash. During our first year of ownership, the loss was $250,000 before salaries for Larry or me or the payments due on the purchase price for the newspaper. Actually we took no salaries, although $4,000 transferred to us each month was carried as salary on the books. It went immediately to the Brown family for installments on the ten-year payout for the purchase price of the paper.

The whole family had become devoted to "the little monster," as Larry lovingly dubbed the newspaper, so-called because it was devouring all our cash. Several times we had lobbed up infusions from our personal pockets to meet payrolls and keep the paper afloat. But it was becoming a really good little newspaper, it was having an impact on the thinking of Anchorage people, and it was fulfilling Larry's hopes and dreams. We felt that it was beginning to be a force for good in this glorious state that our family had come to love. It was a total family operation with all three youngsters participating after school and on weekends.

Working with the talented young folks in the newsroom was one of the aspects of journalism Larry liked best, even though those folks tended to be an undisciplined lot that caused many a headache. In a May 1968 memo he described the situation this way: "The newsroom has been for months in an essentially unorganized condition. . . . By any objective valuation, we are all working for the best newspaper product in Alaska, but it can be made into a vastly better newspaper. . . . I would like to see us undertake bolder and more imaginative ways of telling a story. We should not be shackled to journalism copy-book maxims. I would like to see this newspaper develop into an exciting laboratory experiment in telling how it is. We are not inhibited either by tradition or by any requirement that copy must be written to a formula. A warm, evocative, conversational style is what I most would like to see evolve. I am not suggesting that we fill the paper with wild, antic, far out news copy, but I am suggesting that we communicate directly, honestly, and lucidly with our readers."

Since we did not have any substantial financial resources to fall back on, something had to be done. The telephone book contract, which had supported the paper under the Browns' ownership, was churning out about $10,000 annual profit but that wasn't nearly enough. Trying to solve this problem would preoccupy us in the year to come.

6

In early August 1968, Larry and I and the kids headed out of the Anchorage pressure cooker for our annual vacation in the Lower 48. We planned to take in both political conventions, the Republicans in Miami, where Richard Nixon and Nelson Rockefeller competed for the nomination, and then the Democrats in Chicago in late August, where Hubert Humphrey was facing the challenge of "peacenik" Eugene McCarthy. When we left Alaska that summer, we were unprepared for the seething cauldron in the Lower 48. Young people were rising in protest of the Vietnam War in ever greater numbers, and city ghettoes were unsettled by racial violence.

There were no race riots or massive antiwar protests in Anchorage. The only thing that brought us close to the Vietnam War there was the roar of the hospital planes evacuating the wounded. Dozens of them landed each week for fueling stops at Elmendorf Air Force Base just outside town, en route to hospitals in the Lower 48. From downtown you could see the high-tailed planes taking off and landing at Elmendorf. Anchorage was very much a military town. As we traveled Outside during the summer of '68, we experienced the rising crescendo of antiwar feelings.

In Miami we dined with friends Chuck and Lorraine Percy and witnessed the nomination of Richard Nixon. It seemed odd that Nixon would be the Republican standard-bearer after his stormy exit from politics six years earlier when, after being defeated in his attempt to be governor of California, he bleated to the press, "Now you won't have Nixon to kick around any more." Larry couldn't stand Nixon, had never trusted him since his Red-hunting years as a conservative Congressman. Because of knowing him personally some years earlier, I was more ambivalent.

Over several years, Marshall and I had attended small dinners for Nixon given by Knight Ridder Newspapers founder Jack Knight. Marshall was a Republican. When Nixon ran against Kennedy in 1960, we held a reception for the Nixons at our Chicago apartment just before the 1960 Republican convention. My two memories of that event were of news photographers climbing trees outside our apartment building to get a shot of the candidate, and my daughter Kathy, then six years old, sticking out her tongue at Nixon behind his back as she helped pass the hors d'oeuvres. She apparently sensed something the rest of us missed. Kathy was roundly scolded for her impertinence, but we were secretly amused.

Fortunately the Nixons must have been oblivious of this incident, because when I encountered Nixon a few years later, he asked me out to dinner. It was over the New Year's holiday in 1964, the year after my divorce, and the children and I were vacationing at Key Biscayne Resort just outside Miami. One evening on the dance floor someone tapped me on the shoulder to cut in. To my surprise it was Richard Nixon, who then invited me to join his daughter Julie and his sidekick, Bebe Rebozo, for dinner the next evening. Rebozo drove, Nixon sat beside him in the front seat. I sat in back with Julie, who talked incessantly and bitterly about the way the press had treated her father during the 1960 election. Nixon had lost by the slimmest margin. She was convinced the election had been stolen and she held the press responsible.

When we arrived at a seaside restaurant, Bebe instructed me to walk in with Julie, not Nixon, presumably to avoid gossip since Pat Nixon wasn't along. Pat had stayed up north with the other Nixon daughter, Tricia. As a defeated candidate who then claimed to have renounced politics forever, Nixon was good company and seemed like quite a decent man. In several conversations I had with him over that New Year's holiday, I was impressed with his intelligence and his caring about human rights, the plight of blacks, and the less fortunate. His heart seemed to be in the right places. Now, in 1968, Nixon, the reborn politician, had quite different priorities, the overriding one to get elected president.

Between the two political conventions, Larry, the kids, and I went to the Virgin Islands to relax on the beach. It didn't work very well. We were all edgy over the political situation, and Larry worried about finances at the paper. He hadn't told me yet just how bad the financial problems were, but his discomfort was apparent.

By the time we checked into the Astor Towers Hotel in Chicago for the Democratic Convention, apprehension was mounting. Antiwar protesters were swarming over the city and Mayor Daley was mobilizing his massive police force. The demonstrators were camped out in the parks, a ragged-appearing bunch of people with long hair, their campfires sending a haze over the city. Larry and I wandered through some of the camps, asking questions about why they were there. They were passionate about the evils of the war but most were not the extremists that were being portrayed by the press. They had dignity and a high sense of purpose. We found the parks more interesting than the inside of the convention hall located at the Chicago Stockyards. It had become an armed camp protected by fences and barbed wire. They were cordoned off by hundreds of policemen and national guardsmen with bayonets. Besides, the political suspense was over. Humphrey's nomination was assured and the more interesting story was in the streets.

The protesters were being kept on the Grant Park side of Michigan Avenue by Mayor Daley's Chicago police. One afternoon Larry and I had been talking to some of the young people camped in the park, and decided to cross Michigan Avenue to the Conrad Hilton Hotel. Just then, hundreds of blue-helmeted cops in formation charged up Michigan Avenue toward the crowd that was trying to cross the street. They were swinging their nightsticks, and pushing us bodily back into the park. We resisted, determined to cross the avenue and escape an increasingly hostile situation. We felt helpless, panicky, like victims of a police state. We were jostled and pushed, but I guess Larry and I didn't look much like the protesters, and the police eventually let us through the solid line they had formed. We made it across the street and into the Hilton Hotel, there to encounter vile odors from excrement that protesters had smeared on the walls and tear gas that had been used by police.

We escaped to the Astor Towers Hotel, several blocks removed from the developing violence. The next night, national television showed the blue-helmeted cops at the same Michigan Avenue corner, beating demonstrators who chanted "the whole world is watching." And Senator Eugene McCarthy, who had just been defeated overwhelmingly for the nomination by Hubert Humphrey, was visiting wounded antiwar protestors brought into the Conrad Hilton Hotel's improvised emergency rooms. The triumphant Humphrey lamented the violence and acknowledged that events at the convention would not make the attempt to defeat Nixon in the general election any easier.

~

Back home in Anchorage, emotions about politics had escalated. One of the most contentious primary elections in Alaska history had been taking place in Alaska in 1968, right in the middle of the dramatic Democratic convention week. On election eve, Alaska's four candidates for the U.S. Senate—Alaska House Speaker Ted Stevens versus banker Elmer Rasmuson on the Republican side; former Alaska governor and incumbent senator Ernest Gruening against state legislator Mike Gravel for the Democrats— sparred in a televised debate.

The two Republican candidates were well qualified and ran a mostly polite and traditional race. Lawyer Ted Stevens, with Washington experience as solicitor general in the U.S. Department of Interior, had won the primary and lost the general election for senator from Alaska against Gruening in 1962. He had gone on to win a seat in the Alaska State House in 1964, and again in 1966. Stevens, even then, was notorious for his temper, which would become legendary in years to come. The *Daily News* described Stevens as "speechless with rage" when the "Cook Inlet Republican Club" blasted him just before the election. Stevens sputtered that the Cook Inlet Republican Club didn't even exist.

Elmer Rasmuson was president and chief owner of the National Bank of Alaska, the state's biggest bank, and brother-in-law to Bob Atwood. He had served a term as mayor of Anchorage.

In the election eve debate between the four candidates, moderated by radio personality Herb Shandlin, Stevens accused Rasmuson of using bank property inappropriately for his benefit in the election campaign. Elmer admitted that he had flown in his own National Bank of Alaska plane to get to a political picnic in Wasilla, but said he had parked the plane a half mile away and walked so as not to be using it for political purposes. These were refreshing issues compared to the acrid smoke of battle back in Chicago.

In the debate the four candidates all differed on the Vietnam War. Stevens said the U.S. should blockade North Vietnam and destroy its industrial potential if the current peace talks failed. Rasmuson cautioned against both escalation and withdrawal, and called for a new Asian policy. Gravel said, "We are fulfilling our leadership position in the world" by staying in Vietnam. Only Gruening was unequivocal in his opposition to the war, saying we should fulfill President Johnson's commitment that "no American boys will do what Asian boys should be doing."

Most of the fireworks in this highly spirited contest were on the Democrat side and much of the battle was waged in the *Daily News* newsroom. The grand old man, Senator Ernest Gruening, though extraordinarily vigorous, was in his eighty-second year, and some political pundits were convinced he could not win. Both his age and his passionate crusade against the Vietnam War were seen as serious impediments to a November victory. Anchorage Democratic powerhouses Larry Carr and Barney Gottstein were social friends of 38-year-old State House politician Mike Gravel. The Carrs, the Gottsteins, the Gravels, and *Daily News* executive editor Joe Rothstein and his wife frequently had had Saturday night dinners together and talked politics. These dinners encouraged the insurgent candidacy of Mike Gravel. Gravel was handsome, smooth, and confident. *Daily News* writer Tom Brown described him as "lean-faced, clear eyed, his black hair lightly streaked with gray, and with only a hint of the five o'clock shadow that gave Richard Nixon so much trouble." Brown may have been hinting at some of the credibility problems lurking at the edges of Gravel's character in comparing his five-o'clock shadow to Nixon's.

Gravel came from Springfield, Massachusetts, born of French Canadian parents. The *New York Times* described him as "an adopted Alaskan who drove a taxi in Harlem while pursuing a degree at Columbia University." Gravel had come to Alaska in 1956 and had some success as a real estate developer. Elected to the State House of Representatives in 1962, by 1964 he was speaker of the House. Careers moved fast in Alaska in those days and Gravel was one of the fastest movers around. Joe Rothstein had known Gravel in Juneau when Mike was at the State House and Joe was an aide to Governor Egan. Joe said, "We had a lot of politics in common and then we just kept seeing each other. When Mike said he was going to run against Gruening, I told him he was putting me in a very awkward spot. I loved Ernest Gruening. I felt he was a giant. Gravel said, 'If I can convince you Gruening is not going to be re-elected, would you reconsider?' " Joe had the advantage of looking at all the polling and saw that "there was no way Gruening was going to be reelected" and I hated the idea of the Senate seat going to Elmer Rasmuson. Gravel was a personal friend. So Gravel did convince Joe, and Joe helped persuade Barney Gottstein.

Barney, a leading figure in the Alaska Democratic party, had always supported Senator Gruening. According to Gottstein there were two reasons he decided to back Gravel for the Senate this time instead of Gruening. One was that polls indicated that 40 percent of the people wouldn't support Gruening because of his age. But there was more to it than the age issue, Gottstein told me years later. "I grew up with all the discrimination against the Natives. . . . As a child I remember the Native kids being sent off to the Eklutna school. I was always sympathetic to the Native cause. Gravel became a champion for Native issues. Gruening [initially] made quite a reputation for himself in trying to do something about [the Natives]. But when we got into statehood, he really hadn't delivered on that. Gruening was opposed to the Native settlement act. Gravel supported it."

Barney Gottstein and Larry Carr made an exceptionally strong team. Carr's retail grocery business and Gottstein's wholesale food and beverage operation had worked together since 1953. Both were Democrats in a sea of Anchorage Republican businessmen, so in a sense they merged their political efforts as well. As hefty contributors to Democratic candidates, they wielded strong influence in the Democratic Party. Barney had served as Democratic national committeeman for Alaska. Having Carr and Gottstein behind him, with Joe Rothstein writing pro-Gravel columns in the *Daily News*, gave Gravel a lot of momentum as the primary election neared.

But there was something else that made the big difference in the election outcome. A half-hour highly professional campaign film produced by Washington political consultant Joe Napolitan was shown twice a day on every TV station in Alaska during the last ten days before the primary.

Polls had shown Gruening winning handily over the relatively unknown Mike Gravel until the film hit the air. The film glamorized the Gravel story. It showed Mike and his family struggling through the Depression, and Mike working with the French Underground while in the U.S. Army in World War II. Gruening, in his autobiography, *Many Battles*, commented cynically on the film: "To make sure viewers understood this part of his career, he was shown with the Eiffel Tower in the background. Since he was only eleven years of age when the United States entered the war in 1941 and only fifteen when it ended, he must have been the youngest man enlisted in the Allied cause." Planes carried the film with a projector to every village in Alaska, so Gravel got greater exposure in the state than virtually any politician had ever had. "The primary was fought without issues. . . . It was known that Mike Gravel was depending on a documentary motion picture that would be shown late in the campaign," Gruening wrote.

It wasn't until the film was released the last two weeks before the primary that it was apparent that Gruening was in trouble. The *Daily News* endorsed him in the culmination of detailed endorsement editorials for all state and local offices. Larry believed it was incumbent upon a newspaper to let its readers know where it stood. He felt it was a key element of the press's public service to readers. If they trusted their newspaper, they should be able to count on it to do a thorough job of questioning and assessing candidates for public office. It was a newspaper's democratic duty to share that research with readers, encouraging them to vote and helping them to be more informed when they entered the voting booth. In a glowing editorial tribute to Gruening four days before the primary, the *Daily News* said, "We [endorse Gruening] without reservation. He has served Alaska with courage, wisdom, and compassion for a generation. We consider him well suited to continue representing the interests of our state, our nation, and all humanity. . . . Ernest Gruening has been in the forefront of all the good fights for Alaska."

Among the "good fights" Gruening had fought as the appointed territorial governor of Alaska and three-time elected senator were "the long and heroic battle for statehood, the establishment of the DEW line early warning system against the Soviet threat in 1949," and in Gruening's campaigns against the "pervasive Alaska shipping monopoly," and for "first class citizenship" for Alaska Natives, for improvement in their educational opportunities, development of a viable village economy, and a just settlement of Native land claims."

Capping the editorial was the key issue: the Vietnam War. It quoted Gruening's words on Vietnam: "We inherited this putrid mess from past administrations. . . . This is a fight that is not our fight. . . . The time to get out is now, before the further loss of American lives." Joe Rothstein and Bob Zelnick fought out the Gruening-Gravel conflict on the *Daily News* op-ed page. *Daily News* reporter Bob Zelnick was a passionate supporter of Gruening's campaign during the primary contest while reporting for the *Daily News*, while Joe Rothstein was an avowed fan of Gravel. They squared off against each other on the op-ed page the Sunday before the primary.

On primary day, August 27, the outcome was in doubt, seesawing throughout the night. When it was apparent the next morning that Gruening had lost, he was stunned and for several days refused to concede. Four days later he managed a polite concession statement, congratulating Gravel on his victory by about 2,000 votes. Elmer Rasmuson defeated Ted Stevens by an even narrower margin. The tally was Gravel 18,062, Gruening 15,979; Rasmuson 10,347, Stevens 9,145. Those close margins of victory underlined Larry's theory on the importance of endorsements. Even with the *Daily News'* meager 11,000 circulation, there was an opportunity to have a lot of influence on the state's direction.

After Gruening's loss, Bob Zelnick wrote in a signed column, "Ernest Gruening risked his political life on the great issue of Vietnam and lost it to a pollster, an advertising agency, and an actuarial table," pointing out that Gravel ran the most professional campaign in the history of Alaska. ". . . And of course there was the film . . . one half hour of it . . . pretentious, slick, commercial." It proved, said Zelnick, "the media approach works even in the wilderness." Clearly, even in those days before network television by satellite came to Alaska, election campaigns would never be the same again.

At the time of his concession statement, Gruening said he would support "the nominee of my party." But that would soon change, and

Daily News reporter/columnist Bob Zelnick would be instrumental in that change.

∾

Back in Anchorage in early fall, Larry engaged an old acquaintance and newspaper management consultant, Herman Silverman. A former publisher and owner of the *Sun* papers in Contra Costa County, California, Herman came to Anchorage in October and dug quickly and efficiently into an analysis of the total operation of the *Daily News.*

He had some complimentary things to say about our first year of publishing the paper in his report: "Your people on the staff have done a wonderful job in one year. You have taken a broken-down old newspaper, breathed life into it, and made it an important newspaper not only for your city but for your state. You are offering a fine editorial product. You have increased your advertising substantially. You have started to crack the food field. You have forced your competition to become a better newspaper." But the bad news was yet to come.

Asked by Larry to analyze whether the *Daily News* could succeed in the highly competitive environment, Silverman said in his report that he thought the odds were about 60 to 40 that it could succeed, based on a number of "ifs." They were tough "ifs": "If the *News* is guided by "damned fine management"; if labor costs are reduced by at least $150,000 during the coming year; if revenues in advertising and circulation are increased substantially; if other costs are reduced; and if you collect the revenues on what you sell." Unfortunately the past-due accounts receivable were always way too high.

Larry underlined and starred this sentence of the report: "Don't permit your department heads to overrule your business manager. Don't undermine him." The final two "ifs" were perhaps the most crucial: "If you can bring in additional working capital . . . to carry you over, you will have a chance to build the paper this coming year; and, most difficult of all, if you become a rough, tough manager and publisher. . . . You are going to have to do many things you do not like. You are going to have to be darn cold about firing and cutting costs. . . . You are not going to like firing people before Christmas." It was a harsh but honest appraisal.

The report concluded, "What are the alternatives to the above? You could close the doors tomorrow and lock up. You could sell to a group of local people or Atwood. You could sell to a publishing group. . . ." We weren't ready to seriously consider any of these dire alternatives, so we summoned all our energies to implement the Silverman recommendations.

In the report Silverman suggested one way to build revenues by starting a free shopper that would extend the *Daily News* circulation once a week beyond its meager 11,000. The shopper, named "Anchorage Shopper and Green Sheet," was distributed free once a week on Thursdays, with an initial run of 18,000. It was intended to give *Daily News* advertisers additional distribution, since all ads in the Green Sheet would also appear in the daily paper. The aim was to give advertisers access to every home in Anchorage—"saturation coverage," we said in promotion material—coverage even the *Anchorage Times* did not have.

The shopper was a worthy idea and did bring in more advertising for a while. But it was severely handicapped by chronic distribution problems. Delivering to every home in Anchorage, 32,000 of them, turned out to be more difficult than anticipated. We had to hire extra help to distribute the shopper, and advertisers began complaining they were finding packets of twenty-five or fifty undelivered shoppers in dumpsters around town.

In an effort to expose more people to the improved paper, the whole family pitched in on Thanksgiving morning to distribute thousands of extra copies of the large, ad-heavy Thanksgiving edition, the first paper the *Daily News* had ever printed on Thanksgiving. The union contracts of both papers provided for Thanksgiving and major holidays as days off for ITU printers. But Silverman convinced us that it was an ideal opportunity to secure pre-Christmas advertising and get a jump on the *Times*. Atwood would not produce a Thanksgiving paper because it would require him to pay the printers extra-high holiday wages.

On Thanksgiving morning, after getting the turkey into the oven, Larry and I, Ted, Kathy, and Barbie, were all down at the paper by 4:00 a.m. We fanned out in the dark to various areas to deliver newspapers. So did members of the news staff and other employees who volunteered. We delivered free papers all over town to nonsubscribers, complete with flyers on how to subscribe to the paper. The children and I hit Fairview, one of the poorest sections of town, where many Alaska Natives lived. It was an eye-opener for us. We had never seen the inside of the dingy three-story units, a ghetto of sorts, where many Natives lived.

Another Silverman target for reform was financial control. In an effort to shore up that end of things, Larry hired a new business manager, Bob Robertson, an earnest, competent young man with newspaper experience from Fairbanks. It would be Bob's task to preside over the needed staff cuts in order to reduce payroll by at least $12,000 a month as well as get some kind of handle on other expenditures. In announcing Robertson's imminent arrival, Larry said that Robertson would closely supervise business operations, but "he will have nothing to do with editorial." From his past experience as editor of big-city newspapers, Larry wanted no business-side meddling in editorial matters. The integrity of the newspaper depended on the editorial side being pristine, devoted solely to covering news and serving readers.

The trouble was, the newsroom needed management, too. The apparently indispensable Joe Rothstein had left unexpectedly due to an unfortunate difference of opinion with Larry over events surrounding the Alaska senatorial race. Silverman had convinced us that Larry must devote most of his time to stemming the financial losses. So Larry anointed Stan Abbott as executive editor. Young and inexperienced as Stan was, Larry rightly detected great talent, creativity, energy, trustworthiness, and perseverance in Stan.

In the newspaper business, election years tend to be times of high tension. As the nerve center of the community, all the crosscurrents of public opinion converge in the newsroom. Nineteen sixty-eight was a particularly high-pressure election year and an exciting but unsettling time at the *Anchorage Daily News*.

~

When Larry and I returned from the wars of Chicago, Joe Rothstein had wanted to see Larry right away to ask for a leave of absence. The article explaining Joe's departure ran on the front page of the paper, announcing that Rothstein had been granted a two-month leave of absence to be statewide campaign manager for Mike Gravel: "Rothstein will be completely disassociated from all news and editorial operations at the *Daily News* for the duration of the campaign." This was a blow to Larry. He had come to depend on Joe, not only for the news and editorial page, where he often pinch-hit for Larry, but also for help on the business side. Joe, who owned a small amount of *Daily News* stock he had been purchasing with payroll deductions, was vice president of the paper in addition to executive editor.

Meanwhile, columnist/reporter Bob Zelnick, who simply could not abide Gravel, had been busy. Two weeks after the election, he wrote a bylined news article on page one announcing a write-in campaign for Senator Gruening. The article proclaimed, "Students and faculty members from Alaska Methodist University and the University of Alaska have organized a committee to solicit petitions urging Senator Gruening to conduct a write-in campaign for re-election." The article went on to explain that in conceding defeat to Gravel, Gruening pledged to support the Democratic ticket in November but didn't specifically mention Gravel.

In the next week, articles appeared on the front page of the *Daily News* every day on the progress of the Gruening write-in campaign, which Gruening said he did not initiate but did not disavow. Attorney Allen McGrath had signed on with Gruening to establish the legality of the write-in. Gravel declared the growing write-in movement was "not a legal issue but a question of fairness." One day a prominent front-page article reported on a film starring Ernest Gruening that had appeared on a local TV station. Gruening was shown with a former candidate for the Democratic presidential nomination, George McGovern, charging that a crossover by Republicans into the Democratic primary had caused Gruening's loss.

These front-page articles on the Gruening write-in carried no byline. Some of them were written by Bob Zelnick, who was working feverishly behind the scenes for Ernest Gruening. Zelnick wrote speeches for Gruening while also writing election coverage for the *Daily News*. Today this would be a monumental ethical lapse, and Larry was aware that it was ethically questionable even then. But passions were running so high that he half closed his eyes to Zelnick's dual role.

Interviewed in his ABC News office in 1997, Zelnick said, "My efforts in that campaign were so much exaggerated. All I did was I drafted the original Gruening speech declaring his candidacy as a write-in candidate. I got together some people who were willing to contribute some seed money, including Allen McGrath. The other thing I did was I brought up a couple of advertising executives from California who were committed against the [Vietnam] War and they took things in hand. . . . I probably did some things . . . [that were] rather assertive in seeing the line blurred between opinion and reporting, which I wouldn't do today. . . ."

When Gruening announced he would indeed run a write-in campaign against Gravel and Rasmuson in the November election, Larry pulled Zelnick back from reporting that particular race. In an editor's note appended to an October 7 opinion column by Bob Zelnick, Larry said, "C. Robert Zelnick is a reporter on the staff of the *Daily News*. As a private citizen he participated in the discussions that led to Ernest Gruening's decision to enter the November 5 general election as a write-in candidate. . . . Mr. Zelnick is a vocal partisan of Senator Gruening. His column today is being published in keeping with our stated objective to offer a broad range of opinion on this page."

In the column, Zelnick expounded on the edgy relationship between Alaska's two incumbent senators, Gruening and Bartlett. Although they had worked together for years on Alaska issues in the U.S. Senate, Bartlett, a loyal party man, was supporting Gravel. Zelnick explained that he was told by a former Bartlett staffer that "Bob [Bartlett] has been waiting for ten years to put it to the old man, and this is a chance he never thought he'd live to see." Zelnick continued, "That explanation seems unduly harsh. Senator Bob is a bigger man than that. But a write-in campaign is essentially anti-establishment. Bartlett is one who owes everything he is and has accomplished to the Establishment."

While the *Daily News* was preoccupied with the contentious Democratic senatorial race, the *Anchorage Times* was running banner headlines about Jackie Kennedy's upcoming wedding to Aristotle Onassis and a $1 million bid for an Alaska oil lease. Nixon running mate Spiro

Agnew made a one-day campaign visit to Alaska. As the November 5 general election date loomed, the legal impediment to the Gruening write-in still hadn't been solved. The Alaska state superior court ruled it inconsistent with the Alaska Constitution and lawyer Allen McGrath rushed to the State Supreme Court, which overturned the lower court and approved the write-in on October 22, just two weeks before the election. But valuable time had been lost in the uncertainty, and Gruening was behind in raising money and advertising promotion.

The contest between Republican Rasmuson and Democrat Gravel had become increasingly acrimonious, too. Gravel campaign radio commercials saturated the airwaves with tapes of Ted Stevens' voice strategically excerpted from statements he made about Rasmuson during his unsuccessful primary campaign. "Gutter attacks," screamed Jack White, chairman of the Rasmuson campaign. "These last-minute smear tactics are showing Mike Gravel for what he really is—an overambitious, young, immature man, who is eager to get where he wants by any means. He is no longer the nice, quiet, sincere, young man his film portrays him to be."

Elmer Rasmuson said, "It's like fighting a ghost. There are two Mike Gravels, the real one and the imaginary one" [referring to the new version of the Napolitan film, a reworking of the Gravel primary campaign film, "A Man for Alaska"]. Rasmuson took to calling him "Mike the Myth."

A week before the election Larry wrote the *Daily News* Senate endorsement editorial headlined "We'll Cast our Vote (A Write-In) for the Senator." He wrote, "Our advocacy is based on one exceedingly simple premise: we have in Ernest Gruening a superlative Senator, an exceptional human being. [He] has never compromised principle for popularity, he has not stooped to expediency, he has not been afraid to lay his political career on the line by raising his voice in dissent." Larry also, unenthusiastically, endorsed Humphrey in the presidential race against Nixon.

The *Daily News* also published one of Larry's favorite attention-getters, a "Battle Page": a face-off in which each of the candidates had his last-minute say on the major races accompanied by face-to-face photographs.

At the eleventh hour, Senator Eugene McCarthy flew into Anchorage to make an appeal for Gruening. And the same day, President Johnson called a dramatic pre-election bombing halt in Vietnam, which earned a wood-type banner in the *Daily News.*

Monday, November 4, the day before the election, the *Daily News* ran two exclusive polls, one by Harris and one by Gallup, which showed Nixon just barely ahead of Humphrey, the election neck-and-neck. It also reported a "Target" debate between the three Alaska senatorial candidates. "Democrat Mike Gravel was relaxed and dignified, Republican Elmer Rasmuson was eager to point out differences between his positions and Gravel's. And write-in candidate Ernest Gruening lost few opportunities to lambast both."

But Gruening's was a lost cause. Gravel won over both Rasmuson and Gruening handily, carrying every section of the state. Despite the over- whelming defeat, Gruening won 19 percent of the vote with his write-in, an impressive accomplishment for a candidate who wasn't even on the ballot. In the battle for Alaska's lone U.S. House seat, Republican Howard Pollock trounced Nick Begich in his first try for national office.

Nationwide, Nixon edged out Humphrey in a squeaker. In Alaska he won by only 500 votes, and at *Daily News* press time on election night, it looked like an electoral vote tie might throw the presidential election into the House of Representatives. Election nights were special at the *Daily News.* Larry liked to preside personally over the play of election news. He cleared off the first six pages of the paper for the returns and analysis, explaining in a note on page one how the paper had been rearranged and where readers could find their relocated favorite items.

The children and I were always on hand far into the wee hours on election nights. The entire staff, sports page, women's page editors, some- times even spouses, were pressed into duty to pull together statewide elec- tion results, put them in coherent order, and draw some conclusions. Then, when the paper was finally "put to bed," Larry would break out champagne and we would have a party with the whole staff, while we waited for the first papers to come off the press. There would be an atmosphere of jubilance and accomplishment, a sense of "we actually did it against the odds" that faced a tiny staff: poor communications and limited news sources. Larry congratulated everybody for an extraor- dinary job.

Larry and I usually managed to spend part of election nights at "election central" in the Anchorage Westward Hotel ballroom. There would be a huge board stretched across the back of the room with the latest election returns continually updated. Candidates would hold parties in suites in the hotel and around eleven o'clock, or as soon as the winners became clear, candidate and entourage, winners and losers, would sweep into the ballroom. Democrats and Republicans, supporters, sworn enemies, and hangers-on would all crush into one room. There would be an open bar and convivial atmosphere. Occasionally there was a bloody nose when a frustrated partisan squared off against his opponent.

On election night in 1966, before we had purchased the *Daily News*, Larry and I attended one of these free-for-all gatherings for the first time. Larry was transfixed by the scene and the action. Having presided over election coverage in San Francisco and Chicago, he couldn't believe the way Alaskans all mixed together in the same room on the crucial night, after all the bitterness and name-calling. I think it was one of the things that confirmed his desire for a newspaper in Alaska.

But after the election, bitterness lingered at the *Daily News*. In a letter to Larry written the day before the election, Joe Rothstein resigned from the paper, because "the *News* committed and you condoned acts which I believed to be gross violations of journalistic ethics. . . . First . . . is your handling of the Senate race. I consider your defense of Bob Zelnick's activities beyond comprehension, and I find no mitigation in the fact that he was pulled off the Senate story. I know from our conversation that you saw no ethical problem. For the paper's political reporter to take a central role in organizing and managing one of the candidates in a race is wrong. . . . Your denunciation of Mike Gravel as a celluloid product, your failure to find any redeeming virtue or value in him, I take as a personal insult. . . . You are advocating a politics of despair. . . . You will lose this election no matter who wins because you are against everyone and for no one. And the system will have to continue on without you." The letter continued with this tone for two and a half pages.

Although the letter was addressed to Larry, I replied. Some excerpts from that response are, "Dear Joe, Larry brought home your letter, of course, and I read it with sorrow. I know him—he won't answer it or attempt to defend his position. Nor am I going to try to do that. It isn't such a tremendous surprise that you would be leaving, Joe, but the feeling and tone of it is dismaying to me. You were my first boss. What little I know of newspapering I first learned from you. And a little over a year ago the three of us set our course with such high hopes. . . . I felt that we were proceeding with a remarkably solid front, that we were three and not two and that it was indeed OUR endeavor, three of us.

"That it should have come to this in the course of two and a half years, to the incredibly harsh and condemning words of your letter, Joe, is stupefying. Certainly we claim no monopoly on righteousness or on correct judgments. Larry is as likely to make a mistake as the next fellow. In this first year of owning the *News* we have probably made considerably more than our share. As you well know, the pressure has been colossal.

"I don't want to claim clairvoyance but I told Larry the night you called us in Chicago to ask for a leave for the campaign that this would be the end of our relationship and of your time at the paper. He didn't believe me. But it seemed to me for some time that the political Joe and the newspapering Joe were at war and that this request for a leave meant that the political Joe had won. Which is fine, although you will be missed, not only by us but by the community.

"I happen to agree with you about Larry's allowing Bob Zelnick to handle the Senate race while promoting the Gruening write-in. I thought at the time it was a mistake in judgment, the same kind of mistake I think you made when you asked and received permission from Larry to attend the southcentral Democratic convention as a delegate while remaining executive editor of the *Daily News*. Larry always found it difficult to say no."

I went on to detail some other instances where I felt Joe, too, had crossed the line separating journalism and politics, and told Joe I thought he had greatly escalated Larry's opposition to Gravel. There had been considerable amount of negative information about Gravel that we had and had not used, but Joe didn't know that. I concluded the letter, "That you should want to leave the *News* is understandable enough. Frankly I think you and Larry are just too much alike to make a go of it. You have the same strengths and the same weaknesses. But that it should end on such a note of hostility . . . is to me a small personal tragedy."

A front-page story in the paper announced Rothstein's resignation, quoting Larry: "Joe has made an immeasurable contribution to the growth and development of the *Daily News* over the years. He is an immensely able and talented newspaperman and he devoted his energies selflessly to the newspaper. In resigning Joe leaves much of himself right here because he put so much of himself into the paper. He will be sorely missed, and all of his colleagues on the *Daily News* wish him well."

A few days later Gravel announced that Joe Rothstein would go to Washington to become Gravel's administrative assistant. He would be Gravel's "chief aid and advisor and would be responsible for the management of his Senate office and its operations."

Twenty-nine years later I had a conversation with Joe Rothstein about the *Daily News*, Larry, and Gravel. Except for some correspondence winding up Joe's small stock interest in the *Daily News* and a brief chance meeting on a Washington street, we had had no contact in the intervening years. I saw him over lunch in Washington, D.C., where he had lived for many years. He reminisced about the "Village People" series, which he had conceived and directed in 1966: "I consider that one of the high water marks of my life," Joe said. "I wanted to do a series on who the Natives really were. We ran eleven days, sold out every day, published it in book form, and went through three editions. People were hungry for this kind of information. What I never expected was what it did to the Native community. It put an enormous amount of propulsion behind the land claims, getting them together. At the time I felt that if I never did anything else in my life, I had done that.

"I look at my experience with the *News* as a once-in-a-lifetime event, where essentially there were no rules, no restraints, where a lot of good people got together to do good things. I think Alaska has to be better off today because you kept the *News* going. It became Alaska's voice instead of Atwood."

Then we turned to Joe's acrimonious departure. "I can't tell you how terrible I felt about that," he said. "I felt we had all shared so much; it was so intense and I hated to see it all come apart like that." I asked Joe how he felt about Gravel with the benefit of hindsight. Did he misread Gravel or did Gravel change? He said, "Both. I thought he wanted to come to

Washington to be a senator for Alaska. After we had been here a while, I discovered he really wanted to come to Washington to run for president. It was a constant source of tension between us. All the time he was trying to raise money. It was a very uncomfortable situation. I left him and we stayed cordial for years. Then it got to be embarrassing because people associated me with Gravel. Barney [Gottstein] and Larry [Carr] felt the same way, so we organized an independent committee in 1980 and ran independent commercials attacking Gravel in the primary campaign that let Clark [Gruening, Ernest Gruening's grandson] beat him in the primary election."

What an irony! Gravel beaten for his third term in the Senate by Ernest Gruening's grandson, a defeat mostly caused by attack ads paid for by his staunchest early supporters. In the 1980 general election, Republican Frank Murkowski defeated young Gruening. Gravel, in his twelve years in the Senate, had established a reputation as a grandstander, who espoused many wild and grandiose schemes such as a domed city at the base of Mount McKinley. He had read the Pentagon Papers on the floor of the Senate (an act that most people saw as theatrical but which Rothstein still believes was a noble act in the public interest). The crowning blow was when Gravel nominated himself for vice president on the floor of the Democratic convention. Joe said he went to the movies that night to avoid seeing Gravel make a fool of himself. "I stayed away from the TV coverage as long as I could. It was midnight when I turned the TV on, and there he was being interviewed . . . totally out of control."

Joe turned away from Gravel to a successful political consulting career and then started an international Internet company. Two of his investors were Larry Carr and Barney Gottstein.

But the end of the tumultuous 1968 general election wasn't the end of political tumult in Alaska that year. Governor Wally Hickel took center stage at the end of 1968. Hickel, elected governor in 1966, was a larger-than-life Alaskan character in his own right. He was a big man with big ideas, a can-do guy, who often bypassed the rules and forged ahead just to get things done. When the permitting process for a pipeline haul road became too arduous, he began to carve an ice road on the tundra for access to Prudhoe Bay. The road was stopped by the federal government, and the partially built road became known as the Hickel Highway. In his third year as governor, he had served as one of Richard Nixon's ten surrogate candidates, making speeches around the country for Nixon.

There had been speculation in the national press that Hickel was on Nixon's shortlist for secretary of the interior. Larry and I, on a brief trip to Seattle in December, spent a night at Seattle's Olympic Hotel and found ourselves down the hall from Hickel, who was returning from the Republican Governors Conference in Palm Springs. It hadn't been announced that Hickel would be in Seattle and we suspected something was up. We tried to worm it out of him. "I'm here for some Christmas shopping," Hickel claimed. But in reality he was waiting for the confirming call from Nixon to head for Washington and the announcement of his appointment as interior secretary.

Thursday, December 12, was another one of those blockbuster Alaska news days: two big black headlines dominated page one. At the top of the page, the jarring announcement of the demise of Alaska's junior senator, "Bartlett is Dead." In the middle of the page, "Hickel in the Cabinet." Senator E. L. "Bob" Bartlett, the much-beloved junior senator from Alaska, had been ailing from heart problems but had seemed to be on the mend. Ed Isenson, Bartlett's administrative assistant, a former political reporter at the *Daily News*, made the announcement. There was immediate excited speculation about who the governor would appoint to fill out Bartlett's Senate term. Former state senator Carl Brady, a close Hickel crony, was rumored to be Hickel's top choice, with Ted Stevens, Elmer Rasmuson, and Vide Bartlett, the deceased senator's widow, mentioned prominently. Vide Bartlett would have been a sentimental choice, but she was a Democrat. With a Republican governor doing the appointing, the new senator would very likely be a Republican, the first Republican to serve in the U.S. Senate from Alaska.

The day after Bartlett's death, Bob Zelnick wrote a front-page piece for the *Daily News*, bannered as "Exclusive," stating, "It now appears certain that former state Senator Carl F. Brady will be named" to fill the Senate vacancy. Brady was a prominent Anchorage businessman. He had started the highly successful Era Helicopter Company, which he had recently sold, but he had stayed on as manager. Zelnick reported that

Hickel and Brady had conferred at the Hyatt House in Seattle, and that Hickel had long ago made a solid commitment to Brady that if there were a Senate vacancy, he would get the nod.

Reaction to the Zelnick piece was swift in Anchorage. Most political insiders, although they knew Brady had the inside track, worried that he was not qualified to be a U.S. senator. Hickel dragged out the decision until the day before Christmas, when he finally announced that his choice for the Senate was not Carl Brady but Ted Stevens.

Hickel now claims that Stevens was his choice all along, but that he had to square it with Brady, to whom he had, indeed, made a commitment. Hickel's promise to Brady grew out of Brady's fervent support for Hickel during his run for governor in 1966. On the very day that Bartlett died, and Hickel was in Washington being presented to the world on television along with Nixon's other cabinet choices, Hickel says, "This porter came up and said Bartlett just died. So I told the president-elect, 'Senator Bartlett just died.' And he said to me, 'What are you going to do?' Three people came to mind that quick, and I said, 'Elmer Rasmuson, Carl Brady, and Ted Stevens.' He said, 'Do you have the courage to appoint Ted Stevens?' "

Hickel says he knew then that he wanted to appoint Stevens but that he had made a promise to Carl Brady and he wouldn't appoint Ted unless Carl agreed. "Ted was not a supporter of mine. He didn't even support me when I ran for governor. . . . Ted's a survivor, not a friend, and that was best for the country. The best thing for me would have been to appoint Elmer if I wanted economic interests, or Carl Brady, a forever friend, but I said the best thing I can do for the state was Stevens." Another factor, undoubtedly, was the upcoming Hickel confirmation hearings. Both Nixon and Hickel knew that Stevens was a sharp lawyer and a fighter. From his stint as solicitor general, Stevens was familiar with the ways of Washington, while Rasmuson and Brady were not. Stevens would be a big help in Hickel's battle for confirmation by the Senate.

Ted Stevens and his wife, Ann, were in Mazatlan, Mexico, on vacation, when he received a collect telegram from Hickel saying that Senator Bartlett had just died and was Stevens interested in an appointment to succeed him? The Stevenses flew back to Anchorage to find that Hickel had narrowed his choice down to Carl Brady and Stevens. After a wild series of meetings with Republican leaders and supporters in Anchorage, all trying to influence the decision, Hickel invited both Brady and Stevens to sit down with him at his house on Loussac Drive overlooking Cook Inlet. After a tense pause, Stevens says that Brady broke the silence: "If I were you, Wally, I'd appoint him." "That was it," Stevens said. "Carl and I had been roommates when we served in the state legislature. We each signed a dollar bill and tore it in half and said we are going to remain friends, and that this would be the symbol of our friendship."

The political landscape in the nation had shifted during that momentous year, 1968. Lyndon Johnson's dropping out of the race set the stage for the contentious Nixon years. The assassinations of Martin Luther King Jr. and Bobby Kennedy and the riots at the Democratic convention in Chicago launched a new era of confrontation, violence, and fear nationally. Alaska's political terrain had shifted from a benign Democratic leadership to a split Congressional delegation tilting Republican, with a Republican congressman, one Democratic senator, Gravel, and a dynamic new Republican senator, Stevens.

It had been a tragic, climactic year. And by the end of the year, the *Daily News* itself would be fighting for its life.

7

On his first day on the job in Anchorage, Bob Zelnick was assigned to do a story about the arrest of a young man who had stabbed his girlfriend. Fortunately it had not been fatal. Former lawyer Zelnick describes arriving back in the newsroom from his visit to the crime scene, breaking out his yellow legal pad, and starting to write. Managing editor Stan Abbott ambled over to his desk and said, "What are you *doing?*" Zelnick replied, "I'm writing a draft of my story." Stan said, "You're writing a draft of your story *longhand?*" Zelnick said, "Yeah, I don't type." Stan said, "Oh, yes you do," and rolled a piece of typing paper into Zelnick's typewriter, saying "Of course you type, everybody types." Zelnick recalls, "So I started typing."

Zelnick may have been a reluctant typist, but at reporting he was a tiger. He became our best investigative reporter, political reporter, and legal writer. In the short year and a half Bob was with the paper, he won an American Bar Association prestigious Gavel Award and caused us a libel suit that dragged on for years costing over $50,000. In his valuable prize-winning series, "Justice in the Bush," Zelnick had told of a Nome taxi company that delivered liquor to minors. It turned out there was only one cab company in Nome and it wasn't doing it—individually owned Nome cabs were the booze deliverers. "It was inartistically worded," explained Zelnick later, "but not in any way malicious." Eventually the suit filed by the Nome cab company was thrown out and never reached a jury.

Zelnick, who went on to become a top-level ABC News correspondent and a journalism professor at Boston University, was a bit of a bull in a china shop during his first months in Anchorage. But his aggressive reporting was a spark plug that helped put the *Daily News* on the map. He won the paper its first major national award, and he stirred up the town by digging for the news behind the news. Larry sent him to Oregon and

Los Angeles to cover Bobby Kennedy's primary campaign for president, and dispatched him to Washington to cover the scrappy Hickel confirmation hearings. He wrote about state politics from Juneau, about a complex lawsuit against a dentist whose patients tended to die in the chair, about the controversy over the pipeline route, and extensively about Native land claims issues.

In one political assignment, Zelnick interviewed a conservative Democratic candidate for the State House from Anchorage named Claude Snitzler. Larry wanted recommendations for candidate endorsements in the election. When the *Daily News* published its list of preferred candidates, Snitzler wasn't on it. Poor Snitzler was so angry he sat down to write a furious letter to the editor, had a heart attack, and died at his desk. Characteristically, Larry felt wretched about it and asked Zelnick to write an editorial, saying something nice about Claude Snitzler.

Bob remembers, "He wasn't apologetic about not endorsing Snitzler. He felt there was some little thing we could do at the time . . . that good men seek public office, and the fact we don't endorse someone doesn't detract from their value in running." That was typical of Larry. He believed in some innate goodness in each of his fellow men. "Larry felt he had to listen to everybody, sometimes to excess, that . . . every person is important," Zelnick said. "The things Larry gave me that stayed with me were, number one, a deep recognition of the public service aspect of journalism, and two, the fact that however strong one's ego, the reporter isn't the story. Larry was a very fine human being. . . . I was ennobled by my association with him."

Most of the newsroom felt that way about Larry. Six-foot-five, soft-spoken Tom Brown came from UPI in Helsinki to the *Daily News* so he could work with Larry. In a retrospective conversation about the *Daily News* of the late sixties, Brown said, "This was a place if you got on a story you could actually pursue it without someone worrying whether it was going to . . . make somebody mad, take a week to do instead of two hours. There was the opportunity to dig into things." Brown spoke of how news was what Larry cared about and about his talent for picking good reporters and getting them to work "for what was not high wages," an understatement.

CHAPTER 7

~

There was an extraordinary camaraderie at the *Daily News* during those years. Staff members spent virtually all their waking hours together, and those hours extended far into the night. After the paper was "put to bed" around midnight, they would all go together to the *Daily News* bar of choice, usually the 515 Club or the China Doll, a strip joint that had an upstairs room dubbed the "Upper Yukon River Press Club." Managing editor Tom Gibboney would stay at the paper until midnight when the press rolled and then he would bring papers down to the rest of the group at the China Doll. "Then the night's discussions would begin. That was life at the *News* as we knew it, a wild kind of place," said Gibboney.

Because of the late-night schedule that most of the staff worked and because they were mostly either single or in unhappy marriages, the after-work bar and bartenders played a major role in *Daily News* life. Jiggs was the bartender at the China Doll, and when he later moved to the 515 Club, the group followed him there. "We did our banking at the China Doll," Gibboney said. "We were the consistent daily customers there. We bounced checks, and Jiggs would hold our checks until we got paid. Then we'd pick them up and do the same thing the next week. Jiggs could get you anything, if you know what I mean," an oblique reference to the ubiquitous pot of the late sixties. " He was the kind of character we liked to think we were hanging around with. You could go up this little flight of stairs. Jiggs had to push a button behind the bar to let you up there. It was a bleak room with a pool table. You could smoke pot up there."

Gibboney admits that the staff enjoyed "the seamy side of life." He thought it was the young staff's "vision of what a hard-bitten newsman did. We were the late-night guys. When you got off work you wanted to do something, and it seemed the bar scene in Anchorage was all there was to do. A little pot smoking, and we occasionally went to those after-hour gambling clubs, not very often because we didn't have the money and none of us were that big into gambling."

In late February 1969, a bright young woman, fresh from her master's in journalism at the University of Missouri, joined the staff. Jeanne

Montague, newly married to Harvard-educated Dick Montague, who worked at *Alaska* magazine, drove the highway to Anchorage. Jeanne promptly looked for a reporting job. Dick Montague simply assumed his journalist wife would work for the *Anchorage Times*, since the Atwoods' social circle quickly became the Montagues'. But to her conservative, straight-laced husband's discomfort, Jeanne applied to the *Daily News* rather than the *Times* and Larry, recognizing high talent, snatched her up immediately.

"I couldn't stand the *Times*," Jeanne recalls. "They were so pompous. I read their editorials and they were so off the mark from everything I believed, I said I cannot work for them. I went down to Post Road to a completely different operation, walked in, and felt completely at home, like this is where I'm meant to be . . . wearing this fancy pink outfit that looked like Greenwich."

Jeanne did general assignment reporting, feature writing, a stint as an editorial writer and as Sunday editor. "Larry knew how to nurture talent," Jeanne said. "The *Daily News* was the alternative press of its day. People were fired up, and wanted to make a difference. I felt all the time that what I wrote about could absolutely make a difference in the state. We pushed the envelope, took on causes like gun control, the environment. In Alaska those were quite radical causes. There was a collection of brilliance there that was pretty amazing . . . Zelnick, Allan Frank. . . ." Jeanne threw herself wholeheartedly into the *Daily News* culture, working half the night and playing the rest of the night with other staff members at the 515 and the China Doll. "I still amaze people," Jeanne said, "when I tell them I regularly ate lunch at a topless bar. I don't remember drinking a lot, I was this wide-eyed hanger-on. Most of it was productive journalism."

Predictably, within a few years, Jeanne's marriage to Dick Montague was finished. While she was trying to separate from Dick, Jeanne stayed at my house, hid her car in our garage so Dick Montague, who was prowling all over town looking for her, wouldn't find her. Eventually Jeanne married the divorced Stan Abbott, and as a *Daily News* couple, they would have a major impact on journalism in Alaska for a dozen more years.

Then there was the *Daily News* Flying Club. It was organized by sports editor Bill Fox, who managed to collect enough cash to buy a small older airplane. It was a single-engine, two-person Cessna, and only a few staff members dared go up in it. Tom Brown went up, and press foreman Ken Cope flew it a lot. Some took flying lessons. Larry and I joined, paying part of the tab, but we didn't ride in the plane. And the flying club eventually dissolved, without mishap.

Like many other staffers over the years, Tom Gibboney came to the *Daily News* in stages. He arrived in Alaska in the military, after graduating from the University of Florida and being drafted. He moonlighted at the *Daily News* in the evenings at the end of his day job in the information office at Fort Richardson. He remembers the paper when Joe Rothstein was editor: "He had big fat pencils behind his ear. It was a true-grit type of newsroom, real grimy, small, no windows, no air, with a little window to the back shop."

Gibboney describes how they all loved working with Larry when Larry became editor. Sometimes he'd come in and run the desk. "That was a great thrill for me; kind of scary, too. Larry gave me some compliments sometimes and sometimes he'd throw stuff back. He'd have his bowtie undone, his white shirt, that whole image, always working on that pipe even if it wasn't lit." Tom Gibboney remembered Tom Brown gathering all the facts from the radio wire and whatever source he could find and crafting beautiful, coherent stories. The momentous occasion of the first men walking on the moon was also the first-ever satellite television broadcast of a news event carried live in Alaska. Brown wrote the story from the TV screen as it unfolded. The *Daily News* had its own moonwalk story, not just the AP account. A *Daily News* photographer came to our house on Madison Way to take the front-page photo off our TV screen, which was larger than the one we had at the paper.

It was Gibboney's regular chore to receive the daily packet that came from Chicago by air express. One of Larry's pals at the *Chicago Sun-Times* would see that a daily package of news photos and wire copy was assembled and placed on the Northwest Airlines nonstop flight from Chicago to Anchorage, so we had fresh material that the *Anchorage Times* could not possibly have—even though it was able to afford the regular Associated Press A-wire, the one with coherent newspaper stories unlike our miserable radio wire.

Gibboney remembered how Larry was always looking for, and often found, people in the community who could articulate issues in print. He was dedicated to presenting issues from all sides, even viewpoints he personally loathed. "He stood out in journalism for Alaska because Atwood didn't have that kind of vision. He couldn't see anything beyond the bank."

While the Atwoods may have focused heavily on the bank (after all, Evangeline Atwood's family owned the biggest bank in the state), the bank and monetary affairs were way down the list of priorities for Larry. And by early 1969 we began paying for his inattention to financial detail.

Although the Silverman report had suggested some ways out of our financial quagmire, it had not solved the problem. Some of Silverman's remedies, such as the Green Sheet advertising supplement, actually added to expenses. We were constantly looking for additional investment, and one day two people walked into the office who might have an answer. They were lawyer Bob Goldberg and his prominent father, former United Nations Ambassador and Supreme Court Justice Arthur Goldberg. They announced that they wanted to invest in the *Daily News* because they admired the courageous liberal stands the paper was taking in the face of so much obvious opposition.

Arthur Goldberg was a bristling package of brilliance, arrogance, and liberal idealism. His only son, Bob, had failed the bar exam in Washington, D.C., a humiliating experience for the son of a Supreme Court justice. Bob and his Scottish wife, Barbara, a Harvard Ph.D. in psychology, elected to move to Anchorage to begin a new life. It was evident early on that the younger Goldberg's decision to transplant to Alaska had everything to do with moving as far away as possible from a spectacularly successful, famous, and difficult father. But, at the same time, there was a strong mutual affection between father and son.

We hit it off right away with Bob and Barbara, and were excited by the prospect of having them as *Daily News* investors. We all shared a passion for the cause of Alaska Natives' land claims and a deep concern for the plight of the underdog. And it certainly wouldn't hurt to have an investor in the *Daily News* of the stature of Arthur Goldberg—even though the initial amount would be just $10,000.

Bob Goldberg's path to Alaska was circuitous. It had started at age nineteen when he had a summer job at the *Chicago Daily News* relocating its library or "morgue." He had been told by Eddie Lahey, a revered *Daily News* writer and close friend of the senior Goldberg's, that he should "watch Larry Fanning [then *Chicago Daily News* editor]. He's the real thing." Lahey had told Bob that if he ever had a chance to work for Larry Fanning, he should do so immediately. But Bob had succumbed to the power of his father's influence and sought to become a lawyer instead, graduating from law school in 1967, and clerking for the chief justice of the U.S. Court of Appeals for a year in Washington.

At the low point of his law career, flunking the bar exam, Bob had come to Alaska with the idea that if he couldn't pass the bar exam, he might move to a newspaper career. But after much study and anguish, he did pass the Illinois bar and subsequently the one in Alaska, so the die was cast toward law.

There were other attractions to Alaska. Unlike most immigrants from Russia, when Goldberg's grandfather had come to the United States from Russia, he had crossed the Pacific to Alaska. Bob wanted to find out why. Then he had found the Alaska Native issue compelling: What the future for Alaska Natives entailed, how they would be treated by the government, were all unresolved issues in 1968. That put Alaska on the cutting edge of social justice, issues of deep concern to the Goldbergs.

So when Arthur Goldberg was invited to speak at Anchorage's Alaskan of the Year dinner, which was to honor Wally Hickel, he accepted. Bob remembers that his father was met at the airport by Yule Kilcher, a well-known Alaskan homesteader and character (and much later grandfather to superstar pop singer Jewel). Kilcher had with him a group of Alaska Natives to greet the former U.N. Ambassador in costume and song. As part of his Alaskan of the Year speech, Goldberg gave a strong plea for Native land claims and the future of Alaska's Natives. As a result, the leaders of the Alaska Federation of Natives (AFN), Emil Notti and John Borbridge, approached him to become the AFN lawyer and spokesman for the upcoming land claims battle in the U.S. Congress. Goldberg agreed, and for a few weeks the Goldbergs were invested not only in the *Daily News* but also in one of the hottest issues ever to confront

Alaska, sending associates from his high-powered law firm in New York to Anchorage for meetings with Native leaders. The stakes were not small. At that time, the Department of Interior was recommending a settlement of some 10 million acres of land and $500 million spread over twenty-five years—and the eventual settlement would range far beyond that.

Unfortunately, fuses were short on both sides, and the arrangement with Goldberg didn't last long. Native leaders were not united. What had appeared to Goldberg to be a generous offer—a nominal retainer fee with a percentage of any final settlement—was attacked by longtime Native lawyers out of jealousy and concern for their own fees. Some felt they were being left out of the strategic discussions.

Jack Hendrickson, attorney for the village of Unalakleet, sent a telegram saying that "the village disapproves of the contract with Goldberg because it 'does not offer adequate protection for Natives.'" And Seattle lawyer Fred Paul, a Tlingit Indian who represented the Arctic Slope Native Association, criticized Goldberg for not consulting regional attorneys before preparing his presentation to the Senate Committee on Regional Affairs. He blasted Goldberg for concentrating on the human and social reasons for a generous claims settlement without mentioning the legal basis for a settlement.

As the Native leaders split on the Goldberg matter, the *Anchorage Times* seemed to be reveling in the dissension with huge headlines. Arthur Goldberg's pride was badly hurt and his famous temper flared. In mid-May 1969, he resigned as chief counsel to the Alaska Federation of Natives for land claims, citing derogatory letters and telegrams from "certain lawyers purporting to represent affiliates of the Alaska Federation of Natives." In his message, Goldberg said that the attacks were "entirely lacking in the respect owing to one who has served our country in three of its highest offices."

After that Arthur Goldberg withdrew somewhat from the scene. But Bob and his family settled into Anchorage for a long career in the law, representing Alaska Native corporations that were eventually formed as a result of the passage of the Alaska Native Claims Settlement Act in 1971. And they continued their investment in the *Daily News*, until we were forced to buy them out several years later. A year after the AFN debacle,

Arthur Goldberg ran for governor of New York. On election night, Bob and his family were at his side in a New York hotel. Goldberg lost by a huge margin, and Larry and I, monitoring the election from the newsroom at the *Daily News*, picked up the phone to offer Arthur our condolences. Bob later told us that ours was the only call his father received that night. People don't call a proud and accomplished man when he loses an election.

By late summer of 1969, the stacks of unpaid bills at the *News* were mounting higher. Because there were some improvements in both advertising and circulation, and because we were beginning to build a more competent staff in the business departments, it was difficult for Larry, impossible to trim back the staff and make the drastic payroll cuts Silverman had advocated.

The economy of Alaska was a big factor, too. The North Slope oil boom was just beginning to gather force, with daily excitement in both papers about the upcoming state oil lease sale to be held in September. Fantastic estimates of the oil prosperity just around the corner, of doubling or tripling the population of Anchorage, were enthusiastically fueled by the *Anchorage Times*. It seemed like a poor time to be pulling back and laying off people. Larry and I dug deeply into what remained in our own pockets. I sold the First National Bank of Joliet stock I had inherited from what had been my father's bank. We sold a piece of downtown property that the Browns had bought for a potential new plant. It was easy to sell property in central Anchorage then. The Hunt family of the Hunt Oil Company from Houston, Texas, was buying up every piece that they could lay hands on, providing the price was right. Apparently the Hunts saw Anchorage as the next Houston! We negotiated for a new telephone book contract, since producing the phone book was the one aspect of our business that was actually profitable. Before taking off with the children for a three-week vacation in Spain the end of June 1970, I managed to negotiate a $15,000 loan from a local bank to pay some of the bills while we were gone. Another very helpful $25,000 investment came from my mother, Katherine James.

The purpose of the trip was to provide some desperately needed rest and relaxation for Larry and to show the kids some of the glories of Europe. It was easy in those years to fly to Europe from Anchorage. All the major airlines stopped in Anchorage on their journeys across the pole from Asia to Europe. We chose the Costa del Sol in southern Spain for our beach time because it was cheap. For seven of us, a beautiful cottage overlooking the sea on the grounds of a lovely hotel cost us $7 per day per person! Ted took along an Anchorage East High School friend, Gid Palmer, and Larry's daughter, Judith Hunt, came along, too.

But it was soon apparent to me that Larry wasn't at all himself during the vacation. Usually voluble and full of life, Larry was sometimes withdrawn, taciturn, and argumentative. Something was deeply wrong. Soon after our return I found out what it was. The *Daily News* was in far deeper financial trouble than Larry had ever let on to me. It was characteristic that he wanted to protect me from the dimensions of the problem. Payroll taxes had gone unpaid for some time and there was no money to bring them up to date. The money we had raised just before departure had all gone to pay some back bills, but bills had continued to pile up. We had barely managed the payroll itself.

Larry had always been adamantly opposed to involving the kids in the paper financially. Even though Ted, who had just turned seventeen, had trusts held in a Chicago bank worth many millions of dollars, Larry felt that the newspaper was our decision and our risk. It had become a crusade for us as a family, along with the staff members who felt like family. And we had come to believe that if we were to abandon the newspaper scene to the *Anchorage Times* alone, it would have a devastating effect on the development of the state. Only the perspective that favored the military establishment, the downtown business culture, the oil industry, and excessive development would have a voice in Alaska. Our paper was the lone expression in the state of concern for the environment, or the plight of the Natives, or of the disenfranchised.

In July the *Daily News* began publishing one of our proudest achievements, a thirty-two part series that ran on consecutive days examining, in depth, the potential effects of the 800-mile hot-oil pipeline that was being designed to bring the oil from Prudhoe Bay to Valdez. Tom Brown, who got much of his information from two permafrost experts at the University of Alaska, reported in the lengthy series that the initial design for a nearly all-buried pipeline wasn't going to work. The line would be traversing hundreds of miles of permanently frozen ground (permafrost), and the oil, warm from the ground, would cause the permafrost to melt, threatening the structural integrity of the pipe, possibly causing the pipe to break, and very likely flooding large areas of tundra with oil.

There had been a good deal of environmental writing in other publications about the impact of the pipeline on wildlife, but we were the first, in Alaska at least, to write about the safety of the pipeline itself. The paper received much praise for the series from the environmental community nationally. But the Anchorage business community was wild. Anything that might delay or stop the pipeline would cut into the upcoming oil boom. No matter how true or how justified the reporting, they were vehemently opposed. Even more advertisers boycotted the *Daily News,* calling us "anti-pipeline" and "anti-development."

So as the financial noose was tightening around our necks, we were more convinced than ever that the fearless reporting of the *Daily News* was essential to the future of Alaska. Ted thought so, too. He had moved from his job in the back shop as operator of the Scan-a-Graver, where at one point he had considered joining the union (ITU) because he liked working there so much—until he discovered he would have to be an apprentice for six years. He then worked in the circulation department, undertaking a wide range of assignments, and by summer he was assistant to the sports editor, writing, editing, and enjoying seeing his byline in the paper. He was deeply committed to the causes of the paper and to the fight against Bob Atwood and the *Anchorage Times.*

Ted had a number of large trusts awaiting his majority. The largest held 50 percent control of Field Enterprises, Inc., which then included the *Chicago Sun-Times,* the *Chicago Daily News,* and *World Book Encyclopedia.* The other half belonged to his half brother, Marshall Field V. Since Ted was only seventeen, these trusts were managed by trustees, who included Marshall V; Ed Farley, a longtime friend of his father's; Bailey Howard, CEO of Field Enterprises; and a family lawyer, Howard Seitz, of the law firm Paul, Weiss, Rifkin, Wharton & Garrison of New York. He would not inherit the large trust until he was twenty-five, but a smaller trust, named the Accumulation Trust, had stockpiled the dividends from the large trust, about $2 million per year, and would be available to Ted at age twenty-one. I worried that the millions of dollars he would inherit could be a burden on one so young. Together with that concern and the desperate need the paper had for cash, I talked to Ted about the possibility of investing some of this money in the *Daily News*. He was enthusiastic. So we began a long negotiation with the trustees.

The trustees of the Accumulation Trust were granted the "fullest and broadest discretion" in dealing with the investment of the funds of the trust for the benefit of Ted, the sole beneficiary. They were charged with deciding what constituted Ted's best interests. One aspect they would consider was the high income tax Ted would pay on his Accumulation Trust earnings. Even if Ted's investment in the *Daily News* showed a loss for several years, it would help offset those high tax rates on the rest of his holdings.

Larry was still adamantly opposed to using Ted's money. But the time had come for a stark choice. It was close the paper or seek sufficient financing to give it a chance to succeed. Besides, the stress of the financial situation was affecting Larry's health. He had developed serious asthma attacks and his Anchorage doctor, Winthrop Fish, had put him on cortisone as the only drug that seemed to have any effect.

We had tried every other way to get investment from outsiders to no avail. It was give up the *Daily News* and our way of life in Alaska, or take the plunge with Ted.

Was it right to use Ted's money, and some of Kathy's and Barbara's, with their total consent, for this enterprise? Was it taking advantage of our young children's money? Perhaps. But they were not babies. Each was fully aware of the struggles to keep the paper alive and each was emotionally committed to the paper. In retrospect, was a newspaper, particularly this newspaper in this place, that important? At that period in Alaska history, I believed then, and still do, that it was. Isolated as Anchorage was from the rest of the world, with no other paper of any size or weight coming in from a city nearby, with delayed television news, absenting ourselves from the scene would have left the entire field to the Atwoods. There were merits to the Atwoods' *Anchorage Times*, but not as the sole voice of the state.

To begin with, I personally borrowed $100,000 from Ted's trust, putting up some of the last stock I owned as collateral. It quickly became clear that a larger investment would be needed to make any major impact on the prospects of the *Daily News*. On August 9, 1969, I wrote a lengthy memo to the trustees. Here are some excerpts: "The decision on our part to ask the trustees to make this investment has been a difficult one. At the time we bought the *Anchorage Daily News* and settled our family in Alaska, we determined that we would go as far as we could with the project, knowing that we were undercapitalized, and if, when all our own resources were invested, the paper was not in a profit-making position, we would have to abandon the project. At that time we felt that, under no conditions, would we ever involve the children or their resources.

"Let me go back to the reasons behind our settling here and pursuing this course. Above all we wanted to give these three children, who had had quite an unsettled life up until that time, a secure base and a solid home. Further, we hoped they would become interested in the paper as a family project, that they would have the opportunity to see communications and publishing as an opportunity for public service as well as a fascinating and challenging business opportunity.

"Now, just two years later, as two of the children, Ted and Kathy, are in their teens, it appears that at least part of this plan was almost too successful. Both these older children have become deeply involved with the newspaper and the community. They have worked in nearly every department; they are concerned with every aspect of its operation. They are extremely happy living in Alaska, and they are aware that, if the newspaper did not continue in operation, the family would probably have to move from the state as there would be no appropriate employment for their stepfather, Larry, in the newspaper field since this is his only training."

In the memo I went on to recount the history of the *Daily News* problems. The Field family tradition, I reminded them, was that young people should not receive a large sum of money when too young to handle it with emotional maturity. We had, I pointed out, earlier expressed strong reservations about the first declaration of a dividend on the Field Enterprises common stock, which meant large sums of money would flow to Ted at age twenty-one instead of twenty-five, as intended by his grandfather and father.

I concluded the memo with what was, frankly, my greatest concern: "We ask you to consider, not only the financial prospects of this boy, but the overall prospects for his future. We are fully aware that the request could seem to be a callous "using" of a young man's resources to further our own interests. We have searched ourselves deeply and we do not believe this to be the case."

After much deliberation and back and forth discussion, the trustees agreed to our request. So with our Chicago lawyer, Newt Minow, representing us with the trustees, a new corporation, Alaska Communications Corporation (ACC), was created. It was a "subchapter S" corporation for tax purposes, which had the advantage of using the losses of the *Daily News* to offset the huge gains piling up in Ted's other trusts. A partnership was created between ACC, wholly owned by Ted's trust, and Northern Publishing Company, owned 80 percent by Larry and me, with Locke Jacobs, Bob and Arthur Goldberg, Joe Rothstein, and a few other minority stockholders holding the other 20 percent. Eventually trusts for my two daughters bought out the minority stockholders for $80,000, and Barb and Kathy, who also wanted to be involved, each assumed 10 percent ownership of Northern Publishing Co., Inc.

As some cash infusions came in we could breathe a little easier. But the trustees were rightfully demanding in their overview. Often our advance estimates of cash needs would be short of reality and the trustees would express their discomfort. They sent a team of Arthur Andersen accountants from Chicago to Anchorage to do an audit of the paper. One of the young auditors, Bill Allen, seemed particularly sharp and charming, and he took to Alaska and the *Daily News*. Our business manager, Bob Robertson, an earnest, well-meaning, honest young man, who had done his best to estimate the cash needs of the paper correctly but was often off the mark, and who was worn down by the constant shortage of funds, decided to depart. Larry impulsively hired Bill Allen to be the *Daily News* business manager with the hearty approval of the trustees in Chicago. They must have felt that we would be on sound financial footing with an Arthur Andersen accountant in charge.

Bill Allen would bring a whole new set of worries to the *Daily News*.

8

$900 Million! Alaska's Richest Day" roared the huge black headline. "Here Goes the Money," cried the subheading over a photo of suited couriers carrying heavy briefcases full of cash. The money from the world's richest oil lease sale was to be flown immediately by chartered United Airlines DC-8 to a San Francisco bank so that it could begin earning interest the next day.

Tom Brown's overview story began, "Alaska kept its rendezvous with history Wednesday. It was a long, hectic day of drama, suspense, and the unexpected larded with boredom. When it was over, Alaska was $900 million richer and was embarked irrevocably on an entirely new phase in its spectacular history.

"The drama that will affect the nature and quality of life in Alaska for the foreseeable future was played out before a full house of oilmen, bankers, reporters, policemen, and residents in 656-seat Sydney Laurence Auditorium [in downtown Anchorage]."

The buildup to the September 10, 1969, sale of oil leases on state land had been going on all summer. It was expected to be (and it was) the richest oil lease sale in history, anywhere. All summer, oil executives from around the world in various consortiums had been preparing their bids, surrounded by extraordinary security. This would be a sealed bid bonus sale of 179 tracts of tundra on the North Slope adjacent to Atlantic Richfield's two discovery wells that had proved huge pools of oil lay beneath the surface at Prudhoe Bay. The high-stakes guessing game the oil companies played was the search for the exact location of the producible oil. It was a winner-take-all game. The bid on each tract would be the maximum amount the bidder was willing to pay, accompanied by a check for 20 percent of the total. If the bid was a winner, the other 80 percent was due in fifteen days. Because the Prudhoe Bay field had been discovered on state land, the bonus money went to the state, and so would a 12.5 percent royalty plus any taxes the state might levy.

Oil executives came to Anchorage well in advance to plot their bids. Typically they would reserve a suite at the Anchorage Westward Hotel or at the Captain Cook and then also take the rooms above, below, and on each side, to prevent any other oil company from snooping on their bidding plans.

It had been reported that a sealed "mystery train," in some way connected to the lease sale, had been for several days, under greatest secrecy, running back and forth between Calgary and Edmonton in Alberta, Canada. It turned out that ten oil companies that were bidding together, the Hamilton Brothers group which included Continental and Ashland, had chartered the fourteen-car train at a cost of $10,000 a day. They had installed a bevy of security guards and sixty-five of their top executives. Not even the train crew was allowed in the passenger compartments, and the porters were not allowed off the train from the Friday before the sale until Wednesday morning. Information from an exploratory well being drilled by the group under tightest security ten miles north of the Prudhoe discovery well was radioed to the train, using secret codes, from an airplane circling the drill site. At three o'clock Wednesday morning, the day of the sale, the train's passengers boarded two private planes at Calgary and flew directly to Anchorage to enter their bids.

While we waited for Alaska's Commissioner of Natural Resources, Tom Kelly, to begin, the tension mounted to fever pitch. The sale got off to a dynamic start soon after Kelly read out the first bid. I was sitting in the press section just behind the reporters from London, who had flown in to cover the high-profile British Petroleum bidding team. The first six bids evoked gasps of disbelief. BP, bidding with Gulf Oil, had offered an astounding $97 million on six parcels twenty miles west of Prudhoe Bay at the Colville River Delta—more money in the first few minutes than the total that had been bid at any other state sale. The British reporters from the *Financial Times, London Times, Telegraph,* and others vaulted over the backs of their chairs and ran for the phones to call the news in to their London papers.

The dramatic high point of the day came with one bid for $72,113,000 for just one parcel. The bidders were Phillips, Standard Oil of

California, and Mobil. That figure was astounding enough. But when the next bid on the same single parcel topped it by just $164,000, there were shouts of disbelief. The second group consisted of billionaire J. Paul Getty and the Amerada Hess Company with a bid of $72,022,000, the highest per-acre bid in oil industry history. Starting down the aisle that morning and long after the sale, there were rumors of skullduggery, with reports that a Phillips geologist had sold out his company's data to the Hunt-Amerada-Getty group and "gone south." The close bids were just too much of a coincidence.

Daily News oil expert and business editor Cameron Edmondson wrote, "By racing through the 1,105 bids . . . the state completed the sale by 5:15 p.m., permitting the release of many losers' checks to meet the deadline for East Coast banks. All the excitement was financial. Rumors of planned fires, bombings, and other such disturbances failed to material-ize, probably due to . . . tight security. In addition to a cordon of police and state troopers . . . several suspects were kept under surveillance and a guard was posted on the building. . . ." But there were no threats, only some peaceful Alaska Natives picketing outside the building with signs deploring "$2 billion Native land robbery," "Bad deal at Tom Kelly's Trading Post," and "Oilmen and bankers: Make your checks payable to Alaska's Natives." Some Natives led by fiery Charlie Edwardsen, a Barrow Eskimo leader, were protesting that the state land where the leases were being sold should be Native land. But most Natives were supportive of the sale, knowing that the prosperity it could bring to the state would benefit them as well.

The lease sale put Alaska on the front pages of newspapers around the world. Photographer Dennis Cowall's picture of Tom Kelly presiding over the bid opening was featured at the top of page one of the *New York Times*. He was thrilled when the *New York Times* sent him $100 for use of the exclusive photo—much more than we could pay him. London news-papers bannered the sale. The *Chicago Daily News'* Raymond Coffey wrote about Tom Miklautsch, a Fairbanks druggist, who had bought two small oil leases for less than $5,000 in 1967 and sold them for $5 million. Coffey described the Fairbanks airport as "crowded with bearded, booted workmen carrying heavy parkas over their arms and wearing on their faces the signs of brutal hangovers." The Anchorage airport was another scene entirely—Philip D. Carter wrote in the *Washington Post*, "Anchorage, for one day this week, was the oil capital of the world. The city's hotels and motels were jammed with drawling Texans, crisp Englishmen, and pin-striped New York executives—all in town for the sweepstakes. At Anchorage International Airport, the chartered jets seemed to outnumber the taxicabs."

And Edgar Paul Boyko, Alaska's flamboyant former attorney general, never one for missing an opportunity for press coverage, announced he would sue the state, challenging the award of 33 of the 179 tracts put up for sale. Boyko, with a group of renegade Alaskans such as Pete Zamarello and Neil Mackay, had filed bids on 25 tracts. Boyko (the Browns' lawyer when we bought the *Daily News*) delighted in tweaking the authorities, and his bidding partners would, over the ensuing years, build quite a clip file of being hauled into court in one case or another.

In the next day's *Daily News*, Larry editorialized, "The result [of the sale] was a resounding affirmation that Alaska has taken a giant step forward in its struggle to move from the federal dole to a sound, free-enterprise base. The result offered eloquent evidence that the oil industry rates the North Slope as one of the world's richest petroleum reserves.

"Alaska now faces its real test. Will it dissipate this bonanza in profligate capital spending? Or will it keep its cool, resist pressure for a special spending session of the legislature, and work out, after full public debate, a prudent long-term program?

"Whether it will turn out to be not 'Alaska's Biggest Day Since Statehood' but rather her 'Greatest Day,' will depend on how the state meets the challenge of overnight affluence."

As the excitement cooled over the next days and weeks, many groups of Alaskans made serious efforts to deal with this question.

It was the beginning of the age of consultants in Alaska. One study on Alaska's future, commissioned by Governor Keith Miller, brought in a twenty-four-person team from Stanford University to devise a development plan. In another effort, noted New York petroleum consultant Walter Levy was hired by the legislature to analyze the state's oil potential and recommend ways to optimize it for the benefit of all Alaskans. But the most high-profile of these sessions was convened by the Alaska Legislative Council and its chairman, Gene Guess, a Democratic state representative from Anchorage. Guess brought in the prestigious Brookings Institution from Washington, D.C., a nonprofit research center and think tank, to organize a series of four seminars within a month. The format was highly participative. One hundred Alaskans from all over the state and every walk of life and ethnic background were invited to take part in the exhilarating task of planning the state's future. They were divided into four groups, each designated by a Greek letter. Larry was in Delta group, and I attended most of the sessions at the Anchorage Westward Hotel as his guest. It was a thrilling and unparalleled opportunity. And, understandably, the conference came up with an idealistic, comprehensive series of plans.

Alpha group saw the future of Alaska as, "One which maintains . . . a harmony between man and the natural environment, with strict controls on pollution and environmental degradation; one where the emphasis is on living, not just making a living; one where ethnic, racial, and cultural diversity is a proud and cherished accomplishment; one where discrimination has been eliminated or minimized and where all men are truly brothers; one where the arts, the contemplative life, and other cultural pursuits receive equal attention with material activity; one where the political process achieves a deserved respect through participation of an alert, active citizenry."

Each group made a series of specific recommendations regarding education, welfare, and backing Native Land claims. Delta group wanted to establish an Alaska Academy of Science and Technology. Delta also proposed a cabinet-level Human Affairs Agency to assist the urbanization process for rural peoples. Delta strongly expressed a need for a planning agency with ample input from all Alaskans. Other groups addressed transportation, renewable resources, "avoiding undue influences of special interests," taxation (or the lack thereof), transferring all Bureau of Indian Affairs schools to the state as soon as possible, providing universal health insurance for the whole state, and on and on.

It was a heady experience, planning for a state's future. And it was all based on the sudden acquisition of some $900 million dollars. What no one knew at that time, of course, was that billions more dollars would eventually accrue to the state from oil wealth, and that by the end of the century Alaska's savings account, called the Permanent Fund, would have some $26 billion in its coffers. And still, most of the goals laid out under the Brookings leadership would not have been met. There were exceptions: The BIA Native schools did revert to the state and become a new regional network of rural schools. The celebrated Molly Hootch Case forced the state to provide an education to children in their rural villages, instead of shipping them off to one or two far distant schools. Some of the financial goals were implemented, such as "make available funds to cover guaranteed loans for Alaskans by Alaskan financial institutions for creating Alaskan business."

Probably the greatest impetus of the oil lease sale and subsequent planning efforts was the jump-start it gave Alaskan self-confidence. Prior to the North Slope, many Alaskans felt and acted like second-class U.S. citizens living off the federal dole. The biggest business in Alaska was government, federal government. The Bureau of Indian Affairs, the army, the air force, the Bureau of Land Management, the Alaska Railroad—all were federal programs. By far the largest employer in the state was the federal government. Now, there was an opportunity to change all that.

Two days before the lease sale, Larry and I had had some eminent visitors. Our friends Illinois Senator Chuck Percy, his wife, Lorraine, his daughter, Gail, and son, Mark, had arrived in Anchorage upon completion of an around-the-world tour. Tom Brown reported on page one that Percy made an eloquent speech before a special luncheon meeting of the Anchorage Press Club. He talked about the state's new wealth, and said that Alaska could provide a "luminous example" to the rest of the country by developing its oil resources without ruining its wilderness character. He noted that orderly development could be achieved because of the desire of Alaskans and because oil executives are no longer the "robber barons" of the past. It was indeed a nice speech.

Brown, in reporting it, probably didn't know that Larry Fanning had written it for Percy to deliver! Percy also appeared on the *Daily News* TV program, "Target," where he said many of the things Alaskans wanted to hear from a U.S. senator on the Senate Foreign Relations Committee: "The dependence of the U.S on the Middle East has been lessened considerably. We're more self sufficient within our own boundaries. The possibilities of bringing in oil by sea and pipeline give us the certainty that we have access to resources essential to keep our industry moving." Sweet words to Alaskans!

The Percy visit resulted in some family excitement for the Fannings and the Percys. Sadly, the day they arrived in town, Chuck's colleague, the senior senator from Illinois, Everett Dirksen, had died in Washington, D.C. Because he was a lionized fixture in the Senate and the Senate Minority Leader, his funeral involved heavy formalities at the Capitol and Percy felt obliged to be there. There was no commercial flight that would get him to Washington in time, so we arranged with General Ruegg, commander-in-chief at Elmendorf Air Force Base, for Chuck to catch a ride directly to Washington on one of the military hospital planes from Vietnam when it made a refueling stop at midnight at Elmendorf. The general opened the officer's club to us for Chuck's late-night departure.

We were a motley crew. My son, Ted, drove Mark Percy (who would travel home by commercial jet with his mother the next day) in his Volkswagen Beetle, along with our two new baby kittens. Kathy and Barb were in another car with Gail. Larry and I had the senior Percys in our car. After refreshments and a greeting by General Ruegg at the Officer's Club, we received the signal to proceed to the plane, which was being refueled in a remote corner of the airfield. I'm sure the air force did not intend that our whole three-car retinue travel across the "hot" runways where planes were taking off and landing, but no one told us and that is what happened. Midst flashing red lights and roaring airplanes out across the field our three cars went with the senator. We parked by the hospital plane and Chuck insisted we clamber aboard. So Larry and I walked down the aisles, talking with the wounded GI's, who were mostly happy that they were being flown home from Vietnam. When it was time for the plane to depart, we were on our own to find our way back across the pitch-black field. All very informal for a military affair, but quite an adventure. In his thank-you note to General Ruegg, Larry noted that we were "especially indebted that you put up with that invasion of Percy-Fanning teenagers."

At the same time Anchorage was convulsed by the oil lease sale, another drama was being played out at the top of Alaska, in the arctic ice of the Beaufort Sea. The SS *Manhattan*, a huge ice-breaking tanker specially outfitted by Humble Oil Company (before the company was renamed Exxon), was trying to crash its way through the ice to Prudhoe Bay. The aim was to prove that oil could be shipped through the Northwest Passage to the East Coast by ice-breaking tankers. It demonstrated the conflicting goals of the Prudhoe Bay oil companies, most of which wanted the oil shipped to the West Coast in contrast to Humble's preference for the East Coast. It was a conflict that would be played out in many ways over the next several years.

Two days after the oil lease sale, the 1,005-foot *Manhattan* was firmly wedged in the 14-foot thick pack ice in McClure Strait, unable to move forward or backward. The $40 million supertanker was about sixty miles inside the strait when the jam occurred, the seventh time the tanker had been stopped by clogged ice. It was especially embarrassing to Humble because just a few days earlier, when the tanker had made it safely to Resolute Bay, Humble executives had announced the voyage a success, proving that shipping through the Northwest Passage was feasible. Characteristically, Larry had our own correspondent aboard. He did not accept the limitation that a tiny, struggling Alaskan newspaper couldn't be a player, even in a national or international story. Joe Rychetnik, *Daily News* photographer who was well known as a stringer for *TIME* magazine and other Outside publications, boarded the *Manhattan* at Resolute. He had managed to get his trip financed by *TIME* and was sending us daily dispatches from the *Manhattan* relayed by radio.

When the supertanker finally did break free by turning around and choosing a less ice-packed route, it still had an exciting voyage, as reported by Rychetnik. He described the pack ice as it tumbled to the surface with a roar by the bulbous 148-foot-wide bow, "flipping foot-long fish onto the ice as the ship plows ahead like a giant oceangoing bulldozer." It managed to anchor off Prudhoe Bay, where Humble staged a press event. A ceremonial first gold-plated barrel of Alaska crude oil from Prudhoe Bay was flown to the deck of the tanker accompanied by Governor Keith Miller, Alaska Commissioner of Natural Resources Tom Kelly, and a small press group. Interior Secretary Walter Hickel and Senator Ted Stevens were supposed to be there, too, but the weather closed in and prevented them from making it. Larry was one of the press party. He described it as the most terrifying flight he had ever made, floundering around on a helicopter from Barrow in zero visibility rain and fog, to land on the postage-stamp-size heaving deck of the supertanker.

At the same time all this was going on, the Japanese freighter *Alaska Maru* was docking at the port of Valdez to unload 6,000 tons of 48-inch pipe—the first installment of the 800-mile steel pipeline that would eventually connect the oil wells of Prudhoe Bay with the tankers that would haul them to market. The pipe was also welcomed with ceremony, speeches by Senator Ted Stevens and former Governor Bill Egan. But it would still be a long time before all this would come together. Many obstacles, environmental, practical, and cultural, would still need to be overcome.

The dramatic developments that were gathering to form the Great Alaska Oil Rush were a wonderful counterpoint to the daily grind of making ends meet at the *Daily News* for both Larry and me. There definitely was a connection. We knew that the evidence strongly indicated that with two independently owned and operated newspapers in a city as small as Anchorage, the smaller one would have a rugged time becoming financially successful. But if the economy and population expanded, as it was forecast to do with the development of oil and the building of the trans-Alaska pipeline, we might have a decent chance at survival. We, like other Alaska businesses, were not prepared for the many delays that would hold up the process for several years.

Eager as we were for events to come together that would help the *Daily News* survive, we weren't pulling any punches in our reporting of some of the negative aspects of this development, to the dismay and discomfort of much of the Alaska business community. Because Alaskan business entrepreneurs had experienced such a rollercoaster, boom-bust economy for so long, with much of it controlled by Outside interests, they devoutly hoped that no one would mention the possible environmental downside to the massive development at Prudhoe Bay, the 800-mile hot-oil pipeline to Valdez, or the location of a pipeline terminus and port at Valdez on Prince William Sound. But Larry believed there was information on all sides of this issue that the public must be informed about. The *Daily News* was the only publication in Alaska willing to take on that risky task.

Meanwhile, another controversial issue took center stage soon after the oil lease sale. The Atomic Energy Commission was preparing a live nuclear test on the island of Amchitka in Alaska's Aleutian Chain. A first nuclear test had been carried out there in 1965. In that news-packed autumn of 1969, Alaska would once more be the focal point of a major national news story. The AEC planned on October 2 to explode a 1.2-megaton hydrogen bomb, dubbed "Milrow," in a carefully prepared hole 4,000 feet down on Amchitka Island.

As the day approached, protests mounted, not only in Alaska but also in Washington, D.C., where Senator Mike Gravel churned up a group of twenty-one senators to cosponsor his resolution calling for postponement of the test until a presidential commission could assess the safety of the blast. He also persuaded the Senate Foreign Relations committee to hold hearings, but they disbanded for lack of a quorum. Gravel, with typical grandiosity, likened the AEC's nuclear test program in the Aleutians to Russian roulette, and warned, "What we have now, in essence, is a time bomb on Amchitka, a cavern of radioactive nuclei. A quake in the area could open that chamber. Alaskans would be the first to be hit, then Canada, and finally the mainland U.S."

The *Anchorage Daily News* was restrained but pointed in its opposition to the test. Larry's editorial objected first because the tests could only accelerate the nuclear arms race. The government had never explained the exact purpose of the tests but, as the editorial spelled out, it was clearly connected either to the defensive Anti-Ballistic Missile (ABM) warhead or to the offensive MIRV (Multiple Independently Targeted Reentry Vehicle). We were opposed to both as an unnecessary acceleration of the arms race with Russia. And second, without rousing hysterical fears about radioactivity reaching humans, we were deeply concerned with the geological and ecological effects the blast might have on marine life such as sea otters in the vicinity of Amchitka.

Nevertheless, it was apparent the test would go forward. And it did, without any apparent ill effect. Tom Brown's lead story in the *Daily News* said, "The big bang produced only a seismic whimper." There was no earthquake or tidal wave, and no radiation escaped into the atmosphere or the sea, according to the AEC. Only a 6.5 Richter rating or "a low-level event" in AEC terminology.

Milrow was an anti-climax, but that wouldn't prevent the next and much more powerful blast in the series, Cannikin, from growing into a hugely controversial issue two years later.

With all these news events swirling around us, it was hard to concentrate on the threatening financial issues that had to be faced. But Larry was optimistic that our sharp new business manager, Bill Allen, would help us achieve financial stability. There were problems in nearly every department of the newspaper, but the production disasters stood out. The press constantly broke down, causing massive expense in overtime, which in turn caused breakdowns in the circulation and distribution process. Something had to be done, and Larry started writing to newspaper contacts on the West Coast about the possibilities of acquiring a new press at reasonable (which meant practically no) cost.

What we needed, wrote Larry, was a press that would deliver 25,000 copies an hour with a thirty-two-page broadsheet capacity; a press that could do some color, particularly spot color; a press with a sound, preferably simple control system; a press with a foolproof folder (we were always having trouble with our folder); a press of a model that has "a sparkling record of performance and reliability"; and here was the clincher: a press that could be purchased, dismantled, crated, shipped, erected, and wired for less than $100,000 including stereotype (engraving) equipment.

And he found one! Or so it appeared. John McClelland, owner and publisher of the *Longview Daily News* in Washington state, was converting to offset printing—as most forward-looking newspaper publishers with capital to spend were—and his old press was available. It was a standard tubular thirty-six-page Goss press, about thirty years old, with all the engraving and stereotype equipment we needed. Gone would be the inadequate Scan-a-Graver for producing pictures. We could have all this for $35,000, plus the cost of having it moved and installed, for an estimated total of $70,000. It seemed too good to be true. And it was!

We sent press people to Longview, and made arrangements with the man who had located it for us to break it down and pack it in Longview and install it at the *Daily News.*

There was a lot of excitement in the back shop of the *Daily News* as the pit for the press was being dug and the press installers arrived with a vast number of boxes of gears and parts. We thought we were finally going to be able to compete with the *Anchorage Times* in printing quality, and the whole staff watched in awe as the press was being pieced together.

What nobody told us until some years later was that Longview had planned to junk the press and the rest of the equipment until we came along. The cost of maintaining the thing, once it was installed, was sky high. It looked like a Rube Goldberg contraption with hundreds of moving parts. Since parts for it were no longer manufactured, we had to have a part made specially each time it broke down. And whenever there was an electrical problem, we had to fly in a special electrician from Los Angeles. I remember standing around in utter frustration one night, a big news night, waiting for the L. A. electrician to land at the airport and rush to the paper so we could print that night's newspaper. Still, it did print papers faster, and considering our meager resources it seemed the best we could do. At about the same time, however, Bob Atwood and the *Anchorage Times* were preparing to convert to offset printing, a whole new generation of printing efficiency and readability.

The new business manager, Bill Allen, was in charge of the production department as well as advertising, circulation, and accounting. Only the news and editorial department were outside his purview. But Allen had a quality of attracting young journalists as well as ad sales people and business department folks into his circle of fun and games. He soon became part of the China Doll set. At the same time, health problems assaulted Larry so that he was forced to leave much of the implementation of the new press systems and the financial affairs of the paper to the untried Bill Allen.

An uncharacteristically terse memo from Larry to Bill Allen in February complained, "When I asked you about Feldman [the press erector Larry had hired], I was told two things: (1) that he had reduced his price and (2) that he had been informed we were hiring a new press erector. It's a lousy way to treat people." Larry wrote the original press erector, Jerome Feldman, on February 16, 1970, saying that "For unavoidable reasons I was away from Anchorage and the office from Christmas Day until January 19." He explained that during his absence certain decisions had been made that he found embarrassing, and extended his apologies. But the die was cast, and we had a contract with Bill Allen's choice of press erector, who he apparently thought would be cheaper. The "unavoidable reasons" for Larry's being away was that he had suffered a mild stroke and had been ordered by Dr. Fish to take three weeks of complete rest .

Larry's physical problem, diagnosed as a stroke, came in the midst of one of the more ambitious promotion efforts the *Daily News* had ever undertaken. With barely ten days to prepare, Larry had received confirmation that the American Davis Cup tennis team would play exhibition matches in Anchorage December 22 and 23 on their way back to the Lower 48 from Hawaii. The event's major sponsor would be the *Anchorage Daily News* along with two other sponsors, the Anchorage Racquet Club and Anchorage Community Theater. But the major burden of arrangements would be assumed by the *Daily News*, mostly Larry.

The Davis Cup, an annual competition climaxed by a match between the world's two top male tennis teams, claimed the winners as the world's best tennis players. In 1969 the Americans defeated Romania to claim that title. World-class player (and human being) Arthur Ashe was the star of the group, with Stan Smith number two in rankings. The other members were Donald Dell, captain of the team, Bob Lutz, and Charles Pasarell. They would play two evenings of exhibition matches at the West High School Gymnasium, joined for doubles by Gerald Dubie, a local teacher at Wendler Junior High and Alaska's number one player. (Dubie was, incidentally, my son's tennis coach and friend).

It took a great deal of scrambling to put this event together, complete with homes to host the players, press interviews, and clinics for young tennis hopefuls. The terms of the visit were certainly reasonable: a minimum guarantee of $3,000 or 50 percent of the gross receipts, whichever was larger. There were tickets for $3.50 per person to be printed, publicity materials to be designed, radio and TV announcements to be written, volunteers to be mobilized, receptions, dinners, and sight-seeing tours to be arranged. All at minimal or no cost, and within ten days. Larry, a devout tennis enthusiast, was thrilled with the opportunity to connect these international athletes with the *Anchorage Daily News*. He agreed to be the master of ceremonies, handling introductions, announcements, etc., for the two evening exhibitions. The players would all stay with local families. Tay and Lowell Thomas hosted Donald Dell, the captain. Alaska Methodist University professor and tennis coach Bill Lewis and his family opened their home to Arthur Ashe, and Drs. John and Elizabeth Tower took in Stan Smith. We didn't really have a spare bedroom but we had Stan Smith for dinner, and the kids took him out for a thrilling ride on our new snowmachine, across nearby Otis Lake and into the winter wonderland surrounding it. Snowmachines were a novelty in 1969, still legal in the city, and the lake and woods around Madison Way were full of snowmachine trails where the subdivision Geneva Woods now stands.

The first evening went smoothly, with Larry calling this "a sports event unique in the history of Alaska." He introduced Mayor Sullivan, and Wally Hickel threw out the first ball. The next day Larry stayed home a while in the morning and then called Berchie, his secretary, at the office. In the middle of the conversation, Larry's speech slurred and dropped off. Berchie says I took the phone from him and told her, "Larry's not well."

I drove Larry to Providence Hospital. I was praying all the way, the simple prayer of a Christian Scientist, that man is the perfect, intact idea of God. Dr. Fish met us at the Emergency Room. By that time, Larry wasn't able to speak. The doctor took some tests while I continued praying. Then Dr. Fish asked Larry to write something. He couldn't until Fish asked him to write, "I love you, Kay." He wrote it right away. Fish later told me that often people respond to an emotional idea when they can't do anything else. Soon Larry was moving and talking normally, and Dr. Fish sent us home with the strong admonition that Larry must rest completely for at least three weeks with no work whatsoever. The only way that could be achieved would be to get out of town. That evening we went ahead with hosting the dinner for Stan Smith, but Larry didn't put in an appearance and someone else substituted for him at the tennis exhibition.

Immediately after Christmas, the children, Larry, and I departed for three weeks at Kona on the Big Island of Hawaii, a marvelously restful vacation, unlike any we had had together. Larry rapidly regained his strength and all his faculties. The one cloud was something he said to me one day as we were swimming lazily around the hotel pool. He said, "I've always thought I'd go down one day with a massive heart attack in the newsroom." I implored him, please, not to think that way.

Larry and I did think very differently about such key matters as life and death. He was brought up by a devout Catholic mother, who was widowed when he was only three. Her great hope was that Larry, the youngest of her five sons, would grow up to become a priest. Larry was packed and ready to go off to a Catholic seminary when, the night before he was to leave, he decided that he just couldn't go through with it, that the priesthood wasn't the life for him. Later, he had conflicts with the church's position on political issues and eventually he left the church. That is, intellectually he had left, but emotionally the church, and particularly the church music, had a heavy hold on him. He wrestled all the time, trying to throw off feelings of guilt, which he and I would discuss at length. Larry was a complex man but he seemed to be living out the heritage of the "black Irish." Larry only wrote me a couple of letters during the years I knew him, and unfortunately they were lost. But one of them included a poem he had written about love and life and death. I can only remember the last line: "And death is a dark delight."

My ideas about these topics were quite opposite, and Larry said he envied me for my being able to look at life the way I did. I believed, as a Christian Scientist, that the one God is all and is supremely good, always tenderly caring for mankind. I believed in the power of thought, as reflecting the one infinite Mind, to greatly influence health and harmony. Larry struggled to understand this concept, attended my church with me regularly, and tried to learn to think and pray in a more positive manner. After the stroke incident, while continuing with medical treatment, he redoubled his effort to understand a better way to think about life.

By the time we returned to Anchorage in mid-January, Bill Allen had taken over and had already made some questionable decisions.

9

Slim Randles was a cowboy. There he was when we returned from Larry's rest cure in Hawaii, hired by Stan Abbott to be city editor. Larry loved collecting an eccentric group of people who were good writers for his "laboratory newspaper." Slim was certainly one of those. Originally from California, he had been a professional cowboy for years, competing on the rodeo circuit since he was fourteen. He had roped and bulldogged calves and clung to the backs of bucking broncos. He had been a packer in the eastern High Sierra, taking people into the backcountry on mules and horses. But he had a gift for writing: he wrote a weekly column on rodeo hands for the *San Gabriel Valley Tribune* when he was fifteen, and later took a job at the *Lake Tahoe Daily Tribune*.

A search for adventure and for a young redheaded lady named Connie brought Slim to Alaska. City editor was a desk job that involved putting out the first couple of pages of the paper each night, and it didn't satisfy Slim for long. Soon after Larry returned to his office, refreshed, Slim was talking to him about novel ways to draw attention to the paper, provide good stories for the readers, and, not so incidentally, get Slim out of the office and into the great Alaska outdoors.

Slim had been instantly attracted to dogsledding when he and reporter Linda Billington were given a complimentary ride by one of the PR men for dog mushing. He saw the dogsled as his vehicle to escape from indoor work in the office. So he proposed a publicity stunt that would also make a good story. He would form a sled dog team from dogs in the pound and mush them from Mount McKinley National Park (now Denali National Park and Preserve) to Anchorage along the railroad tracks to Anchorage, a distance of about 240 miles. It would be to benefit the Jesse Lee Home: eight disadvantaged dogs would be making a run to benefit a home for disadvantaged children. It had an appealing ring, Slim thought.

Larry was taken with the idea. It wouldn't cost much, and Slim could write of his adventures every day from the trail. So Slim picked out a ragtag group of eight dogs from the pound and gave them minimal sled dog training. He transported them to McKinley Park by train. In those days, the Alaska Railroad served many cabin dwellers deep in the Interior. All you had to do was flag down the train to get it to stop somewhere near your cabin (most of which were equipped with dog teams), so there was nothing particularly unusual about a dog team traveling by train.

At McKinley Park, Slim's adventure began. He drove the dogs along the railroad tracks, making up to fifty miles a day, and stayed at the railroad section houses at night, where he would call in his day's adventures to the paper. The saga caught on immediately, stirring greater public interest than we could possibly have anticipated. By the second day, Slim had messages waiting at the section houses to call radio and TV stations in addition to the *Daily News*. Slim wrote of each of his sled dogs as individual characters. The two lead dogs were Red and Taffy. Red did much of the hard work, Slim reported. He was a homely part golden Lab. Then there were two huskies, several German shepherds, a Samoyed, and a dog named Nameless that was unpopular with the rest of the team because he had taken the lead and was good at it.

Slim's mushing trip took on a life of its own. One night when he called in his story, Sandy, the young *Daily News* receptionist, answered the phone and said, "Oh, Slim, you're world famous all over Anchorage."

But then disaster struck. One of Slim's dogs was killed. The *Daily News* had sent a small plane to make an air drop of some newspapers and a couple of extra harnesses Slim needed. The package landed about 100 yards off the tracks in the snow, and Slim put on snowshoes to fetch it. While he was gone, the other dogs attacked Nameless and killed him. There was consternation in the newsroom. "We can't tell our readers that one of their precious dogs has been killed by the team," went one line of reasoning. "Yes, we can," said Larry. He insisted that we tell our readers the whole story honestly as a truthful portrait of what happens in life on the trail. We did, and the readers continued to avidly follow Slim and the day-by-day account of his travails.

By this time Slim was a celebrity, more famous than the world-class mushers who were assembling for the annual Fur Rondezvous World Championship Sled Dog Race in downtown Anchorage. Race planners thought it would be a good stunt to have Slim end his trip on Fourth Avenue as a starter event for the race. The only trouble was, Slim ran out of snow at Talkeetna and it didn't look like he could make it. So Stan Abbott drove a borrowed truck to Talkeetna, picked up Slim and his dogs, and deposited them at the end of snow-packed Fourth Avenue for the ceremonial trip finale by dogsled. "We came down the avenue with the dogs. Everybody was yelling and waving. I'd never had that kind of attention paid me before. One old lady yelled out, 'God bless you, Slim.' I had never thought of affecting people like that and I felt very unworthy of it," Slim recalls.

After the event on Fourth Avenue, Larry and I took Slim up to the top of the Anchorage Westward Hotel for a drink. "You're not city editor any more," Larry said. You're a feature writer. What are you going to do for your next trip?"

"I thought he was kidding me, so I said, 'I think I'll paddle a canoe through the Northwest Passage.' Larry said, 'You're crazy. . . . How will you file your stories?' I thought, Holy cow. He's serious." From that time on, Slim's byline was "Resident Adventurer." He did some stories from Southeast Alaska villages. He mounted an expedition to canoe down the Yukon River, but someone stole his canoe off the top of his car before he could even get started.

His next spectacular adventure wasn't paddling a canoe through the Northwest Passage. It was the equally hazardous undertaking of mushing another team of pound dogs from Prudhoe Bay along the length of the proposed 800-mile oil pipeline to Valdez in November. It was billed as "breaking trail" for the pipeline with homeless sled dogs, carrying a quart of Prudhoe oil to Valdez. TAPS, the company formed to build such a pipeline when and if it received Congressional approval, was enthusiastic about helping Slim. It was a good way to keep a positive view of the proposed pipeline in the public eye.

This time Slim filled out his team with several more pound dogs. He scrounged dog food and all kinds of supplies anywhere he could, borrowed an old red sled, and flew with the dogs to Prudhoe Bay. Henry Peck, a *Daily News* photographer, went along to record the scene of the dogs being unloaded and readied for the trip. After a few days to get the dogs accustomed to the drastic change in temperature, Slim started off, eleven dogs pulling his sled. His first stop was eight miles north of a camp called Sag One. A skeleton oil drilling crew with huge augers was there drilling test holes. Slim pitched his tent for his first night on the trail and, to his surprise, was visited by Robert O. Anderson, CEO of Atlantic Richfield (ARCO), who flew out in a helicopter to pay a brief visit to Slim. He brought coffee and took pictures of Slim and the dogs. Not half an hour after Anderson departed, a fierce snowstorm hit. "It was hairy," Slim said. "The only thing that saved me was this horribly ugly sled, nothing esthetic about it but it saved my life. The driving bow was sticking out of the snow, the storm covered everything else. Sixty- to-eighty-mile-per-hour winds and snow blew for thirty hours. I was in this little tent. The dogs were okay except for one who got a line wrapped around his leg and froze it. Eventually it had to be amputated." Slim got frostbite, too. "I have an ear to remind me of the first dogsled trip and two fingers to remind me of the second.

"It's funny how the mind works" [in the deep cold], Slim said. "Mine wasn't working right. The body saves up the warmth of the internal workings and starts shutting it off from the fingers and toes and the head, so the brain doesn't work properly and you do stupid things like wander around in the snow. So I told myself, no matter how goofy I got, I wasn't going to leave that tent." To his intense relief, some thirty hours after the storm hit and with no abeyance in sight, a helicopter from the Sag One Atlantic Richfield camp staggered through to Slim's bivouac. "They shouldn't have flown but they did, and they dug me out, got the dogs out, flew us to Sag One, and stuck me in a hot shower." Slim and all the dogs survived but the expedition was over. ARCO flew them to Fairbanks, where Slim and the dogs ignominiously hitched a ride back to Anchorage in a Weaver Brothers truck. Another failure. Another good story.

Slim went on writing "loser" columns for the *Daily News*. He tells the story of when he hit the Mayor of Anchorage in the belly with a bulldog. Groover was a bulldog that belonged to a group of deaf-mute printers from our composing room. She had become kind of a mascot around the paper. Things were dull around the office one evening, and Groover was begging. So Slim got a towel to play tug-of-war with Groover. Slim could lift the tenacious dog with the strong jaws into the air and swing her around without her letting go. Just then Mayor Sullivan walked through the front door of the newspaper and bam! Groover hit him in the belly, knocking him down. Slim claims that I came out of my office just then and, with a straight face, said, "Slim, I wish you'd be more careful with the bulldog."

There were many more stunts Slim and another crazy fellow, Satch Carlson, thought up. Satch was sports editor, unofficial promotion guru, and sometimes humor columnist. One stunt was the Ugly Dog contest. Slim's favorite dog, Red, was so ugly that sometimes he wasn't appreciated for his true value, Slim thought. So he concocted a multiple-breed ugly dog contest. People submitted pictures of their ugly dog. Lieutenant Governor Lowell Thomas Jr. was one of the judges, along with a few of the town's showgirls. There was a prize for the slowest dog, the dumbest dog, and the all-around worst dog in Alaska. The grand prize was a giant fire hydrant made out of Styrofoam, fabricated by Tom Gibboney's girlfriend. A tiny girl who had painted her huge, shaggy English sheep-dog green won first place. It was an awful-looking dog, but the little girl was very proud to have won the grand prize at the ceremony on the Park Strip.

There was another highly successful Slim promotion in 1974, a few years later. The second year of the Iditarod Trail Sled Dog Race from Anchorage to Nome had just begun with very little fanfare. Long before the race became a national annual event, the *Daily News* had been the prime promoter of sled dog racing in Alaska. That year, the trail was covered with corn snow, which was sharp and devastating to the feet of the dogs. Slim said it was like ice cream salt, like walking on broken glass, and it was cutting up the dogs' feet. The *Daily News* put out an SOS to readers to make dog booties, and printed a pattern for shaping them. Most any material would do, but pillow ticking was recommended as the best. The response was immediate and overwhelming. Thousands of dog booties made by *Daily News* readers flooded in, to be air dropped to the Iditarod racers on the trail, saving scores of dog paws. Dog booties continue to be standard gear for racing dogs.

In late November 1969, the *Daily News* announced another "new" *Daily News* with product improvements such as an expanded sports section, a snowmachine column, and a new morning AP wire service exclusive to the *Daily News* because we were the only morning paper in the state. There would be a reporter dedicated to covering the military, with a weekly military page, a new teen forum, more humor, more in-depth reports. All this was introduced on page one on Thanksgiving Day by Satch Carlson's "Little Man," a cartoon-type character drawn by Satch which was intended to symbolize a people-friendly newspaper. Satch had small round orange stickers made of Little Man, and all staff members delighted in plastering them around town. The volunteer team that was delivering papers on Thanksgiving morning was especially proud of having pasted Little Man on Bob Atwood's front door.

Advertising representative Sheila Paterson remembers that Thanksgiving: "All of us got up early that day. I drove the truck because my arm was broken. It was Bill Allen, Stan, and Tom Gibboney who sneaked over to Bob Atwood's house and put that smiley face sticker on his door." All these antics do sound juvenile, in retrospect. But besides the fact that most of the staff were, indeed, very young, there was a genuine love and intensity of feeling about the *Daily News*. No doubt it was impelled by our deep underdog status. The *Times*, with triple the circulation, at least quadruple the advertising, and a smug, superior attitude, was an ideal target for this talented, creative, energetic group of young people.

Sheila Paterson said years later, "There was a spirit and soul that existed at the *Daily News* . . . and I've never found that since. Not only were we fighting for the underdog, we were literally, in a way, snobs, because to us the *Anchorage Times* was worse than anything in the world. That whole group, it didn't matter if you were in the back shop or if you were a display advertising salesman or classified or in the newsroom. It was all created because of your and Larry's attitude that everyone was important to make the paper fly."

But everyone didn't see it that way, and that included our minority stockholder, Locke Jacobs. Jacobs was always polite, but he asked a lot of sticky questions about our financial status. I tried to keep him up to date, visiting him in his office papered with geological maps and polar bear skins. Locke didn't like the money-losing status of our bottom line and he didn't like our liberal democratic politics at all. One day he was so irritated by one of Larry's editorials he announced he was going to walk down the street and distribute one share of stock in the *Daily News* to each passerby. That turned out to be an empty threat, but he did distribute some of his stock to two business partners and fellow members of the Spit and Argue Club, John McManamin and Willard Nagley. McManamin had been Locke's old boss at the Army-Navy Store. Since Bob Atwood was also a Spit and Argue member and all were partners in Kenai oil drilling, it was possible the intent was to spy on the liberal *News* for the conservative, oil-supporting *Times*. But Jacobs was an independent sort of fellow and it was more likely a mix of curiosity about the *News* and the desire to make mischief.

In any case, now that Ted's trust was invested in the *News* and some New York lawyers were involved, it became a high priority to remove these loose-cannon, salty Alaskans from such close proximity to the financial dealings of the paper. Bob Atwood undoubtedly knew we were losing money, but it didn't seem necessary for him to have access to all the details. Negotiations began to buy out the minority stockholders. A stockholders' meeting was held in attorney Jack Roderick's office. Ted Stevens' former law partner, Roderick had replaced Stevens as our attorney, friend, and advisor since Stevens went to Washington as a U.S. senator. Two lawyers from Paul, Weiss, Rifkin, Wharton, and Garrison, the New York law firm that represented Ted's trustees, came to town for the event. Larry and I were there with Jack Roderick. Jacobs, Nagley, chewing on his corncob pipe, and McManamin, dangling an unlit cigar from the side of his mouth, were clearly enjoying the opportunity to play the role of the naïve country boys who had every intention of taking the city slickers to the cleaners. In reality they were as sharp as New York lawyers. They knew "the suits" wanted them out badly and that the cards were stacked in favor of the corncob pipe and unlit cigar.

After playing their role to the hilt, making it clear that they knew they had us in a tight spot, they settled for $5 per share, a pretty good price for shares in a corporation that was losing money at an alarming rate. They signed a stock sale agreement that, for $75,000, bought out Nagley for $37,000, McManamin for $10,000, and Jacobs for $26,000. It was a great relief, but I must confess that I was kind of sorry to see Locke Jacobs go. He was a challenge and kind of fun.

At the same time, we bought out the Goldbergs and the few remaining shares held by Joe Rothstein. My two daughters, Kathy and Barb, purchased the minority shares, so now it was totally a family affair, a partnership of Alaska Communications Corporation, totally owned by Ted, and Northern Publishing Co., owned 80 percent by Larry and me, 20 percent by Kathy and Barb. It seemed like a workable arrangement for the future of the newspaper.

But we were in for a dizzying round of personnel changes that nearly upended the whole newspaper. Bill Allen, who we had brought aboard with such high hopes and the great confidence of Ted's trustees, had made some sudden, unexpected decisions in connection with the installation of the new press. But he answered the questions of the trustees so well, his monthly financial projections were so professional, and the trustees seemed so happy with him, we tried to close our eyes to the worrisome signs. He had a tendency to make flat statements that couldn't be supported by facts.

He did do some good things. He instituted sound systems; he wrote a beautiful procedural manual (most of which was never implemented), he put us on the computer, and he got the bills out on time (something no other business manager had achieved). But he also authorized a useless and costly market survey that cost $2,500 without consultation with Larry, fouled up the all-important telephone book contract, and filed our quarterly IRS withholding reports one day late, costing us $1,000 in penalties. So despite Allen's almost godlike status in the newsroom and throughout the building and his high standing with the all-important trustees, it was evident we had to let him go.

At the paper we announced Allen's departure as a resignation to "do other things." Bill was going to hang his shingle out as a consultant in Anchorage and continue to work with the paper on a consulting basis with no line responsibilities. That soon changed as reports surfaced that

Allen had told people that he (1) would be going to Chicago to work for the trustees; (2) was going to work for the Field newspapers; (3) had invited Ted to go motor-biking through Europe with him that summer. In fact, he did go to Europe after a driving trip to the Lower 48 with Stan Abbott.

One of the things we'd given Bill Allen high marks for was the good people he had hired. Notable among these was Bill Armstrong as controller. He seemed a godsend as Allen departed, leaving everything in a snarl. With solid business school credentials and about to be awarded his CPA, he seemed well qualified to take over many of Allen's responsibilities. Larry announced that I would come aboard full time as assistant to the publisher, working with Armstrong in the accounting area and signing all checks. Accounting was a strange role for me, but we had been burned enough by the outflow of cash. As an owner of the paper, I would be more motivated than most to keep an eagle eye on the bucks.

A triumvirate would assume Bill Allen's general manager role: Stan Abbott, executive editor in charge of all news function, Bill Armstrong in charge of all accounting, and a newcomer, Dave Stein, sales manager in charge of all advertising and circulation sales. Dave had recently moved to Alaska from the Salem, Oregon, *Statesman-Journal,* where he had been a top account executive handling many of their major advertising accounts. He had studied business administration at Oregon State University, and had been a management trainee at Montgomery Ward. It was a slim business background, but Dave had a quiet, open quality that inspired trust and he did have a good grasp of the basics.

Bill Armstrong, unfortunately, began quickly to exhibit signs similar to what we'd just been through with Bill Allen. But he wrote some heart-wrenching memos to Larry about what needed to be done at the *Daily News,* where he soon felt overwhelmed. A telling line in one of his memos portended impending events. "The ultimate P&L responsibility can't be delegated to anyone but is one of the 'evils' of owning your own business. The delegation of this authority has been . . . a factor in moving the last two people that had it to actual or near nervous breakdowns."

By this time we had begun to understand well why Blanche Brown had kept all the money matters under such tight control, why she had even counted the pencils. The simple fact was that, while exceptional news reporters were attracted to and intrigued by Alaska, stable business-side people were extremely hard to come by. In our dire need as the two Bills mercifully disappeared from view, we hired a longtime, well-known Anchorage CPA, Eivin Brudie, to help us out in finding an accountant we could trust. Brudie came in each month to close the books, and he found Lurlyne Allen, an accountant he had worked with at the Evan-Jones Coal Company in Palmer, Alaska. When that coalmine closed down, she had transferred to a gold mine in Nevada, but she was eager to return to Alaska.

When Lurlyne settled in at the *Daily News* building on Post Road, we knew we had finally found the right person. She was calm, cheerful, familiar with Alaskan ways, and no amount of chaos seemed to unnerve her. With Dave Stein and Lurlyne, we felt the ship beginning to steady itself.

Understandably, Ted's trustees were disturbed by the amount of turnover and instability. We always needed more money and we always had piles of unpaid bills. One of the trustees, Bailey Howard, was also CEO of Field Enterprises, and he and Ted's half brother, Marshall, arranged to send us some temporary help in the form of a tightly wound bundle of energy and business expertise named Jack Crosby. Jack was an Alabaman who had done trouble shooting of various kinds for the Fields for years. He had been with Marshall Field & Company and taken on a host of assignments for Field Enterprises, and had an MBA from Harvard Business School. Jack came in a consulting role. First commuting from Chicago and finally bringing his wonderful wife, Sarah, and two of their children to Anchorage for a six-month stint, Jack inspired respect around the paper.

The first thing Jack did was write job descriptions for the senior management team including Larry. (I escaped as too lowly on the chart). He quickly determined that Dave Stein was the one hope to become an effective general manager, and began training him for that role. Jack and Sarah virtually became family members to us—Sarah, always motherly and caring, and Jack, the courtly southern gentleman. Soon after their arrival, Jack wondered to me why I didn't stay home and bake cookies like Sarah did. (She did bake marvelous cookies.) But I could forgive Jack that because his motives were so genuinely good.

With Armstrong and Allen gone, Lurlyne on board, and Jack Crosby working with Dave Stein, I withdrew happily from the accounting department and tried to take some of the load off Larry, particularly in dealing with the public. We were having plenty of trouble in that area. Larry reflected the dimensions of the problem in a memo to me and the department heads, lamenting a series of "silly and unfathomable breakdowns in communication." It ran to such things as a date to send a photographer to cover a ribbon cutting. No photographer appeared, infuriating the ribbon cutters, who were counting on our coverage.

I worried over all the stress these things plus the financial woes were causing Larry. Even though he avowed that he had never been happier in his life with the "little monster," his asthma was growing worse, sometimes keeping him sitting up all night. Larry was never one to blow off his frustrations. He always kept a calm exterior and you had to know him well to discern his inner turmoil.

I responded to his "silly and unfathomable breakdowns" memo with a lighthearted one: "In searching for my identity here I have taken the liberty of creating a new title for myself—and thereby becoming a department head, entitling me to attend department head meetings. I am now Chairman of the Nitty Gritty Department. It is abundantly clear that the staff of this newspaper is spectacular on the BIG STORY but appallingly bad on all matters of nitty gritty." I went on to explain about the irate morticians I'd been dealing with. The obituaries just weren't getting into the paper because something else was always more important, in somebody's judgment, and would replace them. Mr. Kehl, the undertaker, complained that when he called in an obit, whoever answered put his hand over the phone and tried to get someone else to take it.

It was an ongoing dilemma. The hot-shot young reporters were always after the big story. I would plead with Larry to just hire a couple of mediocre reporters who would be content to cover unexciting news that matters to people.

About the same time, one of our hottest-shot writers, Tom Brown, had just won a coveted national award, the Thomas Stokes Award for best writing in the U.S. or Canada on development, use, and conservation of natural resources. It was for his examination of challenges to the environment that building the pipeline would involve. Larry took enormous pride in such national recognition of our tiny little paper in the frozen North.

By mid July, with the help of Jack Crosby, we had begun to make the cuts in newsroom staff that Larry was so reluctant to make but were so necessary. Six bodies that included some of our more visible writers were eliminated, among them Satch Carlson, an expensive and unnecessary luxury. Then there was Luc Smith, a reporter who had sidelined himself by going to Washington, D.C., ostensibly in search of a story but without authorization, installed himself in an expensive hotel, and billed it all to the *Daily News.*

But that summer we also took on a new hotshot. His name was Allan Frank. Loaded with talent and energy, Allan wore the air of an unexploded time bomb. With long curly hair that stood out at right angles from his head, Allan arrived in September wearing a shaggy fur coat down to his ankles. We called him "the critter." He resembled an abominable snowman.

Allan Frank was the son of Morton Frank, the publisher of *Family Weekly* magazine. Earlier in the year, Larry and I had gone to New York to see Mort Frank, to talk him into letting the *Daily News* subscribe to *Family Weekly* for its Sunday package. Since the *Times* did not have a Sunday paper, we calculated that building the Sunday issue was one of our best routes to creating enough circulation to attract advertisers. Still, at only 17,000, the biggest of the Sunday supplements, *Parade,* wouldn't touch us, and we knew we'd have to persuade Frank that it was worth the trouble of shipping *Family Weekly* to Alaska for 17,000 readers. We hit it off right away with Mort Frank. His goals for newspapers were similar to ours, and before long he had bought into the Alaska mystique and agreed to send *Family Weekly* to Anchorage, assuming the complex logistical problems could be solved.

Family Weekly debuted in the *Daily News* Sunday, April 6, to much fanfare, the first Sunday supplement to appear in the state. But only two weeks later the dreaded logistics reared their heads. We had to run a front-page box apologizing for no *Family Weekly* due to strikes and shipping problems in the Lower 48. The missing magazine finally appeared in the paper the following Thursday.

While we were in Mort Frank's office, he brought in his son Allan, who had just graduated from Columbia journalism school. From the first moment, being around Allan Frank was a dramatic experience. He had no sooner sat down than a telephone call came in from his sister announcing that the house across the street from the Franks' Greenwich Village residence had just blown up and burst into flames. It was the home of Kathy Wilkerson, a member of the radical Weatherman group, and it made front-page news. A bomb-making exercise had literally blown up in the faces of the radical group. Wilkerson managed to escape into years of hiding and exile. The incident was a good conversation-starter, and in the process of talking with Allan about news and the *Anchorage Daily News*, Larry, discerning Allan's talent, energy, curiosity, and intelligence, suggested he might consider applying to us for a job in Anchorage. In July Allan did exactly that by letter, and was soon on his way to Anchorage.

When Allan first arrived in town in September, we put him up for a spell in our house on Madison Way, where he immediately bonded with both my daughters and Larry's daughter, Judith Hunt, who lived nearby with her son Hal and baby Peter. Before long, Allan had become close to all three, forming a brief but serious relationship with Judy before moving on. Allan asked Larry how he did in writing his letter applying for a job at the *Daily News*. Larry said, "Except for one split infinitive, it wasn't too bad."

Antics at the China Doll Bar were in high gear in late 1970, and Allan Frank quickly became a leading member of the Upper Yukon River Press Club. He tells of walking in to the paper one morning with a hangover from a late night at the China Doll and taking a call from reporter Andy Williams, who was at the Crow's Nest atop the Captain Cook Hotel in downtown Anchorage. Williams had just seen a plane crash at the end of the International Airport runway. In his little Volvo, Allan "hooked onto" the back of a fire truck, got into the airport, and found the crashed charter plane that was carrying soldiers to Vietnam. He actually acquired a mild case of frostbite from the foot-deep snow while pacing off the distance between the plane and the end of the runway in his loafers. It was about a mile but he didn't want to guess. Be exact, he had learned in journalism school. But "I lost track because my feet were so cold about 1,000 steps into it, I had to start over." He remembers the smell in the morgue, the first time he had seen burned human remains. And he counted the bodies. "I learned then one of the critical rules of journalism. The *Anchorage Times* said there were 48 dead. Our story said 47. We were right." The rule Allan said he learned was you can always add bodies but you can't subtract them. "Don't kill off any more bodies than you've counted." Allan's first story won the *Daily News* Best Spot News Story of the year from the Alaska Press Club.

Working with raw talent like Allan Frank and watching it mature and flourish was one of Larry's great delights. He was in his element with people like Bob Zelnick, Tom Brown, Stan Abbott, Allan Frank, and another new hire at the end of the year, Molly Bowditch. Molly had been a researcher for *TIME* magazine, tangled with the gender policies of Time-Life, and called from the bottom of the Grand Canyon to ask for a job. Larry said that anyone who can find a payphone at the bottom of the Grand Canyon he had to have.

But the downside of the picture was still rankling terribly. As the financial accounting improved and the true picture emerged, we found that at the end of September 1970, the net loss for the past year was $495,000. Much of this went to repairing or replacing a decaying production facility. The "new" press had come online the end of May, and was certainly an improvement over the old one. But it wasn't nearly as romantic. I wept the day the press erectors carried the old press out to the junkyard. In a way it symbolized our family's dreams, which had become so much harder to realize than we imagined on that giddy day three years earlier when we had posed for pictures standing by that wonderful seventy-five-year-old press with its brass rails.

Understandably, Ted's trustees wanted a first-hand accounting, a meeting with us and with Ted. So the end of June, we all went to Chicago for a meeting with the trustees, where Ted could talk about his commitment to the newspaper and that, yes, he wanted to continue supporting it.

While in Chicago, Ted approached his father's long-time secretary, Doris Burkland, then working for a third generation of Marshall Fields, Ted's brother Marshall, and asked if she could get him a blind date. He specified an interest in blondes. It so happened that Doris knew a family with four beautiful blonde daughters. The date with the one selected, Judi Erickson, was an immediate and long-term success, so much so that Ted made a spontaneous decision to attend Northwestern University in Evanston, Illinois, that September so he could be near Judi. In August Larry, Barb, and I went back to Hawaii for a little more rest and relaxation for Larry, while the two older kids went to Adventure Unlimited camp, a riding and climbing camp in Colorado.

As we continued to grapple with the core problem of the newspaper as outlined by executive-on-loan from Chicago Jack Crosby ("reduce expenses and increase revenues"), Larry's asthma grew worse. He was constantly on cortisone now and Dr. Fish was emphasizing that it wasn't good for him. In December Larry drove across the country with Ted in his new Audi and abruptly and unilaterally took himself off cortisone. He was a wreck when he got back to Anchorage, but soon stabilized again as we headed into the most frigid January and February we had encountered since we had come to Alaska.

10

It was a quiet January 1971 in Anchorage. The city descended into a deep freeze, 20 to 30 degrees below zero. The snow glistened and crackled. The trees were thick with hoarfrost. The Chugach Mountains behind the city looked like giant cream puffs, and across the inlet 180 miles loomed Mount McKinley, often bathed in pink light. A great orange sun dangled low in the sky for a few hours each day. Fires burned in nearly every fireplace, even ours. Larry wasn't much of a fire builder but it did make the house so cozy. Larry was actually home some evenings instead of always at the paper. He seemed much improved since returning from his drive with Ted. As a family we watched our favorite TV programs, the "Smothers Brothers," "Laugh-In," "Mission Impossible." It was a special family time.

In early February, a longtime journalist friend of Larry's came to town from New York. Steve Fischer was with *Scientific American* magazine and was heading to the North Slope to do a story. He was obviously not prepared for the weather he would encounter there, so Larry loaned him his marvelous dark green arctic parka and a pair of winter-weight trousers. The evening before Steve was to fly to the slope, we took him out to dinner at Nikko Gardens, Anchorage's favorite Japanese restaurant for special occasions. I loved Nikko Gardens. I had written the first piece about it when it opened in 1966, detailing the loving care with which each rock for the garden had been sent from Japan. How the little waterfalls had been crafted and how the tables had wells under them so that you seemed to be sitting on the floor but you really weren't. Two couples, special friends Jack and Martha Roderick and Bob and Barbara Goldberg, went to dinner with us. It was a happy evening.

The next morning Larry and I quarreled over breakfast over the most inconsequential thing: whether Larry's pants needed to go to the cleaners before we loaned them to Steve. I said they should. Larry said it wasn't necessary. The kids set off for school, bundled up against the frigid morning, and Larry and I both headed for the paper.

He and I and Dave Stein had just begun to go over the finances that morning in the regularly scheduled weekly meeting Jack Crosby had set up before he left town. Larry excused himself to go to the restroom, and when he came back said he'd like to postpone the meeting so he could lie down for a little while. He complained of a pain in his chest. He lay down on the couch in his office for a few minutes, seemed to feel better, but decided he should call Dr. Fish. I watched Larry's face become paler as he talked to Fish. The doctor told him he had probably had a heart attack and should come down to the Emergency Room right away. Within a few minutes Larry had another, very sharp pain and was lying on the couch again. While I stayed with Larry, Berchie, his secretary, called Dr. Fish and asked him to come to the office. Fish said that wouldn't do any good. He wouldn't have anything to work with there. He told us to get an ambulance and bring Larry to the Emergency Room at Providence Hospital.

So we called 911, and pretty soon the ambulance came right up to the outside door of Larry's office. As they loaded Larry onto a wheeled stretcher, he asked where his glasses were. I assured him that I had them. As he was trundled out the door he said, "Well, I'll be damned." I've wondered since just why he said that. I think it was because what he had envisioned was actually happening, just as he had outlined it. I rode in the front seat of the ambulance, praying all the way, as it screeched its way to Providence Hospital. The doctors had me wait just outside the Emergency Room so they would have room to work on Larry. After an hour or two I left for a moment to make a phone call. When I returned the doctors who had been working so feverishly on Larry had relaxed and were no longer at work. I thought he must be better. Then Winthrop Fish came out and said simply, "He departed, Kay."

It was as if the breath was knocked out of me for a moment. Then I rallied. This was the time to prove what I deeply believed, that life is permanent, spiritual, and can never be lost, regardless of appearances. I knew that Larry, although no longer visible to me, would go on being and doing his good work, that nothing spiritual and permanent could really change. I got into the car and went to Madison Way to tell the children, who were home from school by that time. That was perhaps the hardest thing of all. They had lost one father just four and a half years earlier, and now they had come to love this new one very much and now he was gone at the age of fifty-six. Ted was particularly helpful, I remember. He went down to his room and came back with some citations from the Bible and *Science and Health*, which he thought would help us all. And they did. Next I had to tell Larry's daughter, Judy Hunt, who was in the midst of giving a piano lesson at her house a few blocks away. And then I had to tell the paper.

Dave Stein came to the house to pick me up. I don't remember much of what happened next, but Dave remembers driving me to the paper, wondering how I could hold up. He said, "You were creating strength even for me at that point." I don't remember anything I said to the assembled staff. It was late by that time and the day staff had mostly gone home, so I talked to the newsroom and some production people. Dave said that I told them what had happened, that I knew it was a terrible loss to them as well as to our family, that I was grateful for the four wonderful years I had with Larry and was going to dwell on the good times we had together, and that this paper was going to survive. Although I hadn't the slightest idea how any of this would be achieved, I said that we were all going to pull together and depend on one another to make it happen.

The news traveled fast and calls started to pour in. I made it clear to people who called that I didn't want a lot of Larry's friends and family coming in from the Lower 48. That was a selfish act. He had such great legions of friends who wanted to come to pay tribute to him, but I felt that it might be overwhelming. The truth was, I knew I just couldn't handle it. I later learned that some of Larry's friends, business associates, and family from the Lower 48 were deeply hurt that they were not invited to come to Anchorage for the memorial service held a few days later. Larry's son, Michael, and his wife, Jill, came, of course, from Seattle, but not his brothers. Chuck and Lorraine Percy simply jumped on a plane from Chicago and came without asking. They remembered how Larry and I had been on hand when their daughter Valerie was murdered. Since they were Christian Scientists and I felt they could share in my way of thinking about this event, I was glad to have them. Another journalist friend who adored Larry, Dean Schoelkopf, then working in Minneapolis, simply showed up.

The next day, after the kids and I had somehow gotten through the night, a very sober Stan Abbott and Tom Brown came to see me. Tom had flown in immediately from Juneau, where he had been covering the legislature for the paper. Both were deeply shaken. The purpose of their call, besides extending sympathy, was to implore me to keep the paper going. I said that it never occurred to me to do anything else, that more than anything I wanted to keep our dream alive. But I said I would need a lot of help, and asked them if they would jointly head the news operation, Stan the newsroom itself (which he actually already did), and Tom the editorial page. They agreed.

The next days are a blur. People coming and going, flowers, masses of letters, calls from all over the country. The memorial service was held at St. Mary's Episcopal Church. Bob Hahn, our friend and a lawyer for the paper, who was also First Reader of the Christian Science Church, officiated, reading selections from the Bible that the kids and I had selected. It was standing room only. I remember virtually the whole *Daily News* staff being there, including the deaf-mute printers communicating by sign language. At an informal reception at our house afterward, Senator Chuck Percy took to the phone, calling advertisers and community leaders to tell them that the newspaper would go on under my leadership.

At a time like this, as many others have discovered, there is nothing to do but go forward. The kids went back to school. I went to the paper. I wrote a memo to the staff, thanking them on behalf of Ted, Kathy, Barbie, Judy, and me for "your expressions of sympathy and understanding and for renewing your dedication to the goals of this newspaper." I told them that I had received a call from (former) Senator Gruening, who said, "This event is a calamity for Alaska." And that it was our job, all of us together, to see that this was not so.

"No one can take Larry's place," I said, "but I intend to do what I can in active participation at the paper and still fulfill my essential responsibilities at home. . . . I expect to spend part of each day at the office. It is as yet unclear to me what, if any, title I should take." I concluded the memo, "Larry told me many times that this paper was the most satisfying thing he had ever done. We thank you all for giving so much of yourselves, sometimes under difficult circumstances, to make it so. I think Larry knows that we will keep the colors aloft."

Just how, I had no idea.

Kay and Larry Fanning at the Post Road plant, early in their ownership of the *Anchorage Daily News* (date unknown). COURTESY OF THE *ANCHORAGE DAILY NEWS*.

▲▲ Kay's first home in Anchorage, 3023 Madison Way, in College Village (date unknown).

▲ Larry Fanning and Kay Fanning at Portage Glacier, Alaska (c. 1966–1971).

Kay Fanning, editor of *Alaska Living* magazine, the *Anchorage Daily News* Sunday magazine, at her desk (c. 1966). PHOTO BY WILLIAM L. FOX III. COURTESY OF THE *ANCHORAGE DAILY NEWS*.

▲▲ Family picnic at Sand Lake in Anchorage. Kay Fanning is on the right, with (from left) Kathy Field and Barbara Field, and Hal Hunt and Peter Hunt, the children of Judith Fanning Hunt, Kay's stepdaughter (late 1960s).

▲ Kay Fanning with Anchorage Mayor Jack Roderick (early 1970s). COURTESY OF JACK RODERICK.

▶ Larry and Kay Fanning admire the printing quality of one of the first Sunday papers to come off their new press on Post Road, the *Anchorage Daily News* (date unknown). COURTESY OF THE *ANCHORAGE DAILY NEWS*.

◄ Kay Fanning in the trans-Alaska pipeline during the height of the pipeline's construction (1976). Kay is sitting inside a "Snoopy," a welding cart that travels inside the pipeline. PHOTO BY NEAL MENSCHEL. COURTESY OF THE *ANCHORAGE DAILY NEWS*.

▲ Kay Fanning at the *Anchorage Daily News* newsroom at 200 Potter Drive with (left to right) Jim Babb, Bob Porterfield, and Howard Weaver, winners of the 1976 Pulitzer Prize for Public Service, a first for an Alaska newspaper. COURTESY OF THE *ANCHORAGE DAILY NEWS*.

◄ The *Anchorage Daily News* welcomes the new press on Potter Drive (April 1979). Left to right, top: Executive Editor Stan Abbott, John Redding, Clay Haswell; on the ladder, Jim Wright; on the floor holding the newspaper, Don Howson, then Lurlyne Allen, Jerry Grilly, and Kay Fanning. COURTESY OF THE *ANCHORAGE DAILY NEWS*.

▲ Kay Fanning, with C. K. McClatchy (left), and Jim Lanane (right), president of SII Computer Company, on the startup night of the new *Anchorage Daily News* press on Potter Drive, April 1, 1979. COURTESY OF THE *ANCHORAGE DAILY NEWS*.

▲▲ Howard Weaver (left), Kay Fanning (second from right), and Senator Ted Stevens (date unknown). COURTESY OF THE *ANCHORAGE DAILY NEWS*.

▲ Kay Fanning, with (from left) Bob Atwood, publisher of the *Anchorage Times*; Lew Williams, *Ketchikan Daily News* editor and publisher; and Stan Abbott, executive editor of the *Anchorage Daily News* (date unknown). SOURCE UNKNOWN.

◄ Kay Fanning, Barbara Field, and Judith Hunt in front of the house at 2001 Stanford Drive, Anchorage (1979).

▼ Kay Fanning aboard *The Observer* at Tracy Arm near Juneau, Alaska (July 1981).

▲▲ Kay Fanning, editor and publisher of the *Anchorage Daily News*, looks over the first copy of the Sunday edition, right off the press (February 1, 1981). Photo by Fran Durner. COURTESY OF THE *ANCHORAGE DAILY NEWS*.

▲ The *Anchorage Daily News* staff outside the Potter Drive building, celebrating reaching 50,000 circulation (October 5, 1982). COURTESY OF THE *ANCHORAGE DAILY NEWS*.

▲▲ Kay Fanning, president of American Society of Newspaper Editors (April 1987–April 1988) introducing President Ronald Reagan at the ASNE convention, on April 13, 1988, at Marriott Hotel, Washington, D.C. PHOTO BY JIM MARKS.

▲ Kay Fanning with Oscar Arias, Nobel Peace Prize winner (c. 1984). Photo by W. C. Dannenbrink. COURTESY OF THE *CANANDAIGUA* (NEW YORK) *DAILY MESSENGER.*

◄ Kay Fanning in a pensive moment (date and location unknown). SOURCE UNKNOWN.

▼ Kay Fanning (right), with husband Amos (Mo) Matthews and Martha Roderick, wife of former Anchorage mayor Jack Roderick, on the Top of the World Highway to Dawson City, Yukon Territory, Canada (August 1993).

▲▲ Kay Fanning on the Alaska Peninsula looking for bears (fall 1983).

▲ Kay Fanning with Mount McKinley (Denali) in the background (1996).

▲▲ Kay Fanning at the Petersville Mount McKinley (Denali) overlook (August 1997). From this spot, Alaska artist Sydney Laurence painted many of his works of Mount McKinley.

▲ Kay Fanning (right) and husband Mo Matthews at Circle Hot Springs (August 2000).

PART II
Kay as We Remember Her

Kay and Larry Fanning met Ted Stevens before he was a U.S. senator and national figure. When they first met him in 1967, Stevens was an Anchorage lawyer who lived in a log cabin in town with his wife, Ann, and their children. His participation in the successful purchase of the Anchorage Daily News *was crucial.* **Senator Ted Stevens** *(Republican) has served in the United States Senate since 1968.*

When Kay and Larry Fanning asked that I represent them in their negotiations to buy the *Anchorage Daily News*, I believe they came to me because of their friendship with Fred Seaton, publisher of the Hastings, Nebraska, *Tribune*. Seaton had been my boss when he was secretary of the interior during President Eisenhower's administration, and I was assistant to the secretary and later solicitor of the department. Secretary Seaton had a great interest in Alaska, was a strong supporter of statehood when he was in the U.S. Senate, and he knew most of Alaska's editors and publishers.

It's my recollection that Kay, Larry, and I met in 1967. My law practice was in Anchorage, but that was the year of the devastating Fairbanks flood, and there was a special session of the State Legislature, where I served as House Majority Leader. During that session, I returned to Anchorage on several occasions to meet with Norm and Blanche Brown as well as with Kay and Larry. They brought their friend Newt Minow, a former FCC commissioner and a lawyer, to Anchorage to help in the arrangements for the sale. Because I had been the attorney for the *News*, not the Browns' personal attorney, I was somewhat of a middleman in the negotiations.

Kay and Larry's purchase of the *News* in 1967 was viewed positively by my friends in Anchorage. We had survived the earthquake of 1964 and Anchorage was beginning to grow. Even Bob Atwood, publisher of the *Anchorage Times*, appeared to welcome Kay and Larry into our state's new community. Larry's experience as an editor of San Francisco and Chicago papers promised to bring a measure of "big city" prestige to Anchorage.

Events in our lives and in our state were cascading quickly in the year after Kay and Larry took the helm at the *News*. Alaska's Senator E. L. "Bob" Bartlett died. Appointed to succeed him, I went to Washington, D.C., in December of 1968.

It was truly a time of turmoil: oil was discovered at Prudhoe Bay. The battle began to construct the pipeline. Settlement of Alaska's Native land claims was obviously necessary before a pipeline could be built. That problem would have to be solved with landmark legislation never before considered or approved by Congress. That augured yet another Congressional battle. And our state's land grants could not be selected until those claims were settled.

Kay took a deep interest in these problems of her new state, and the *Daily News* stepped up to the plate and did a fine job of covering the issues that consumed us. I remember she attended early meetings at my home to discuss and seek solutions to the concerns that statehood brought about. I was pleased that Kay and Larry believed that the *Daily News* should give full support to the Alaska Native Claims Settlement Act passed in 1971.

While the *Daily News* and I often did not agree on issues, that disagreement did not stand in the way of friendship. Kay made sure that the paper provided the opportunity for healthy debate for readers. The paper's pages, through Kay, gave voice to Alaskans, many of them new to our state and who brought new ideas to the Great Land. In our young state, whether you agreed with them or not, there was a place for new thoughts and new ideas that might help to achieve the goals of statehood. Kay provided that place in the *Daily News*.

I will never forget the *Daily News*' editorial after our aircraft crash in 1978, in which my wife, Ann, and four others perished. It was warm and tender, written by a person who knew and loved Ann and who understood the impact of such a loss. Those words meant much to me and my family.

With Kay's total involvement in the paper after Larry's death, and the U.S. Senate taking a good chunk of my time away from Alaska, we didn't see each other regularly after those first few years of the paper's publication. When Kay would come to Washington on business, we'd often meet briefly in my office. When I was home, there would be occasional short visits and meetings with Kay and the editorial board of the paper.

We had some lively evenings together during the campaign of 1996, when my wife, Catherine, and I rented a condo just two doors away from the one Kay and Mo Mathews bought after their marriage.

We'd talk some about the early days, but by that time Kay had begun her association with the *Christian Science Monitor*, so our discussions broadened. Because I was raised by my Christian Scientist grandmother, our visits were often more philosophical, and sometimes more related to national issues than our early times together when our state was new.

When she went to the *Monitor*, Kay was front and center on the national stage as the editor of one of our nation's prestigious dailies. Despite the fact that she was now a national figure, I was proud to see that she remained a true Alaskan in many ways, particularly because she continued to champion the rights of Native Americans.

She may have been a gently reared city girl, but long before she came to Alaska, Kay possessed the Alaska spirit. With the determination and strength and fearlessness she exhibited when she came to our Great Land, a young mother with three young children, she proved the inspiration for many young Alaskans, particularly those who worked for her on the *Daily News*, to believe in their convictions, and to work hard to make their dreams come true.

~

Ted Stevens was not the only lawyer to assist Kay and Larry in purchasing the Anchorage Daily News. *They sought help from outside Alaska from their attorney, Newton Minow, who flew to Alaska from Chicago to offer counsel.* **Newton N. Minow**, *attorney and author, was chairman of the Federal Communications Commission during the John F. Kennedy administration.*

Indomitable! A big word. But Kay Fanning was big—big in courage, big in determination, big in idealism, and big in her contributions to our country. Indomitable is the right word to describe Kay, who was so exceptionally resolute in achieving her goals. I have been around a long time, and have met many people. I never met anyone who could match Kay's steadfast commitment to the highest standards of journalism and citizenship.

I first met Kay in Chicago in the 1950s. Later, in the sixties, Kay married my friend Larry Fanning, who had been the managing editor of the

San Francisco Chronicle, executive editor of the *Chicago Daily News,* and editor of the *Chicago Sun-Times.* Before her marriage to Larry, Kay decided to move with her children to Anchorage, Alaska. Kay needed legal advice for her family, and Larry recommended me. I became the family lawyer almost forty years ago. After Kay married Larry, he moved to Alaska to join Kay and her children, and we remained close friends.

One day, Kay and Larry called me to come to Alaska to help them purchase the *Anchorage Daily News.* This newspaper was then the struggling, second newspaper in Anchorage, a city not large enough to support two daily papers. I worked with Kay and Larry's local lawyer, Ted Stevens (now the senior U.S. senator from Alaska) to represent them in the negotiating and purchase. I believed the *Daily News* would not succeed, and recommended against the purchase. But Kay and Larry were confident and determined, and they became the owners, publishers, and editors of the *Daily News.*

Sadly, Larry died within a few years. Kay had to decide whether to continue alone or close the paper. She decided to carry on, struggling each year. Her editorial standards and courage led the *Daily News* to journalism's highest honor, the Pulitzer Prize. We worked out a joint operating agreement with the dominant paper, the *Anchorage Times,* persuading the Department of Justice to approve the transaction under legislation protecting failing newspapers. But the joint operating agreement did not work.

The sale of the *Anchorage Daily News* to the McClatchy organization resulted in a first-class operation, fulfilling Kay and Larry's dream.

One day, Kay called to say she was leaving Alaska to return to the Lower 48 because she had accepted a new job. I told her I knew what the new job would be. Kay asked, "How could you know? It is a secret!" I said there was only one job that could persuade her to leave Alaska, and that could only be editor of the *Christian Science Monitor.* Kay said, "You know me so well that you are right; I will become the editor of the *Monitor.*"

Kay brought new energy and promise to the *Monitor,* maintaining its high standards and increasing its influence on American policies. Her colleagues in journalism recognized her leadership by electing her president of the American Society of Newspaper Editors, its highest honor. For women journalists, this was an exceptionally important landmark in the history of achieving equality in their profession.

Kay's contributions endure. She helped Alaska grow and benefit from a first-class newspaper. She helped the *Christian Science Monitor* maintain and enhance its high standards. She led her colleagues in journalism to recognize their essential role as the fourth estate. And she showed all of us how to reach our goals, fulfill our dreams, and remain true to our ideals.

~

It is unlikely that Kay would have ever made the decision to move to Alaska and start a life that was so very different from the one she had been living in Chicago if it hadn't been for her college friend, Tay Thomas, and Tay's husband, Lowell. Tay's enthusiasm for Alaska and her assurances that it was a wonderful place to raise children had a profound effect on Kay. Here, Tay recounts her memories of Kay's first visit to Alaska and her days as a new resident of the state. **Tay Thomas**, *author and longtime Alaskan, is the wife of Lowell Thomas Jr., who served as lieutenant governor of Alaska from 1974 to 1978.*

Kay Woodruff and I seemed fated to live in close proximity. Although she grew up in the Chicago area and I on the East Coast, our parents owned winter homes in southern Florida. Jupiter Island was known as a wealthy community that shunned outsiders, but the houses were unpretentious and shielded from the one narrow road by thick undergrowth and trees.

We seldom met during those early years because school vacations rarely coincided, but I knew her parents, and Kay's picture, as a much-adored only child, was everywhere in their home.

When we both entered Smith College as freshmen in 1945, we greeted each other as longtime acquaintances. But even our four years there were a continuation of separate paths: different courses and friends. By the time we were seniors, however, we had begun to meet regularly for coffee in one of the Green Street cafes. We were making plans for travel after college, hopefully as part of jobs we would both seek at the *National Geographic* magazine.

The next contact, a year later, was in the form of wedding invitations— one from her to me and mine to her—the same date 800 miles apart. She married Marshall Field Jr. while I married Lowell Thomas Jr. Our common goal had not changed, but just the means by which we would travel about the world. I was not too surprised when, on our honeymoon to Hawaii, Lowell and I encountered Kay and Marshall in Honolulu, sitting at a table next to us at Trader Vic's. We had all heard that Hawaii's Mauna Loa volcano was erupting in spectacular fashion, so we put our heads together and decided to rent a boat in order to watch the lava flowing into the sea. When we said goodbye, we promised to keep in closer touch, but then followed a lengthy period of years with no contact at all. We were both traveling extensively and starting families as well. Kay had three children while I had two.

Lowell and I moved permanently to Alaska in 1960, but then lost our home to the 1964 earthquake. My article for the *National Geographic* on that catastrophic event fulfilled that Green Street dream. I cannot be sure whether it triggered Kay's memory or not, but one spring day just a year later, when Lowell and I had started building a new home, I received a phone call from her. It was 1965, and fifteen years had passed with no contact at all, so I was stunned when she came right to the point. Could she and the three kids come visit us in Anchorage during their upcoming spring break?

Of course I was delighted; in those days no friends traveled so far just to visit, and tourism was in its infancy. However, I tried to talk her into waiting until summer. I was anxious for her to see Alaska at its best, and that was definitely NOT during "spring breakup." At that time most of our streets were still unpaved, and so during April we drove or walked through deep mud. Dirty snowbanks revealed all the discarded old tires, lost boots and gloves and paper products from the previous fall. And while the "Lower 48," as Alaskans refer to the rest of the states, were enjoying flowering trees and daffodils, we had to make do with gray pussy willows.

However, nothing would deter Kay. She had already selected her arrival date in early April, and she could hardly wait to join us on a northern adventure. Needless to say, neither of us noticed the dinginess of our surroundings; we were too busy catching up on fifteen years of news in both families. In a way, it was like being back on Green Street again, as we gradually moved on from my glowing reports of life in Anchorage and our kids' excellent public schools to talk about the future.

Kay had recently been divorced and felt she wanted to leave Chicago behind. She might even look for a house in Anchorage. Within a week of her arrival she and the children were driving about with a real estate agent, and a day later we were given a tour of their new home. Within four months, they had returned again, this time followed by a moving van. They were quickly joined by Kinka, a German shepherd puppy from the same litter we had just acquired a dog.

Life was full of fun for both families that year as we all went camping, fishing, hiking, and then skiing together. However, the day came when Kay felt the need for more personal challenge, and she applied for a job as a reporter at the *Anchorage Daily News*, at that time a small morning daily newspaper dwarfed by the evening giant, the *Anchorage Times*.

Later, Kay returned briefly to Chicago to marry a longtime friend and editor. Larry Fanning came back with her and they purchased the *News*, running it together for a few years. Then Larry died suddenly of a heart attack, leaving Kay to run it alone, eventually turning it into Alaska's largest newspaper.

~

As close friends of Kay's, Jack and Martha Roderick witnessed her transformation from an Outsider to a true Alaskan. The long battle that Kay fought to keep the Anchorage Daily News *alive forged her identity as a strong Alaskan pioneer in the realm of journalism. Jack and Martha Roderick were perhaps her most supportive friends throughout that long struggle.* **Jack Roderick,** *author of* Crude Dreams: A Personal History of Oil and Politics in Alaska *(1997), has been a resident of Alaska since 1954. He was Kay and Larry's lawyer in the late 1960s and served as Anchorage Borough Mayor during the 1970s.*

Kay Fanning and her three young children came to Alaska in 1965, to find an exciting new life. Shortly after arriving in Alaska, she wrote to her son's trustees: "Alaska is a new country where people worn from the battles of the 'old country' can find a fresh start and, hopefully, make their fortune as well as enjoy a cleaner environment." She did not make a fortune in Alaska, but she did get a fresh start and also found her own self in this "new" country.

During the nearly two decades Kay lived in Alaska, she, Mo [Kay's third husband, 1983], Martha, and I took many trips around the state each summer. We'd go to the most remote places in Alaska we could find: Brooks Camp, Camp Denali, Valdez, Jay and Bella Hammond's home on Lake Clark, up the Petersville Road all the way to "Vicinity," to Halibut Cove, McNeil River, along the Denali Highway, Chicken, over the "Top of the World Highway" to Dawson City, down the Yukon River to Eagle, to Slana, and up to the mine at the end of the Nabesna Road. We went across the river on the old, single-seated tram to McCarthy and Kennicott in the beautiful Wrangell Mountains, and on our last trip together, in the late summer of 2000, we visited Arctic Circle Hot Springs and walked along the shore of the Yukon River. We slept out, hiked, got stuck several times, and communed with the bears. Kay loved travel in Alaska.

One of my fondest memories of Kay was on one of our trips up the Petersville Road, near Talkeetna. I can still see her sitting on top of the tundra munching crackers. We had hiked up off the Petersville Road onto the ridge where Sydney Laurence had painted most of his canvases of the great Denali. As we gazed out at the mountain, I remember thinking how much Kay had become part of Alaska. She had come from the sophisticated and crowded urban Midwest to this rather simple and open place. In so doing, she had come to love Alaska, its newness, its sense of adventure and possibilities. Most of all, I think, she loved the feeling of adventure and freedom.

When Larry and Kay bought the *Anchorage Daily News* from Norm Brown in 1967, my family and I were preparing to go to India with the Peace Corps. When we returned a year later, Ted Stevens was in the process of being appointed to the U.S. Senate by Governor Hickel. Ted and I had practiced law together in the early 1960s, so he asked me to take over his law practice. Among his most important clients at the time were Larry and Kay Fanning and the *Anchorage Daily News*. I became their attorney. Larry was then editor and publisher of the *News*, while Kay served as reporter, editor of the twenty-four-page Sunday magazine, sometime columnist, advertising salesman, and assistant to the publisher. With Larry's sudden death in 1971, she was catapulted into the number one job at the *News*. Few thought she could handle it.

Larry had built an outstanding team of young investigative news reporters, but most of the entire financial support of the paper was coming from Kay's son Ted's trust fund. And, understandably, the trustees were nervous about Kay's ability to take over management of the *News*. The paper's circulation had only nominally increased during the previous four years under Larry's leadership, and none of the few large retailers in Anchorage had increased their advertising in the *News*, at least in any significant amount. Bob Atwood's *Anchorage Daily Times*, the state's leading newspaper, remained a worthy and formidable competitor.

When Kay took over management of the *News* in 1971, Anchorage was suffering from a financial shock. The pipeline that was to bring crude oil from the North Slope to market had been delayed by the secretary of the U.S. Department of the Interior. A freeze had been placed on all federal land disposals. The major oil companies that had discovered more than 10 billion barrels of oil at Prudhoe Bay several years earlier needed a pipeline right-of-way on which to lay their pipe. Congress could lift the freeze, but it first had to settle the land rights of the Alaska Native peoples. The delay was causing local banks and businesses to suffer serious financial troubles. Most Alaskans realized that something "big" had happened on the North Slope, but little economic growth in Anchorage could be expected until pipeline construction began. Anchorage's economy was stymied. The *News* was caught in the stalemate.

I was mayor of the greater Anchorage Area Borough at the time. Our municipal government spent most of its time planning for the coming of construction workers and equipment. That would not begin to happen until the spring of 1974.

Meanwhile, Kay had to find a way to keep the *News* afloat. That same year, 1974, she and Ted's trustees agreed that the *News* should enter into a joint operating agreement with Robert Atwood's *Anchorage Daily Times*. Under the agreement, the *Times* would take charge of all circulation, advertising, and production for the *News*. For two years, the joint operation limped along, with circulation and advertising revenues for the *News* dropping drastically. Finally, the *News* filed a lawsuit, followed by arbitration, resulting in the *News'* receiving some needed cash from the *Times* but not enough to put it on its feet. The *Times* kept the Sunday edition, and the trustees decided the trust had suffered enough.

Kay's *News* was now in worse shape than before. To help keep the paper afloat and to survive, Kay organized the "Committee for Two Newspapers." Loyal readers began soliciting subscriptions and advertising from their neighbors. Good effort but not much financial help. She then solicited money from individuals. Most of these were from Outside, but the Bristol Bay Native Corporation gave her some financial support. Not enough, though, for the *News* to stay alive. Finally, she approached C. K. McClatchy in Sacramento, who came north, liked what he saw and heard, and, eager to own and operate a statewide newspaper in a growing state, bought the *News* from Kay's family.

In one of her early reports to the trustees, Kay characteristically said what she believed a newspaper should be. "It is not primarily a business but a public trust—truly the fourth estate, whose responsibility is first and foremost to report the news responsibly, to be watchdog over government, to provide a forum for all sides of the issues, and to spotlight areas of injustice." She stayed true to this credo.

Kay remained with the *News* until 1983. At that time, she left Alaska to become editor of the *Christian Science Monitor*. Though living in Boston, she kept her home in Anchorage, where she and Mo spent most Christmases and summers. Our travels together were uninterrupted. She was a woman with "graceful tenacity," as one admiring writer put it. I don't believe anyone else could have saved the *Daily News* as she did. In the process, the little girl from Joliet, by way of Chicago, finally came home.

～

Kay believed that the Jay Hammond era in Alaska politics promised a new age for Alaska in terms of environmental enlightenment. In turn, Governor

Hammond credits Kay with inspiring him to stick to his ideals for the state despite often strenuous opposition. Here he discusses the effect of her influence on his style of governing. **Jay Hammond** *was elected Alaska's governor in 1974 and reelected in 1978. For many years until his passing in 2005, he lived the Alaska dream in a log cabin on remote Lake Clark. He is the author of* Tales of Alaska's Bush Rat Governor *(1996) and was an accomplished bush pilot and trapper.*

Reflections on Kay Fanning induce a warm, if sad, glow of how deeply she's missed by all who were privileged to know her. Of the media multitude with whom I've crossed paths (or collided), Kay most nimbly and gracefully traversed that fine line between bias and objectivity, fact and fiction, sense and nonsense. In the process, she proved so elusive a target that slings and arrows some would launch her way usually fell far short. Others were deflected by her shining armor of credibility, compassion, and character. To me, Kay was the Joan of Arc of journalism. So highly respected was she by even her foes, I can't recall anyone ever bad-mouthing Kay. Of course I was not privy to comment made during war councils held in the bunker of her major competitor, the *Anchorage Times*. Moreover, so busy was I dodging their missiles myself, I might not have detected collateral damage inflicted on Kay.

I came to know Kay while sharing the trenches during the onslaught endured from two formidable, irate behemoths: the *Times* and the Teamsters. She was targeted for having the temerity to challenge the *Times'* credibility and to expose Teamster connivance. I, for having made the imprudent suggestions that we should comply with the law and evaluate alternative pipeline routes to avoid construction delays and vastly increased cost overruns should our failure to do so propel us into court.

Though later these proved to be valid concerns, in those years the *Times* and the Teamsters were by far the biggest political guns in the state. Both were determined that only a pipeline route to Valdez be considered. Those who disagreed did not affront them without being targeted. Though both guns have long since been spiked before they were silenced, I like to think I helped Kay survive their barrage; just as I know she helped me.

Kay Fanning was an inspiration to all who knew her. She compelled one to try to "play above one's head." Certainly every action I contemplated taking while in public office was first mentally laid upon the yardstick she held over one's head to see how it measured up to her standards. Forgive me, Kay, if those standards may have sometimes been beyond my floundering leap. However, without the guidance, support, counsel, and inspiration of folk such as you, I'd have been hard pressed to even get up off my knees.

As one of the most admirable people I've known, Kay's departure leaves in its wake a great smoking crater, which all the fond memories, high esteem, and affection cannot begin to fill.

~

To augment Jay Hammond's personal recollections of Kay, we asked Alaska journalist **Pete Spivey** *to interview Governor Hammond about Kay. Having worked on two Florida newspapers, Spivey drove to Alaska in 1980 with the hope of joining Kay's "inspirational battle" to keep the* Anchorage Daily News *alive. Two years later, Kay asked him to write a small article on the business page announcing that the* News *had surpassed the formerly dominant* Anchorage Times *in circulation. In 1982 he left the news, and now works as a freelance editor/writer in Anchorage.*

Jay Hammond: It was in the wake of Watergate, and people were very much turned off on traditional politicians, and I guess I was perceived to be the most improbable and nontraditional of all. I don't know how long prior to the campaign of '74 that I had met Kay. I'm sure I had met her before that. But anyhow, I had been familiar with the *Anchorage Daily News* hierarchy, but I actually became most familiar with Kay early on in the campaign. I was not the darling of the Republican Party, although I had filed as a Republican.

So early on, I had no great party affiliation or strings attached, and I was kind of hanging out there in limbo, and apparently, after talking to Kay about some of our mutual concerns, she stepped forward and played a very significant role in breathing life into the Alaska Independents for Hammond.

There were several editorials that at least gave me credibility and, to a degree, sanitized my image beyond what the *Anchorage Times* was trying to lay on me. I got in trouble (with the *Times*, specifically with owner/publisher Robert Atwood) by asserting that some growth and development wasn't necessarily healthy. We had malignant as well as beneficent growth. What's the distinction? I stated the distinction is that healthy growth requires that it is environmentally sound, something the people want, and can pay its own way. And unhealthy growth does not meet those criteria, and if doesn't, I'll oppose it.

Well, as usual, I alienated both ends of the spectrum. Ardent environmentalists—all they heard was that I'll support growth under certain circumstances—and at the other, that I'll oppose it, so as usual, I alienated both, about equally I guess. But Kay quickly, and certainly more fairly, was able to decipher my verbiage, and subscribed to it as well.

She, along with myself and others up here, knew that we were on the cusp of pipeline development and oil development that would change the face of Alaska immeasurably, and that we should husband our resources to at least prevent total desecration, which too often had been the case. The World Bank called me up (after the Permanent Fund and dividend programs were established in law) and told me, "We have looked at every state and nation at how they've handled their oil wealth, and concluded that Alaska did by far the best job." And they attributed it in largest measure to the dividend program.

The reason, they said, was because the dividend program provided transparency. Transparency in that people, if they received a direct discernible benefit that rises or falls on the prudence or magnitude of investment in their oil wealth, will pay heed to what the politicians and those in power are doing with their wealth. The genesis of that concept was something that Kay bought into very early on.

[Before running for governor, Hammond, as mayor of the Bristol Bay Borough in southwest Alaska had failed to convince his constituents to create a fund to pay dividends to residents from taxes on the incredible wealth generated by the Bristol Bay fishery—most of which went outside the state—and also to use the fish tax to reduce residential property taxes. He was again frustrated later on by failing to convince the Alaska Native hierarchy to create such a fund and dividends from at least part of the $1 billion their various village and regional corporations were due to receive from the federal and state governments under the Alaska Native Claims Settlement Act of 1971. He believed that by not doing so, they not only put their wealth at jeopardy but also splintered their political strength.]

I got into this with Kay, explaining how I was determined, if elected governor, to take another shot at it, to make sure our oil wealth didn't go the same route. I proposed then creating what I called Alaska, Inc., the same concept as Bristol Bay, Inc. That we create an investment account, conservatively managed, that would spin off dividends, equally to each and every individual. I probably would not have run for governor . . . save the possibility of doing something along that line. I conveyed that to Kay, and she was entranced with the Alaska, Inc., idea and encouraged me to pursue it further.

When I was elected, I created the Alaska Public Forum. It was designed to go around the state . . . and my intent was to showcase the Alaska, Inc., idea. Back then there was very little support. Kay understood the premise, and she encouraged me to pursue it, and I think it was something that captured the imagination of certain elements of Alaskans who otherwise would have been in the opposite camp.

Kay wrote an editorial or two. We discussed it at some length, and she could see the merits of it. I think a lot of people were surprised at the moxie and intellect she brought to the *Daily News,* and many others greatly underestimated her. I virtually deified Kay Fanning. And of course, by contrast to her opponent, the *Anchorage Times,* her appeal doubled in my quarter.

Kay was one of the lone voices that dared to come out of the woodwork and support me, this, "posey-sniffing swine." There are odd things that occurred. Not only was there the turnoff on traditional politicians in the wake of Watergate, but the concerns of many up here—"What's going to happen to the state?"—with all this involvement in oil and pipeline construction, and so forth. A lot of the folks were concerned about how it would impact the well-being of the state. And of course, on one hand, you had the *Anchorage Times* thumping me over the head, asserting I was determined to build a big fence around the state and put it in a huge national park and throw away the key. Of course, I made things worse by appearing before the Anchorage Chamber [of Commerce] and referring to that by saying that there's a rumor this would occur and Hammond would throw everybody out of work. I said this was absolutely ridiculous; you folks have absolutely nothing whatsoever to worry about. In the first place, your community doesn't deserve park status. It's already degenerated beyond acceptable eligibility. Boy, you can imagine the heartburn they had when I was elected.

But Kay probably perceived more clearly what I was up to and why, and was able to articulate and sanitize and or interpret my hieroglyphics or garblings in a manner that no other media folk were doing up here. She helped me immensely. I have said many times there are few people to whom I owe virtually the majority of the reasons why I was elected, and certainly one of them was Kay Fanning. I've even come to forgive her for it.

I was miserable the first few years as governor. I would go in and kind of muse on that with Kay, and she would tell me to keep in there plugging and maybe you'll prevail, things are turning your way. And they did.

Kay pierced through much of the diatribe that was coming from the *Anchorage Times* and the Teamsters. Every week there would be a yellow paper out with Jesse Carr (now deceased, then the powerful boss of the Alaska Teamsters Union), instigating, ultimately, a recall petition, which at one point, since I was so miserable in the job, I felt I wanted to sign it myself. But Kay bucked up my spirits and gave me a lot of moral support at the time, when it was sorely lacking in many quarters.

[Besides supporting Hammond's spirits, Kay Fanning also oversaw publication of a *Daily News* series about the Teamsters Union's political power and heavy-handed bargaining tactics. The series won her newspaper the 1976 Pulitzer Prize Gold Medal for Public Service. It also increased the animus between the union and Hammond; there were even threats against him. Hammond remains skeptical about the threats, but the Alaska State Troopers were concerned enough at the time to increase his security coverage and insist that he wear a bulletproof vest during a couple of public events.]

Kay and I were mutually "bombed" by the Teamsters for the articles she had done, so we had a common ground there that brought us together, too, that was a major source of mutual admiration . . . or fear, I'm not sure which. Kay was a haven of peace and support at a time when things were not going my way at all. She never seemed to falter in her support.

[A time came when Hammond could offer important support for Kay Fanning's struggling newspaper, centered on the placement of state-paid advertising in newspapers. The ads were a considerable source of newspaper revenue; they sought private contractors to provide services to the state, covering the gamut from office supplies to major construction projects.]

Bob [Clarke, Hammond's director of communications] was the guy who came to me one day and he said, "Do you realize that 99 and 44/100 percent of the state advertising is going to the *Anchorage Times*, your vigorous opponents?" Of course, my commissioners, many of them Republicans, were oriented against the *News*. I called a cabinet meeting, and I said, "For any community that has more than one newspaper, from henceforth, thou shalt advertise in that paper which provides the best rates." The *News'* rates were far better than the *Times*. The argument [against Hammond's declaration] was that there is so much more circulation [by the *Times*] . . . but people who are interested in advertising and those jobs, they're going to subscribe to both papers or at least not let somebody reading the morning paper [the *Times* was an afternoon paper] beat them to the punch, so that argument was specious.

Bob came to me later and said, "They still ain't doing it." Then I laid down the hammer on them and said, "Thou SHALT do it!" They did. Kay, at the time, was hanging by her fingernails financially. I know it helped her. I'd like to think that we were symbiotic in our aid and abetment for a worthy cause. I know the advertising turned around in Anchorage 180 degrees, and all the state ads went to her. It didn't endear me to Atwood.

[Even as Alaska's economy was being superheated by the oil industry's development project, and by the legislature's frenetic spending of oil revenues after the pipeline began transporting oil from Prudhoe Bay in 1977, Hammond was still being strongly criticized by the *Anchorage Times* as the "no-growth" governor.]

Alaska grew without precedence during the "zero-growth" Hammond years, not because of my efforts, but in spite of them. But Kay took the position of "What's going on here?" I remember her doing one editorial essentially saying that "Hammond's being charged with stifling growth and development at a time when Anchorage is about to sink under the capital projects" . . . and all the stuff that was going on here. The *Times* lost a lot of credibility, I think, by constantly hammering that "Hammond's going to throw everybody out of work." She would take them to task—counterpoint those types of editorials. Did it more than once. That was very heartening, because at times after I'd read an *Anchorage Times* editorial, I'd fear stoning in the streets when I'd come back to town. So she, no doubt about it, played an enormous role in not only salvaging what small reputation I might have had and sanitizing the Hammond image, but also salvaging my sanity. Wonderful lady. Never known anybody like her.

~

The image of the newly arrived Alaska journalist Allan Frank with his long, frizzy hair and shaggy sheepskin coat was indelibly etched in Kay's memory. Nicknamed "the critter" by the family because of his appearance, Allan appeared to have been born with that curious combination of energy, curiosity, skepticism of authority, and the ability to be in the right place at the right time that makes an excellent reporter. His account of the Anchorage Daily News *investigation of the massage parlor industry in Anchorage forms an essential and humorous chapter in this history.* **Allan Dodds Frank** *followed his reporting job at the* Anchorage Daily News *with a career in broadcast journalism. He lives and works in New York City.*

I was a student at the Columbia University Graduate School of Journalism in New York City when I met Kay and Larry Fanning at my father's office in midtown Manhattan on March 6, 1970. It turned out to be an auspicious day.

A vast student strike about the war in Vietnam was under way, and the bickering was so widespread that my father and I were barely talking. He was convinced that my classmates and I were in the process of destroying our careers before they began. And we thought he and many of his colleagues, especially the World War II veterans, were missing the mark about how different the war in Vietnam was from the big one against the Nazis and their fascist allies.

I was supposed to meet with my professor of media management that day to talk about what I was going to do with the rest of my life. But he cancelled because one of his sons and daughters-in-law abruptly gave birth to the professor's first grandchild. Since this was long before cell phones, I then went to a pay phone since I was in the neighborhood and called my father, who was the publisher of the Sunday supplement called *Family Weekly*. He said, "Why don't you join me for lunch and hang around. A really interesting couple who run the feisty number-two newspaper in Anchorage are coming in, and you ought to meet them."

So we had lunch, which in those days was at least two scotches and a big hunk of red meat, and went back to his office. In came a legendary Chicago and San Francisco newspaperman (my father had filled me in at lunch) named Larry Fanning. He was in town judging the Pulitzer prizes and was accompanied by his wife, a beautiful, charming woman named Kay Woodruff Field Fanning, who had moved to Anchorage after splitting from Chicago. The two were madly in love and Kay had told Larry, "You said you really love me and would follow me to the ends of the earth. Well, I'm there, in Anchorage, Alaska."

Together they had taken over the *Anchorage Daily News*, then a small 13,000-circulation daily located in a sheet-metal one-story building at 133 Post Road, not far from the entrance to Fort Richardson. The old press was so slow that it took more than four hours to print the paper, and if the headline had to be big, the press used wooden type. When there was a potentially libelous mistake or an egregious misspelling, the press would be stopped and a hammer would be applied to flatten out the lead, leaving a mysterious but innocent blank spot on the offending line of type.

Anyway, back to New York and my father's office.

Larry and Kay wanted *Family Weekly* for the Sunday paper in order to compete against the much larger, ultraconservative *Anchorage Times*. Even though the *Anchorage Daily News* was really too small to be a *Family Weekly* newspaper, my father was charmed by Kay and Larry and by the notion that *Family Weekly* could be in all fifty states. The conversation then turned to me, and I began asking about Alaska and life there.

Then the phone rang. It was my sister, Marilyn, saying the Wilkersons' house, across the street from my father and stepmother's townhouse at 25 West 11th Street, had just blown up. Instantly, I launched into an analysis. It must have been the Weather Underground, a violent faction of the Students for a Democratic Society, I said.

The Fannings were intrigued. After a little of my play-by-play, Larry said, "Why don't you come work for me?" I, of course, said, in the politically incorrect fashion of the day, something like, "Don't be ridiculous. I understand there are not even any girls there."

Kay took this canard and shredded it, saying something to the effect of, a "There are lots of smart, pretty women there if you can handle strong independent women."

The conversation continued, as I chainsmoked. Finally, she said, "Besides, cigarettes are cheaper there."

I was hooked, and the day I arrived in Anchorage after driving from New York, Kay and Larry put me up. When I arrived at their house in the late afternoon, Kay and her friends, Ann Stevens, the wife of the new U.S. Senator Ted Stevens, and Tay Thomas, the wife of Lowell Thomas Jr., were making my bed to welcome me to Alaska.

I stayed with the Fannings for a week or more until I found my own rental, a one-room trailer not far from the Brief Encounter Lounge and the Glacier Pilots ballpark.

From the moment I arrived, Kay made me part of her family, for better or for worse. And as she did with all of us at that little paper, she relied on her faith as a Christian Scientist to get her through all the bad behavior she had to put up with on the frontier.

Following are just a few of the highlights of the overwhelming generosity of spirit that made Kay such a great person, and a great newswoman.

A few months after I arrived in September 1970, Larry died of a heart attack at the newspaper. I had just left for my first vacation to go to a newspaper convention in San Francisco with my father. I remember talking to Kay and giving her my condolences, while offering to write something. I remember her telling me that the man whom I had replaced, Bob Zelnick, had just filed a splendid, long piece and wired it from Washington, Night Press Collect. "Just the way Larry would have wanted it, she said."

Kay quickly learned the ropes of running a newspaper the hard way. First she wanted quality, encouraged it and nurtured it. Somehow she understood that the collection of screwballs in her employ were actually creative and caring and would produce. But I am sure she quietly prayed for excellence.

Like a good baseball manager, she was totally aware of tradition. The first election night after Larry died, she set up a bar in her office for all the reporters and editors to celebrate getting the edition to bed after the returns were in and the type was set. She was a teetotaling Christian Scientist, but she felt it was a memorial to Larry and an act of affection for her staff.

And like all great editors, she had the smarts and instincts to back her reporters to the hilt even when they were under fire from the biggest guns in Alaska. I remember a story about misdoings at the Alaska Fish and Game Department and some big-time poachers. A reporter named Dan Gross did most of the work but another reporter and I also were on the story. When the newspaper got sued, Kay immediately enlisted one of the best lawyers in town to defend us. Gross took the witness stand and the reporter's version of the Fifth. And Kay, who was prepared to have me and my other colleague testify, did her best to keep the process servers away, and hid us in the hotel across the street from the courthouse just in case we had to appear,

Then there was the time in 1972 when I was at the Juneau bureau covering the Alaska legislature. She came to Juneau to lobby the legislature against some bill that might have forced Christian Scientists and others who did not believe in medical care to take their children to doctors. She never interfered in my coverage nor did she ask me to take any special interest in her activities. A few months later, however, when the circulation guy in Juneau quit, she did prevail on me for two weeks to spend my lunch break picking up bundles of 1,000 newspapers daily to deliver to our outlets in Juneau. That, she said, was important.

And when the international press corps converged on Anchorage for the historic meeting between President Nixon and Emperor Hirohito, Kay was ready. She somehow got on the VIP line at Elmendorf Air Force Base and handed Nixon a copy of the paper's special edition. A picture of that exchange, to the everlasting chagrin of Bob Atwood and the *Anchorage Times*, ran around the world.

Perhaps my favorite memory of Kay, though, revolves around her handling of a special investigation she commissioned on organized crime and massage parlors that proliferated around Anchorage as the buildup for the pipeline began.

Most of the reporting was done by the youngest reporter on the staff, Anchorage native Howard Weaver, and me. We cruised all around Anchorage for months late at night, recording license plate numbers at massage parlors, then looking them up during the daytime at the Division of Motor Vehicles. We laid out a map of who worked where and who owned or controlled each of these mysterious places. We began to get a feel for the Anchorage underground, which went way beyond the education the staff was getting nightly at the Club China Doll, one of the greatest strip joints ever (which deserves a motion picture itself).

Anyway, the months went on despite our exceedingly small staff and Kay wanted the goods. She wanted us to be able to prove that sex and drugs could indeed be purchased at these establishments, but she did not want any of her reporters engaging in illegal activities. So we came up with a plan to use a private investigator we knew. Kay allocated a small budget of $250 for this escapade. That was big for the paper at the time, since we routinely had to get permission to call the Lower 48.

But the private eye turned us down, so we went to plan B. We enlisted a guy from the back shop to be our undercover man. Naturally, he ran into the toughest hooker in Anchorage, who immediately smelled a rat, took his money, did not deliver complete sex, and failed to come up with hard drugs.

Dismayed, Howard and I tried to figure out how we could come up with proof. So together we went after midnight to a place called Kay's Oriental Massage, where we suspected the madam [of being involved in all sorts of questionable activities]. Howard and I were doing fine with one of the madam's employees until the madam herself appeared. She realized who we were and insisted that we were trespassing. I cited various public accommodation laws and she called the police.

Immediately on their heels came Herb Shandlin, then a TV newsman who was renowned for cruising Fourth Avenue late at night listening to his police scanner and carrying a camera. So when we got hauled out, it was on television, and one of the Anchorage cops who detested the liberals at the *Anchorage Daily News* tipped off the *Anchorage Times* to our arrests.

It was difficult for me to use my one phone call at 4:30 or 5:00 a.m. to call Kay, but I did, and she and Stan Abbott, the editor, came down to bail us out. To say they were unhappy would be an understatement. But they stuck with us, even after a dispiriting incident when we left a file box of our meticulously annotated three-by-five cards on the roof of Howard's Volkswagen bug as we drove away from the paper and they spilled down the bank toward Turnagain Arm as we rounded a corner near the waterfront.

Kay's only demand: We had to do the series right away, now that the *Anchorage Times* knew what we were doing. She was right, of course, and it was a great series, one that laid the initial groundwork for Howard and my successors to win the Pulitzer Prize for Public Service for investigating the Teamsters.

I could go on about Kay's graciousness and integrity forever, but just remembering the little moments is enough for me. Who else could have forgiven me for taking pictures of her sixteen-year-old daughter Kathy in front of the competing newspaper or keeping her seventeen-year-old son Ted out drinking with the actor Jack Lemmon at a series of seedy bars and strip clubs until 5 in the morning? Or lighting up a cigarette the moment I crossed the threshold out of the Christian Science Church one Sunday after I had gone there as a guest of her family.

Kay Fanning was, in life, the character Katharine Hepburn and Grace Kelly always tried to be in the movies.

Kay Fanning was a good friend to many and strongly believed in the value of mentoring aspiring journalists. Many of those she helped went on to have distinguished careers in journalism. Kay had a fascination with all the goings on in a frontier town like Anchorage. So it was natural that she would become a friend and mentor to Kim Rich, an aspiring writer and young journalist. **Kim Rich,** *who had grown up in Anchorage, was brought up by her father, Johnny Rich, a notorious member of the Anchorage underworld. She later wrote of her life in her successful and intriguing book,* Johnny's Girl: A Daughter's Memoir of Growing Up in Alaska's Underworld *(1993). Kim Rich still lives in Anchorage, and is a writer, teacher, and mother.*

On my desk rests a photograph of Kay Fanning. She's sitting in the newsroom at the *Anchorage Daily News,* in a dark suit and a strand of pearls, with her hair styled as she always wore it, off the shoulders, swept up and back. She exudes the qualities that defined her—poise, warmth, and intelligence.

I keep the picture where I can see it to remind me of a cherished friend.

I never got to work for Kay when she headed up the *Daily News* newsroom. By the time I entered the newsroom in the mid-1980s, with my freshly minted bachelor's degree in journalism, she had already moved on to the *Christian Science Monitor.* Her legacy and influence could still be felt throughout the newsroom, though. She would return occasionally to visit and, with awe, I would watch her walk through the paper.

Her reign and the talented staff she attracted had become the stuff of legend. With a cadre of energetic and fearless reporters, Kay took on the powers that be in Anchorage in the early 1970s, an old-boy's network that included powerful *Anchorage Times* publisher Robert Atwood and Teamster leader Jesse Carr. She took them on and she beat them, winning a Pulitzer Prize to boot. I envied those who knew and had worked for Kay.

Then one day I was introduced to her and we became friends.

It was in the spring of 1987, around the time I was writing a newspaper piece about my father, murdered underworld figure Johnny Rich. The story became the basis of my book, *Johnny's Girl.* Ironically, my dead father was my link to Kay.

Early in my reporting, I researched clippings in the *Daily News* morgue. There I found dozens of stories written about my father and his illegal activities, and eventually, his murder. I was surprised to see stories by my boss, Howard Weaver. I was writing about my father in part to solve a host of personal mysteries. There was much about my father I didn't know, and some of the answers were in the library of the *Daily News*. I felt an odd sense of my life coming full circle. It was as if I was meant to work there.

I wrote a three-part series about my father, titled "Family Secrets," which ran in October of 1987. Soon I began getting calls from film producers and book agents. Kay and Howard helped guide me in making some of the most important career decisions of my life. Before long, I was under contract to write *Johnny's Girl*, and unfortunately, I had to leave the newsroom to do so.

I frequently turned to Kay for help during the research and writing of my book, a process that took nearly four years. When I finished, I gave her an advance copy for her to review. She agreed to write a blurb. In part, this is what she said: "As editor of the *Anchorage Daily News* during the years we reported extensively on the activities and death of Johnny Rich, I find this book a riveting and truthful tale of the seamier underside of Alaska's oil boom years. . . . Kim . . . miraculously manages to tell her very personal story of growing up among strippers, gamblers, prostitutes, and criminals. . . . Somehow this perilous, unorthodox childhood seems not to have tarnished Kim, who has emerged as a strong woman and a gifted writer."

I don't know about gifted, or any of the other complimentary things she said, but I do know that her words came to mean a great deal to me.

I eventually moved to New York City to attend graduate writing school at Columbia University. Now and again, my husband-to-be, Bill Large, and I began getting together with Kay and her husband, Mo Mathews, for dinner or sometimes a leisurely Sunday brunch in Boston, and then later, in Anchorage. No matter how busy Kay was, she always made time to see us. I know we weren't unique. I'm sure she made time for all of her friends. Her loyalty and commitment to others is what made her such a remarkable person.

Somewhere along the line she became a mentor to me. I turned to her for advice and counsel on writing, publishing, and all career matters. She was my role model. I trusted her instincts and valued her opinion. I always felt gratified that she cared about me. It mattered more than I can say. In a way, she became not only a good friend, but also like a valued relative, an aunt, or even like a mother. Mine died when I was nine. As an adult, I missed her more than ever. Kay helped fill the void—an older woman I could look up to and who could guide me.

She also introduced me to a polite world of thank you notes and mannered discourse. I grew up in the rough and tumble atmosphere of Anchorage. My parents weren't around long enough to teach me things like how to send a thank you note after a dinner party. Kay did so by example. Yet she wasn't snobby or pretentious. Quite the contrary. I still remember how delighted I was one morning when Kay called to thank me for having her and Mo to dinner the night before. She then asked about two other friends—a man and woman—who had also been there. Both were single and she thought they'd make a nice couple. "Do you think there's a chance for romance?" she asked.

I gave her my assessment. We then laughed, and for a half hour or more, chatted like a couple of girlfriends.

When Bill and I married, and bought our first home in Anchorage, we would have Kay and Mo over for dinner whenever they were in town. We became tied in other ways, too. Mo's daughter-in-law ended up being represented by my literary agent, who, for some time, wanted Kay to write her own story. He was convinced, as I was, that Kay was a major figure in contemporary journalism.

Later, when Kay was working on her own memoir, she would contact me for advice or to talk about her progress. I felt—and still do—honored that Kay would call. Yet it made sense. Though we came from opposite sides of the track, we shared an unusual connection and bond to each other and to Anchorage's colorful, modern history. Having already written my own memoir, we also frequently talked about that process and what she was going through.

I looked forward to Kay's trips to Anchorage and always made time in my schedule to see her. I couldn't imagine her not being around. And then one day, a *Daily News* reporter friend called me on my cell phone to tell me Kay had died.

I was coming out of the Federal Building downtown, having just attended a swearing-in ceremony for a Mexican woman friend who had finally achieved U.S. citizenship. I reached my car in a parking lot across the street. I leaned against the door, stunned by the news. I hadn't even known Kay was ill. I had last seen her a few months earlier for dinner. Bill and I happily shared the news that we were pregnant. Kay was thrilled for us. I looked forward to sharing my foray into motherhood with her. But sadly, not long after that dinner, I lost that pregnancy. I was uncertain how I was going to tell Kay.

She hadn't told me, or many others, it seems, of her own illness. For me, it just seemed too heartbreaking to disappoint her with my own news. As for Kay, I can't imagine she'd want to burden anyone with her disease. That wouldn't be like her. She was always upbeat, positive, and full of energy. I can't imagine her not well.

I cried a great deal at her passing. I wondered how I would fill the place she occupied in my life. Bill and I worried that we would lose touch with Mo.

Thankfully, that didn't happen. Mo remarried Pam, a wonderful woman I have since become friends with. I like to think Kay would like things this way. She'd especially like the other news in my life. Bill and I went on to to have three children: three beautiful daughters, all of whom I know Kay would have adored.

I still miss her. I miss talking to her on the phone, hearing about her work, her asking about mine. But then I look at her photo on my desk and I feel the presence of my dear, wonderful friend.

〜

Barbara Goldberg was a longtime friend of Kay's from outside the world of journalism. Kay valued Barbara's down-to-earth honesty, sensitivity, and perceptiveness. **Barbara Goldberg**, *a native of Scotland, is the wife of former Anchorage attorney Robert Goldberg. She now lives in rural Virginia.*

I met Kay for the first time in January 1968 in the famous old Chart Room of the Anchorage Westward Hotel. Bob and I had arrived in

Anchorage only a day or two before, he for job interviews, I seven months pregnant with our first baby and not at all sure that this was where I wanted to be. Bob's father was still in public life at that time and very well known. Bob was determined to come to Alaska as a completely private person to begin his career as a lawyer on his own merit. It was too much to hope for. Someone, we never knew who, spilled the beans, and we found ourselves the object of much curiosity. I was beginning to feel like the newest exhibit in a zoo by the time we were invited to a Saturday night dinner with cocktails beforehand.

The Chart Room was a famous Anchorage meeting place. It was dark, richly decorated, warm, a large room that still felt intimate. An enormous amount of important Alaska business was initiated, conducted, and probably concluded in the Chart Room. It is now, unfortunately, long gone, but that evening it was packed.

We were introduced to a whirl of strangers that evening, but although the names have stuck with me—for some reason I'm very good at remembering names—the faces were (and remain) a blur, at least until I was introduced to a very pretty woman in a pale blue dress. We were just beginning to chat when a waitress brought over a tray of brimming wine glasses which we both declined, but for different reasons, she because of faith, although I didn't know that then, I because of pregnancy. It is no exaggeration to say that she is the only person from that evening who left a lasting impression on me. I remember her smile, her open friendliness, and the very distinctive timbre of her voice.

Kay had presence, and a great deal of it came from a natural, almost innocent elegance that had no pretense about it. She was interested in everything, a clever, animated person of resolute character. She was also kind.

Through the many years that followed, I came to know her not as one of her closest friends but certainly as a friend, She was someone I liked, respected, and was always glad to see. Many of the occasions were jubilantly happy, as when the newspaper she loved so much and fought for so vigorously won a Pulitzer Prize. Some were very sad. We had a dinner with her and Larry Fanning the evening before his sudden death. It had been a convivial, predictably stimulating time, Kay and Larry both at their sparkling best. In dealing with the shock of his heart attack, Kay was calm, sad, but sustained by her deep beliefs. It happened that Larry and I had spoken about life after death during the dinner and Kay asked me to tell her, in as much detail as I could, what we had said. Her questions were searching and precise as she dealt with her personal, but not spiritual, crisis.

I think that some lives are connected, and Kay's life was connected with ours in ways that I don't really understand but just accept. Perhaps it is only that we cared deeply about many of the same things and that our years in Alaska were among the most important of our lives. The last time we met was at our home in Virginia about a year before her death. She was writing a book about Alaska and wanted to interview Bob. She and Mo arrived just after lunch, and we spent almost four hours talking and reminiscing. It amazed me because at that time, Bob was recovering from a severe injury and was rarely able to cope with visitors, far less converse with them. That visit was a breath of sanity and hope during a very difficult time.

We learned of Kay's death in the Seattle Airport. Once again that Alaska connection was there. Bob was about to be honored at the Alaska Federation of Natives (AFN) convention in Anchorage. It was the purpose of our visit and his first return after his near fatal injury. He was still not very well. We bought a copy of the morning paper as we sat waiting to board our flight, and read about Kay with a sense of disbelief. Later, at the convention, when Bob received his award, he chose to speak not of his own work, but at some length about Kay, her friendship, her immense contribution to Alaska, her memory. It was terribly important to him that the convention recognize her work and her life. It was his first public address, very moving to me, who was the only listener who knew what a huge effort it was on his part, but also a poignant, powerful reminder of Kay's absolute trust in the sacred healing power of life.

In a world that is increasingly fearful and spiritually meager, I find much of Kay's wisdom sustaining.

We are so glad to have known her, and shall never forget her.

~

In the gallery of colorful Anchorage Daily News *characters, ex-cowboy Slim Randles was perhaps the most vivid of all. Slim's adventures on behalf of the*

Anchorage Daily News *were, according to Kay, textbook examples of Murphy's Law in action—but probably made better reading because of that. His byline in the* Anchorage Daily News *back in the 1970s said "Resident Adventurer," and he was, making frequent long-distance trips and visits to remote Native villages as part of his job as feature writer. After moving to a cabin in the bush in 1971, he wrote a weekly column for the paper until 1978.* **Slim Randles** *now lives in New Mexico, where he writes a syndicated newspaper column, "Home Country," and a monthly column in New Mexico Magazine. He has authored fiction and a nonfiction book.*

I always thought Kay Fanning had the nervous system of an astronaut. No matter what the deadline pressure or hassles of the day, she sailed through it with a smile, and it drove us nuts sometimes. About the only way you could tell things were getting tough was when she would brush a wisp of hair back into place. Our impression was that it would take more than a sauna to make her break a sweat.

I held a strange position at the *Anchorage Daily News* during her tenure, because I wrote a column, went on occasional stupid dangerous trips, and filled in whenever someone needed me. Thankfully, they needed me enough to make me feel part of the *Daily News* family, an honor I cherish these thirty years and many long miles later. We believed, under the direction of Larry Fanning, and later under Kay, that we were somehow knight typists of the Alaska roundtable, off to challenge evil and illiteracy in the Great Land. Foolish, of course, but we fooled ourselves enough to have a great time doing it. I'd ride all night and starve to death for Larry and Kay Fanning. And did, on occasion.

I saw one side of Kay one weekend when she and the kids came up to my cabin, twelve miles from the nearest road, north of Talkeetna. She enjoyed herself bringing in firewood and collecting freshwater mussels from a nearby lake. That same weekend, she arranged for a classical pianist friend to play an impromptu concert for all the old sourdoughs in Talkeetna.

The one incident I recall most vividly, however, was the evening I flattened the mayor of Anchorage with a bulldog. Back when the newsroom was down in Anchorage's Industrial Gulch, the Fannings saw nothing wrong with reporters and editors occasionally bringing a dog or two to work. I had a bunch of sled dogs out at the cabin and brought one in a few times. Others had a pet or two. After a deadline-tension dogfight one evening, pooches were banned from the newsroom.

This ban, however, did not extend to Groover, a hell-for-stout female English bulldog weighing about fifty pounds. Groover belonged to several of our print shop guys, who shared a house.

They also shared deafness, which in the days of extremely noisy hot-lead printing wasn't uncommon. Communicating by sign language, the roar of the presses didn't bother them. One night their house caught fire and Groover went around and woke each of them and got them out of the house in time. She was a hero, and as such, was accorded the honor of being the only official *Daily News* pooch allowed in the building.

On evenings after deadline, or when we were waiting for an accident to happen out on the highway, we would tell Groover to go get her towel and we'd have some fun. She had an old red press rag about the size of a dishtowel, which was hers alone, and had a knot tied in the end of it. This towel was her delight, and ours, too.

She'd disappear back into the pressroom, and emerge packing this rag in her mighty jaws and present it to whomever had requested it, which person was, at that instant at least, her new permanent best buddy.

Groover's buddy would then hold the end opposite the knot, swing the towel, and Groover would leap up and clamp down on the knot with those steam-shovel teeth and hold on, as she was swung in a circle about two feet above the floor.

On this one night, I found myself with nothing to do but wait for news, so I was swinging Groover happily around in a circle just inside the front door of the building. In through the door strode Mayor George Sullivan, the glad-handing portly leader of Anchorage's city fathers. Ol' Groove caught him amidships, right in the flying spinnaker, and Sullivan was slammed back against the door and slid to the floor. Of course, he immediately smiled and shook my hand, waving off my apology. He was definitely a politician and this had taken place in front of a dozen reporters.

But his touchdown was rather loud and it brought Kay out of her office. I knew I was in for it. Kay saw Sullivan and smiled politely. She was holding some papers and had her glasses down on her nose. "What happened?" she asked.

Some snitch in the newsroom said, "Slim hit the mayor in the belly with the bulldog."

Without batting an eye, Kay looked at me and said, "Slim, I do wish you'd be more careful with that bulldog."

I promised I would. And my love and respect for Kay Fanning was such that, although I've bitten a few politicians since with a typewriter, I've never again given them the bulldog treatment.

∼

The story of the Joint Operating Agreement with the Anchorage Times *is one of the more complicated and intriguing episodes in the history of the* Daily News, *and an essential chapter. In many ways, it is a tale of what to avoid in such an arrangement. But without the Joint Operating Agreement, the rest of the story of the* Daily News *might never have taken place.* **Suzan Nightingale** *worked for the* Anchorage Daily News *as a reporter and metro columnist from 1975 to 1980. In 1982 she became a full-time columnist for the paper, and from 1985 to 1990 she was editor of the editorial page. She passed away in 1996. The following excerpt is from an article originally published in* The Buying and Selling of America's Newspapers, *edited by Loren Ghiglione (R. J. Berg & Company, 1984).*

The Fannings' brand of journalism was something new for Anchorage. In a state where it is not unusual to take a gun on a camping trip for protection, the *Daily News* editorialized in favor of gun control. And when the city was just beginning to realize the economic benefit that could come from North Slope petrodollars, the *Daily News* took a long (thirty-two-part) critical look at the effects of the trans-Alaska pipeline—a sharp contrast to Atwood's enthusiastic pro-development policy. Another in-depth series in 1969 looked at the quality (or lack of it) in the bush justice system. It was quite a jolt for readers used to the former owner's more conservative editorial policy, and it was not the sort of copy designed to engender warmth in the hearts of advertisers.

"We got," Kay Fanning said, "a rude awakening very quickly. I think Larry was convinced, and so was I, that all it took was good people to put out a good product and put it over the top. We thought we'd hire very good reporters and have a lot of good news and everybody would want to buy it. The old mousetrap. It was probably naive. We took editorial positions which were not compatible with the general Alaskan viewpoint."

If the advertising dollars did not come their way, several national reporting awards did. Both the bush justice series and the "Oil on Ice" series won national honors, the former an American Bar Association Gavel Award, and the latter an Edward J. Meeman Award, a Thomas L. Stokes Award, and a National Headliners Club Award. But despite Larry Fanning's renown as an innovative editor—he encouraged a new columnist named Ann Landers while executive editor of the *Chicago Sun-Times* before becoming editor of the *Chicago Daily News*, where he encouraged another young columnist, Mike Royko—he was not an experienced businessman.

The new press from Bellevue, Washington, had just been installed when Larry Fanning, trademark bow tie untied and shirtsleeves rolled up, suffered a fatal heart attack at his desk in February 1971. He was fifty-six.

Already dealt the blow of Fanning's death, the paper—subsidized by Kay Fanning's son's (Frederick "Ted" Field) trust—continued to lose money. Although Fanning says she "never considered anything but keeping the paper going," former reporter Elaine Warren remembers "an impending sense of doom" heavy over the newsroom after Larry Fanning's death.

The following fall, Morton Frank, publisher of *Family Weekly* and a mutual friend, approached *Anchorage Times* publisher Atwood, seventy-four, to sound him out on a possible joint operating agreement with the *Daily News*. Gradually, talks commenced. "It was a closely guarded secret," Fanning recalls. "I used to meet Atwood in parking lots so people wouldn't see us together. Our advertising and circulation was tenuous enough without raising fears."

An agreement was finally reached, and Fanning and Atwood approached the Justice Department. Under federal guidelines, the *Daily News* had to qualify as a failing newspaper, "which we had no trouble doing," Fanning recalls dryly. "There was no hearing." When official approval came, the *Anchorage Daily News* and the *Anchorage Times* entered into the first Joint Operating Agreement since passage of the Newspaper Preservation Act legalizing such partnerships.

On August 1, 1974, the Joint Operating Agreement (JOA) was publicly announced, to take effect the following December. Spirits high, the *Daily News* moved from its sardine-can-like offices (appropriately located by the Port of Anchorage) to a breezy office with a view of Mount McKinley across the alley from the *Anchorage Times*. Under the agreement, the *Times* would handle circulation, advertising, and printing; the *Times*-owned *News* office was exclusively a newsroom. In nailing down the bargain, Fanning had signed away the Sunday morning paper to the *Times*. It had been responsible for 40 percent of the *News*' ad revenue. It was the only card Fanning had left to play.

"I had mixed feelings about it," Fanning says, about the JOA. "It meant everyone at the *Daily News* lost their jobs except the editorial department. But there was simply no alternative." Unlike many other joint operating agreements, where an independent, third corporation is formed to administer the agreement, the Anchorage JOA was to be administered by the Anchorage Times Corporation. "I wanted it to work, but in my heart I knew it wasn't a very good JOA," claims Fanning. "It lacked an essential element, which was profit pooling. They weren't really accountable to us in any way. We had no control over our own business affairs, but if there was a loss, we had to pay up."

(Atwood refused to grant an interview for this chapter, questioning the ability of a former *News* reporter to write it objectively, but over the years he has repeatedly taken offense at Fanning's comments about the JOA, saying if he had wanted to sabotage the *News*, he simply would not have entered such an agreement.)

By June 1975, Fanning was "deeply concerned. Circulation was going down and there was no sense of mutuality about the project." The *News* was losing "an increasing amount every year." Atwood meanwhile contended the

News, which lacked the *Times'* emphasis on community news and had scared off some advertisers with its pro-consumer orientation, was "unsaleable."

But, determined to carry on the investigative tradition Larry Fanning had started, Fanning freed three reporters to work full time on an in-depth look at the increasingly powerful Teamsters Local 959. In December 1975, their findings were published in a weeklong series, "Empire," which outlined the scope and power of the Teamsters, and how the organization was using its sizable trust fund. Five months later, in May 1976, "Empire" won the Pulitzer Prize for Public Service. The *Times* printed a congratulatory editorial, and a beaming Atwood presented Fanning with a huge engraved loving cup at a subsequent Chamber of Commerce luncheon. The happiness was short-lived.

Within months, Fanning's son, Ted, decided to stop subsidizing the *Anchorage Daily News*. He had injected $5 million of his inheritance in the *News* since 1968. When, at twenty-five, he decided to pursue other interests, trustees of the Marshall Field IV Trust agreed.

So, in October 1976, five months after receiving journalism's highest honor, the *Daily News* laid off five staffers, leaving it with five reporters to cover Alaska's four time zones. The belt-tightening started in earnest.

In a front-page editorial entitled "A Message to Our Readers," the *News* said it was facing "a severe financial crisis. We need substantial community support to continue."

A "Committee for Two Newspapers," consisting of community supporters, was formed to encourage subscriptions and advertising. Although committee members represented a spectrum of political ideology, many were liberals who expressed concern about balanced coverage of such issues as the pending Alaska Lands Bill and continued oil development if the *Daily News* faded from the scene. Committee members visited local advertisers, talked on local shows, and even set up circulation booths in local shopping centers.

Small circulation gains followed, but the financial picture continued to worsen. In the two years since the JOA took effect, home delivery of the *News* declined, from 11,600 to 7,580 copies, according to *News* figures.

On February 9, 1977, deciding "there literally was no other recourse," the *Anchorage Daily News* filed a $16.5 million lawsuit against the *Anchorage*

Times, claiming breach of contract and unfair competition. The two newspapers' cases might best be encapsulated by their page one headlines announcing the suit. The *News* read, "*Daily News* Sues the *Times*—Breach of Agreement Cited." The *Times* read, "*News* Suit Follows Ultimatum."

The *News*, claiming the *Times* had not lived up to obligations assumed in the joint operating agreement, said the *Times* had violated both the Clayton and the Sherman Antitrust acts by attempting to "monopolize, control, and dominate" Anchorage's newspaper market. The *News* alleged that the *Times* influenced potential subscribers to buy the *Times* and employed joint advertising rates that discriminated against the *News*. Potential *News* advertisers, phoning the number listed for advertising, were greeted with the salutation, "*Anchorage Times*," and *News* ads were offered as an "add-on" buy to the *Times* ads, the suit charged. The *Times* flatly denied it had violated the contract, calling the lawsuit the result of a *Daily News* ultimatum.

Atwood said Fanning had demanded he must either relinquish control of the *Times* Corporation or be replaced by an independent manager who would report to a committee, whose members could not be a majority of *Times* representatives. The other demand, according to Atwood, was for the *Times* to give the *News* a share of *Times*' profits. Atwood maintained that nothing in the JOA guaranteed the financial solvency of the *News*, which he said consistently failed to pay the *Times* monies owed.

Not surprisingly, relations became less cordial. Much of the town literally chose sides. At least one member of the Committee for Two Newspapers resigned. Even social events felt the tension, with hostesses carefully telling Fanning when the Atwoods were expected to arrive so she could make her appearance at another time.

Eight months later, Atwood announced his intention to terminate the JOA, saying the *News* owed the *Times* $300,000. But a U.S. District Court judge ruled the *Times* could not unilaterally block the agreement without submitting the debts to arbitration.

As the battle heated up, the *Times* cited nonpayment of debts and evicted the *News*. On moving day, the *Daily News* staff left one thing standing in the center of the *Times*-owned office—the loving cup Atwood had presented a year earlier.

In June 1978 a panel of arbitrators found that Atwood had "directed his employees to do their best to make the joint operation successful and to fairly allocate the revenues and the expenses of the joint operation." But the panel said Atwood had erred in the allocation of some costs under the joint operating agreement, inappropriately charging some items to the *Daily News*. The *News*, according to the arbitrators, did not owe the *Times* money, but it had violated part of its portion of the agreement by failing to purchase computerized newsroom equipment compatible with the *Times'* equipment. Both sides claimed victory and prepared for the sure-to-be-costly court fight ahead.

The following September, though, after months of negotiations—and the certainty of even costlier litigation in the future—both papers announced an out-of-court settlement. Under the terms of the settlement, the *Times* paid the *News* $750,000 and agreed to print it at no cost until March 31, 1979, when the joint operating agreement would terminate. Again, both sides claimed victory. (Atwood called it "good business practices to pay the *News* $750,000 instead of spending that much or more . . . for lawyers, accountants, and the other expenses of court trials and appeals.")

The divisive fight was finally over. But the *News*, now lacking both young Field's subsidy and the Sunday paper, was even weaker than when it entered the JOA three years earlier.

Meanwhile, Fanning, who had kept the paper afloat by acquiring donations from East Coast liberals concerned about environmental coverage and loans from such diverse sources as Alaska's Bristol Bay Native Corporation and Patricia Hewitt, the Illinois heiress to the John Deere farm equipment fortune, was faced with a familiar dilemma: money. Armed with $750,000, she had six months to purchase a press and production equipment, assemble a composing room, and organize advertising and circulation departments. "It quickly became apparent that three-quarters of a million dollars wasn't going to go very far," she said.

But Fanning was also armed with an unwavering Christian Science faith that repudiates the possibility of failure. ("Christian Science has saved this paper before," she once told a staffer over lunch, "and it will save it again.")

Refusing to entertain the possibility of folding (at least in front of staff members), Fanning ordered the press and composing room equipment. But blending pragmatism with her optimism, Fanning also started looking hard for an investor. A multimillionaire in Kansas City expressed interest, "but he didn't know anything about newspapers, and I wanted to deal with someone who knew what they were getting into. And anybody who knew the kind of losses we were sustaining didn't want to come in here because they didn't have the vision McClatchy did."

Newspaper consultant Jim Smith, who had been the business manager for the *Sacramento Bee*, suggested McClatchy Newspapers. Long a political and journalistic force in California—it owned the *Sacramento Bee*, *Fresno Bee*, and *Modesto Bee* triumvirate—the McClatchy organization was looking to expand its horizons beyond central California.

Exhausted by the lengthy fight behind her and mindful of the uphill battle ahead, Fanning made plans to spend Christmas with her mother in Florida. Prompted by Smith's suggestion, she telephoned McClatchy before she left town. Could she make a detour and stop in and see him on the way to Florida? Although the two had never met, they knew of each other. Fanning knew of McClatchy's sound reputation (and profitable newspapers), and he "was vaguely aware they were having problems" in Anchorage. In an afternoon stopover, Fanning presented her case. McClatchy listened politely.

The next week, chasing off the Alaskan chill with the Florida sun, Fanning continued to mull over the possibilities of saving the *News*. She convinced herself McClatchy was exactly what the *News* needed. She telephoned him again. Could she stop in on the way back to Anchorage? This time McClatchy expressed more detailed interest, but said his organization would want to acquire majority interest, "very much an emotional hurdle" for Fanning at the time, "but compared it to oblivion, to the paper folding. What I would have loved was them putting up all the money and me keeping majority interest," she laughs now. "Who wouldn't?" She tentatively accepted the initial terms.

A week later McClatchy, accompanied by Erwin Potts and a team of advisers, was in Anchorage, visiting the Chamber of Commerce, shaking hands with the mayor, and talking to advertisers. McClatchy was impressed with the potential for the only morning paper in Alaska and with the spunky fight that had been put up to save it. Over lunch, Fanning and McClatchy finalized their agreement and shook hands on it. "I think some people thought we were crazy to do it that way," Fanning recalls, "but there was a basic sense of trust."

On January 17, 1979, less than a month after Fanning's initial phone call, the board of directors of McClatchy Newspapers purchased 80 percent of the *Anchorage Daily News*, Kay Fanning retained 10 percent, and her two daughters, Kathy and Barbara, retained 5 percent each. Neither Fanning nor McClatchy will reveal the purchase price, although $250,000 plus the *News'* debts remains an oft-repeated figure. Says Fanning, "There wasn't much money that changed hands, but they repaid all the loans with interest." Says McClatchy, "Every year that we lose money, it's like a purchase price." Under the purchase agreement, Kay Fanning would remain as publisher for three years, with an option to renew her contract.

"I think CK ought to get either the credit or the blame, because he really was more intrigued by it than anyone else," says Potts. "I was intrigued, but wary." McClatchy claims to have trouble putting his finger on the facet of the *Daily News* that intrigued him, but associates suggest it was a combination of forces.

After years of working his way up the company ladder as a reporter and editorial writer, McClatchy, fifty-five, had just become president and chief executive officer, taking the corporate reins from his strong-willed aunt, Eleanor McClatchy. Unlike Eleanor, whose grandfather had purchased the infant *Bee* in 1857, McClatchy did not want to limit his interests to the state capital and the farm-rich San Joaquin Valley to the south. Then too, the *Anchorage Daily News* was a respected liberal paper in a state where environmental concerns were strong. Without its voice, some important stories likely would not get told. Although McClatchy and Fanning had never met, both had longstanding establishment newspaper family ties and knew of each other. And finally, there was the bottom line. Alaska, with its oil development, growing population, and long-range prospects, was a young market with a lot of potential. The *Sacramento Bee* had just gone from an afternoon to a morning paper, and McClatchy's people believed strongly in the *News'* "morning factor."

"We were carried along by our do-goodism, but there were project costs, and it seemed to be a doable project," says McClatchy.

Back in Anchorage, Fanning triumphantly broke the news to her staff, emphasizing that the McClatchys were not a chain, but a family. The staff had two questions. Were new people going to be brought in? And were they going to call it the *Anchorage Bee*? Yes and no, respectively. What Fanning did not tell the staff that day—and has never told the staff to this day—was that, if McClatchy had not purchased the News, she would have folded it in mid-January.

McClatchy remembers his goal as being "to save the paper with the least expense and the least commitment. But the more we looked at it, that didn't seem to be the road to success. It quickly became apparent to us that the initial pro forma we'd made to keep the thing afloat was unrealistic. We had to add staff, and we had to add more space for the news." It was that key decision—McClatchy's February decision to not just save the *Daily News*, but to resurrect it as a totally new, much-expanded product—that has apparently made all the difference.

With weeks to go before the *News* started publishing with its own (not yet arrived) press, McClatchy decided the "new" *News* would never have fewer than thirty-two pages, and would, from day one, be marketed as a complete newspaper instead of the add-on buy it had become.

An aggressive general manager, thirty-one-year-old Gerry Grilly, was recruited from his post as Sun Coast Division director of a chain of Florida shoppers and weeklies owned by the Tribune Co. Graphics; circulation and advertising experts from McClatchy's Modesto operation were temporarily reassigned to the *News*, formulating a new layout, new logos, and new features.

"They wanted to make sure that everything that was available for money was locked up—wires, syndicated columns, syndicated comics," recalls Haswell, now writing a novel in Vermont. "We bought five wires and sixty-three syndicated columns and forty-four comic strips."

Meanwhile, a new plant had to be found. Deciding that Anchorage's downtown real estate was prohibitively expensive for the amount of space that would be required (a press, plus newsprint storage, in addition to personnel), McClatchy bought an unfinished warehouse in a new industrial park on the southern outskirts of town, where most of Anchorage's new growth is centered. Offices and newsroom space were built into the cavernous building; carpet was laid; and an artificial, lower ceiling was installed.

As the staff continued to put out the "old" paper, still printed and delivered by the *Anchorage Times*, the *Daily News* formed new advertising and circulation staffs to prepare for startup.

The last week of March, a skeleton staff, working off card tables and folding chairs in the rapidly evaporating downtown office, continued to put out the last of the old *Daily News*, while colleagues moved into the new plant across town, familiarized themselves with the new agony of composing on computer terminals, lived on cold, delivered pizza, and started stockpiling features for the new, thicker *Daily News*.

But the cold pizza and the long hours were forgotten when, in the early hours of April 2, the staff watched the first press run. Hours later, as the sun rose over Anchorage, a new *Daily News* was on the streets.

To make sure the community saw its new product, the *News* made Anchorage an offer more than 12,000 families could not refuse: a free one-month subscription. Not only did the new circulation department have to take off from a dead stop, it took off running. "Circulation just exploded, says Grilly. "I remember one day we had 1,000 starts. We had starts in areas where we didn't even have carriers. Sometimes a start took two or three weeks."

With the cold, dark Alaskan winter mornings, delivery had always been one of the *Daily News*' weaknesses. So, in addition to the tried-and-true Disneyland Contest employed by many papers, the *News* implemented a "Carrier Winter Bonus." Under that program, any carrier who stayed on the job for five months with a good record got his choice of a bicycle, a stereo, or a black-and-white television. "The first year, we paid better than 200 carriers," says Grilly. "It assured good delivery. We were so concerned about delivery, collections were really taking a back seat." It was a back seat that was to return to haunt the *Daily News*.

"The main problem we've had since day one is to be able to prove our circulation and readership," says marketing manager Mark Hamilton. "With Audit Bureau of Circulations (ABC) audits, they're auditing history.

It's a disadvantage to a paper on the grow. We've had circulation and not had audits to back it up until recently."

Although "auditing history" has been a concern, woefully inadequate circulation records in those booming months after the transition created their own problems. Thousands of nonpaying subscribers took advantage of the *Daily News'* one-free-month offer. But when it came time to transfer those free customers to paying status, literally thousands of willing readers fell through the cracks. Although at least half the "free" readers opted to continue their subscriptions, the *Daily News* did not have the paperwork to prove it.

So in June 1979, when the *Daily News* was loudly proclaiming 25,000 circulation, ABC auditors were able to confirm only about 12,000—a direct result of poor record keeping in the circulation department. "When the auditors came in, we didn't have a proper audit trail," says Grilly. "We had just taken an adding machine and totaled all the checks up and made a deposit. When he wanted to trace an individual audit to individual subscribers, we couldn't do it."

The ABC auditor gave the *Daily News* a choice: It could either accept his solution—take the three-quarters of that audit year maintained properly by the *Times* under the JOA, divide the total by three, and use it as an average circulation figure—or be suspended. The *Daily News* swallowed hard and accepted the 12,000 circulation figure. "He said he understood how it had happened because he had never seen a newspaper grow so fast," says Grilly, "but he had no choice but to penalize us."

Not surprisingly, *Times* advertising salespeople pointed out the discrepancy, leaving many advertisers uncertain about the *News'* circulation claims. "Certainly if I was a competitor, I'd go out there and plant the seed of controversy," says Grilly matter-of-factly. "But we carefully prepared a dialogue and went out and explained what happened to us. For the most part everyone understood. When our [June 1980] audit came out, it verified our third quarter of 1979. So now we could say, 'See, we were telling you all the time.' "

When the circulation discrepancy came to light, the *News'* inexperienced circulation manager, a twenty-one-year-old who had been in charge of the *News'* street boxes before he was promoted, was promptly replaced. The new circulation manager was Tim Whiting, a graduate of the *Akron Beacon Journal* circulation training program. Whiting set about organizing the department, and the next time ABC auditors asked for paperwork to substantiate *Daily News* claims, they got it. By September 1979 verifiable circulation had doubled to nearly 25,000.

"McClatchy has done the only thing we couldn't do under the joint agreement," *Anchorage Times* general manager William Tobin told the *Washington Post*. "He's changed the paper. And he's had some degree of success because of it."

Indeed, change had come so rapidly to the *Daily News*, it made some people suspicious. Although many businesses leaped at the *News'* aggressively discounted ad rates, Anchorage's number-one advertiser, J. C. Penney, was one business that still hung back. "I had some very difficult times believing some of their numbers," says Penney's Anchorage marketing manager Doug Rush. "Circulation wasn't based on anything. It was based on giveaways. My feeling was, 'Let's wait and see what the other advertisers do. Once they got off the special programs, were they going to stay with the *News*?' As the retailers went off the special rate program and on the regular rate, they were staying with the *News*—and that's how we made our decision. The *News* may be a viable force in the market, and we should be a part of it."

Clay Haswell, the former managing editor, agrees the *News* is more business conscious under McClatchy. "There's no question at all in my mind that the paper took a lot less risks after the purchase than they did beforehand," says Haswell. "Let's face it, it's a lot easier to be a liberal paper when you're broke. If nobody's advertising in you anyway, there's no one to really antagonize. Before the purchase, I don't remember a single conversation when we were concerned about antagonizing an advertiser. Boy, I remember just loads of those conversations after."

Haswell cites a business story that was held for days because its subject was a major supermarket chain—a business still refusing to advertise in the *News*, despite ardent wooing. The story outlined how the chain was buying milk from Seattle, causing serious financial hardship on local dairies in Alaska. "The story ended up waiting for at least two days," says Haswell. "The truth of that is Kay Fanning just sat on that story and would not let it go for two days."

In the end, the story, substantially softened, ran, but Fanning openly acknowledges she took special care with it. "In a sense, that's true. But we have, over the years, had certain areas or people that we seem to gravitate toward making goofs on. We seem to have had an absolute genius for the Carr-Gottstein people [owners of the supermarket chain] for getting it wrong. Although I feel that 90 percent of the time we get it right, whoever we're writing about, Barney Gottstein gave us chapter and verse of mistakes we'd made about him. It was a case of, 'For crying out loud, get it right. Let's make sure it's right and it's fair before we get it out.'"

It was, says Fanning, one example of the McClatchy influence. "One of the few directives I ever received from the McClatchy people was that we be perceived as a fair, accurate paper by the community. Rightly or wrongly, we were perceived as anti-business by the community, so there were, indeed, a number of sessions in which we discussed that, that we didn't want to go out of our way to antagonize the business community."

There is more business coverage these days—mug shots of award-winning salespeople, short briefs on career promotions—in addition to hard-hitting business news (such as possible conflicts of interest in legislative support of Alaska's young farming industry), and complete stock listings.

It is indicative of the expansion of the news product as a whole. More news, more features, more sports, more graphics, more business, even a community news tabloid complete with Cub Scouts and Miss Alaska Teen, not likely candidates to appear in the "old" *News*. There's a weekend opinion section now, a television magazine, and a *Daily News*–produced general interest magazine, *We Alaskans*.

Such expansion is a direct result of space and people provided by McClatchy money. "I think there's a pretty clear understanding that the paper has to serve a variety of interests to make money in order to exist," says then managing editor Howard Weaver.

It is a decidedly different philosophy than the *News* labored under before the McClatchy acquisition. With only five reporters and an extremely limited news hole, the paper opted to leave the baton-twirling photos to the *Times*. "I think we decided we couldn't do everything, so what we chose was politics and enterprise," says Weaver, one of the Pulitzer-winning "Empire" team.

The *News* today does have broader appeal. More international and national news (important to Alaskan readers thousands of miles from the Lower 48), and more local news of all sorts, including breaking news as well as general interest features.

As part of the "new" *Daily News*, McClatchy created a strong weekend package for Saturday. It included comics, the TV log, a weekly magazine, a travel section, and book reviews—all the trimmings of a traditional Sunday paper, twenty-four hours before the *Times'* Sunday edition comes out.

In November 1980, the *Anchorage Times* responded by taking its Saturday afternoon paper to Saturday morning. As a two-month introductory offer, it reportedly offered Saturday morning advertisers 50 percent off pickup ads that ran any other day of the week. (The *News* had been offering a variety of reduced rates. When *We Alaskans* was launched, advertisers were given a two-for-one offer.)

But in February 1981, the *News* kicked off its own Sunday paper.

The decision to go Sunday was mandated by the concept that "advertisers didn't accept you as a complete newspaper until you fill the hole," according to McClatchy Newspapers executive editor Frank McCulloch. But the *News* kept its strength in its Saturday package, designing the Sunday product to be "brisk, easy reading, guaranteed to get you away from your breakfast table in fifteen minutes."

Bob Porterfield, one of the *News* reporters who won the Pulitzer in 1976, told students at Yale in 1981 that, "When the McClatchy chain bought into the *Anchorage Daily News*, they made a big infusion of cash. But it intrigues me that a newspaper that was a boat-rocker and a bush-shaker until 1978 and was very committed to investigative journalism is not doing that now. They say they want to build advertising before rocking the boat."

Porterfield says his remarks, printed in *Editor & Publisher*, were part of a speech on investigative reporting and were taken out of context, a key omission being his stated faith in Kay Fanning's pledge to refocus on investigative reporting once the paper has conquered the challenges of expansion.

"It ended up being harder to do [investigative reporting] after they were in than before, because they were making so many other demands [on local coverage]," says Haswell.

News staffers disagree, reciting numerous examples of investigative work in recent years. "With McClatchy, our newspaper has realized more resources for investigative reporting than ever before, and we've pursued more than a dozen projects in the past several years—investigations that any paper would be proud to claim," insists Abbott. Those investigations range from a series on inhumane pit bull gambling to the state's largest arson-for-hire case.

When the 1981 Alaska Press Club Awards were handed out, the *News* won the top four awards for series (there is no "investigative" category, per se), including a series on the legacy of a state supreme court decision on bush schools; the mixing of politics and business by a prominent state senator (who was not reelected); the power and influence of the state supreme court since statehood; and the long-range development plans for Mount McKinley. When the awards banquet was over, the *Anchorage Daily News* had walked off with thirty-two of the fifty-four awards it qualified for in statewide competition. (The next day the *Times* carried the story, "*Daily News* leads the pack in journalism honors." The *News*' aggressive advertising department promptly reprinted the *Times* story and headline and circulated it to advertisers.)

In December 1981 the *News* ran a twenty-nine-story series, "The Village People," about the ten-year ramifications of the 1971 Alaska Native Claims Settlement act and what it has done to the politically and economically emerging bush population. Seven reporters were freed full time to work on the project, spending weeks at a time in the Alaska bush. It is the largest project, both in scope and time and money, the *Daily News* has ever undertaken. It is the kind of project that could not have been carried out without McClatchy money.

"It cost us tens of thousands of dollars," McCulloch says of "The Village People." "Anywhere else, it would have cost hundreds of thousands. I think dollar for dollar, it's the best paper McClatchy produces, journalistically. Somehow the staff and its management absorbed the diversion of those hours with no additional expense."

Unlike the three California *Bees*, the *Daily News* writes all of its editorials locally, and sometimes, they are 180 degrees from the *Bees'* editorial positions. Probably the most important example was in the papers' positions on the Alaska Lands Bill. The *News* endorsed the state's "moderate" bill; the *Bees* backed the more "restrictive" environmental bill. No pressure was ever brought to bear on the *News* to conform, though Fanning tried to change McClatchy's mind about the *Bees'* editorial.

So what is it about this reincarnation of the *Anchorage Daily News* that appears to be succeeding where others have failed? Well, millions of McClatchy dollars provide one obvious answer. ("The one frightening aspect is that McClatchy has more millions than I do," Atwood told *Newsweek* magazine, "and he's apparently willing to blow them.") But *News* executives say it is more than just dollars.

"It's a rather complete, broad formula," theorizes Grilly. "I think we put out a package that was entirely different from what existed in this community and entirely different from what the *Anchorage Daily News* was. It was complete, packaged for the reader, well-written, extremely well-balanced, objective. And we packaged it so it was easy to read. That's the number one reason. Then you've got to get the paper delivered on time. We promoted it. We told them we were different. Then after we told them, we went out and asked them what they thought. We try to stay in tune with the readers' thoughts and needs, and we tailor our package according to our findings. We have had the guidance of McClatchy. They're certainly not here every day, but when we do strategic planning, they're involved. We've learned from their mistakes, and their expertise. As long as it's smooth sailing, they leave us alone."

~

Howard Weaver, *a native of Anchorage, began writing for the* Anchorage Daily News *during his junior year at East Anchorage High School in 1967. Between 1972 and 1995, he was a reporter, columnist, and editor at the newspaper and worked on both of the* Anchorage Daily News *Pulitzer Prize–winning series, "Empire: The Alaska Teamster Story" (1976) and*

"People in Peril (1989)." He is now managing editor, news, at McClatchy Newspapers in Sacramento, California.

The *Anchorage Times* and *Anchorage Daily News* were rivals from the moment the *Daily News* was launched in 1946. But between 1974 and 1978, the papers were also partners. During those years they operated together in a kind of loveless marriage, united by contract but never in spirit, in an endeavor to preserve the smaller paper by combining business operations in a more efficient operation.

Although *Anchorage Times* publisher Robert Atwood declared in repeated public comments and sworn court testimony that he'd agreed to the arrangement only out of friendship and neighborliness, many of the auditors, accountants, and arbitrators who later examined the deal found it often disadvantaged the smaller paper.

Atwood said he'd always done what he could to make it work. If that was so, Fanning must have wondered why the agreement failed to meet its own stated intentions, or to match similar newspaper deals in other cities that worked profitably and well for both sides. Out of all the similar newspaper agreements that had ever been tried, why was this the only one where things got worse for the smaller paper after it turned operations over to the big guy?

Fanning later bundled those questions into a $16.5 million breach-of-contract lawsuit against the *Times*, and its outcome would reshape the state's media landscape forever. The legal process that sorted out that dispute was messy and full of conflicting testimony. Because it was settled by an out-of-court deal, no final judicial determination was ever made, but the weight of the evidence supports the concerns that drove Fanning to court in the first place.

A contemporary, November 1977, news account of a court hearing on the lawsuit set the stage for the final confrontation: "Robert Bruce Atwood, publisher. Proud and powerful, silver-haired and confident. His newspaper, a dominant voice in the community and state, brings in something like $100,000 net profit each month. Katherine Woodruff Fanning, publisher. Tailored and coiffed, a respected prize-winner. Her newspaper, its life or death hanging on a judge's weekend verdict, has cost her family millions. She has seen single months with losses exceeding $100,000. Locked now in court, it is difficult not to frame their struggle in almost epic proportions. They sat at opposite sides of the old, dark-paneled courtroom, surrounded by the gladiators of the law, who do battle at their will. It was a scene of money, power, and pride. Reputations and occupations hang in the balance. The contest has turned friends into enemies, and the tension generated by that transformation crackled across the room.

"The room was full of three-piece suits and calfskin briefcases. The *Times'* Bill Tobin crossed blue-suited legs to display a shiny black patent leather loafer. Kay Fanning, in a plain brown suit one day and a plain gray one the next, pushed against carefully styled hair absently with one hand."

The testimony Fanning and Atwood traded in federal court, November 21–22, 1977, offered a rare public expression of their long and ultimately bitter fight about doing business together. Atwood would declare that entering the deal was the biggest mistake of his life, but the evidence argues differently. History would show that his fatal miscue was the decision to make Kay Fanning fight her way out of the deal.

At the time of that November court encounter, each side was still couching some remarks in polite tones. "I invited the *News* in to live with us in our household," Atwood testified. "The *News* was accepted into our family as one of our own."

If so, it proved a very dysfunctional family, indeed.

Other JOA's provided incentives for the big paper to behave—for example, by calling for profit-sharing pools or by creating genuinely third-party management that operated in the interest of both. The *Times-News* deal had neither. "As we all know, we did not bargain from a position of strength in 1974," Fanning's lawyers would remind her two years later.

Instead, the *News* gave away not only business control, but also its most valuable asset: the state's only Sunday newspaper. Especially with that plum, the deal was highly advantageous for the *Times,* by appearance much more a hard-headed business decision than an invitation to join the family.

In one respect, the JOA worked splendidly. As intended, it did pre-serve editorial independence for the *Daily News,* so much so that in May 1976 it became the first Alaska newspaper to win the Pulitzer Prize for

Public Service, journalism's highest honor. Yet five months later, the paper went public with news of insolvency: unless things changed, Fanning declared publicly, the paper would fold.

She would testify later that she had invested everything she had in the cause, and that her son, Frederick "Ted" Field, had invested another $5 million before declaring that he could spare no more. Atwood attorney Donald Holbrook would say in court that the case involved "a situation here where a woman seems to be obsessed with a newspaper, small newspaper, very small, one of the smallest in a situation where we have a two-newspaper town, $6 million in family money down the drain."

Holbrook's condescending characterization drew a sharp rebuke from the court, but his arithmetic was about right.

Depositions and in-court testimony painted the battle in sharp terms—a "Humpty-Dumpty relationship" beyond repair, Atwood called it—while the subsequent arbitration explored intricacies of things like "cost-sharing algorithms" and the allocation of circulation expenses.

But no single version of the truth ever emerged. Anchorage newspaper readers could be forgiven if they had trouble following the process in their local dailies. For example, on the morning of June 23, 1978, a *Daily News* story on arbitration findings quoted Kay Fanning saying, "There is no question but that this is a victory for us." Later that day, the afternoon *Times* quoted Atwood saying, "There is no question but that this is a victory for us."

On balance, though, the arbitration findings were a considerable boost for the *News*. As the morning paper reported, the three-person panel of local lawyers found the *Times* "acted contrary to the agreement" and "breached the agreement" on numerous instances.

Just three months later, the lawsuit ended with an out-of-court settlement. In a joint statement, Atwood said his decision was entirely economic; Fanning declared that the deal would enable her to establish a separate plant and continue publishing uninterrupted.

In retrospect, it's apparent that the *Times*' handling of the JOA represents a rare phenomenon in business: a truly fatal error that changed the shape of things forever. Atwood had it within his power to guarantee the *Times*' dominant position in perpetuity, but instead forced Fanning into a different course that finally would leave nothing of the *Times* but a fading memory. [The *Anchorage Times* folded in 1992.]

If the *Times* had operated the JOA in a way that returned even a tiny profit to Fanning, she probably would have accepted that and run the *Daily News* as a permanently subservient, number-two newspaper. "It had not been our desire to try to make huge profits on the *Daily News*," she testified in court. "All we wanted to do was break even and stay in business and be able to run a newspaper."

Letting her do so would have guaranteed that the *Times* would always remain the state's dominant newspaper. As the controlling partner in the deal, it could have ridden the coming economic boom to record earnings, taking not only its own profits but a share of those generated by the *News*. What's more, the money that both sides spent on the ensuing competition—surely more than a $100 million—could have been pocketed as profits, instead.

But instead, the *Times* backed Kay Fanning into a life-or-death corner, and the genteel lady from Chicago partnered up with a quiet California newspaper company and came out swinging. It would be years before the final chapter was written, but the fate of Atwood's *Times* was sealed the day he forced Kay Fanning's hand. Before the story was over, the *Anchorage Daily News* would emerge as the biggest newspaper in Alaska history, a two-time Pulitzer Prize winner with unmatched reach throughout the state.

The venerable old *Times* would be gone forever, reduced to a half-page of commentary carried in the winner's paper.

∾

As Kay herself observed, the year that the Anchorage Daily News *won the Pulitzer Prize in 1976, when she was at the helm of the paper, was both the best of times and the worst of times. It was exciting because winning the prize provided the official confirmation of worth that the* Daily News *had long craved. But winning the prize coincided with the worst of the paper's financial problems. The Pulitzer for the series "Empire: The Alaska Teamsters Story," however, enabled Kay to raise the money needed to keep the paper going until a final resolution could be worked out.* **Howard Weaver** *is a former* Daily News *reporter and editor. In his second contribution to this book, he gives insight into that heady experience of being part of the team that won the News its first Pulitzer.*

When you win a Pulitzer Prize, people naturally start asking, "What's it like?" The answer is complicated, of course, but over the years I've settled on a short response that's both honest and economical: "It's like lightning striking."

On May 5, 1976, that lightning struck in Alaska for the first time. A ringing telephone in the second-floor newsroom of the *Anchorage Daily News* conveyed the unimaginable news that a tiny, struggling daily on the edge of North America had won not just a Pulitzer, but the celebrated Gold Medal prize for Public Service. The paper was among the smallest ever to have captured that award, its staff one of the youngest. The journalistic excellence and community service that had animated Kay and Larry Fanning in buying the paper and sustained her in preserving it had been stunningly confirmed.

Only weeks after that proud moment, the paper announced that it stood at the brink of bankruptcy, soliciting community support for survival. A few months later, about 40 percent of the newsroom staff was laid off for lack of money. The replica gold medals distributed to the writers seemed accompanied by a distinctly bittersweet taste, yet the prize held within it the seeds of one of the country's most improbable newspaper success stories.

Within the next fifteen years, the editor and publisher who launched the prize-winning project would depart to edit an international newspaper; her fledgling little daily would go on to eclipse its longtime rival to become the state's largest paper; and the *Daily News* staff would learn, by winning another Pulitzer in 1989, that lightning really can strike twice.

Perhaps the portent of such success glimmered deep in Kay Fanning's well of perpetual optimism on that sunny day in May, but none of the rest of us had a clue.

Even before we published the project called "Empire: The Alaska Teamsters Story," the odds seemed stacked against us. For starters, our subject had somehow attracted the attention of a competitor that probably didn't even recognize we were playing the same game.

One good thing about being local: when somebody from out of town shows up and starts asking questions, chances are you'll hear.

That was the good news. The bad news was that what we heard was this: the mighty *Los Angeles Times* was in the state—a whole *team* of reporters, people said—and they were covering the same ground our little paper had been laboring over for months.

Just how powerful was the Alaska Teamsters union? How wide open were things in Alaska during those Klondike–Dodge City days of trans-Alaska pipeline construction? And what about these rumors of organized crime?

Bob Porterfield and I had been asking those questions for a couple of months already by the time we heard the *Los Angeles Times* was in the state sniffing around. Dispatched by Fanning and directed by executive editor Stan Abbott, we'd set out to examine pervasive rumors about the wealth, power, and operating technique of Alaska's most potent labor union. By that point we'd uncovered reams of previously unreported information, but very little of it would fit under the kind of "Union Goons Rape State" headline that some twenty-four-year-old reporters, like me, might have imagined.

Alaska Teamsters Local 959 had a reputation that encouraged such speculation, to be sure. You could hear the stories at any legislative watering hole in Juneau, any lawyers' luncheon in Anchorage, or any union bar in Fairbanks. But you sure couldn't find anybody to quote. By that time, Porterfield and I had learned first-hand the truth of the old newsroom cliché: those who talk don't know, and those who know don't talk—not for attribution, anyhow.

But I suppose it's easier to be bold when your newsroom is 2,300 miles away; when the *Los Angeles Times* team got back to California, anything they had learned, they shouted. On November 18, 1975, the paper featured a bold, front-page banner headline: "Crime Wave Strangles Alaska." Their lead: "Widespread lawlessness, a helpless government, and the stranglehold of a single Teamsters Union chief severely threaten a state crucial to the nation's future energy independence."

As we read that, our own investigation was still weeks away from publication. "Crime Wave Strangles Alaska." Damn. Sitting in the newsroom in my hometown, I wondered, how we could have missed a thing like that?

But we labored on in the paper's Fifth Avenue newsroom, a bright, newly constructed space with the ambience of an insurance office, leased from the rival *Anchorage Times* under an agreement by which it managed everything but our journalism. Two of our dozen staffers had been working on the project nearly full-time for months, and a third had recently joined in, which obviously strained remaining editors and reporters even more than usual. It seemed somehow symbolic when the electricity failed one evening near deadline; a gas-powered lantern augmented Anchorage's waning autumn twilight, and we kept writing.

As publication day approached, I tried out one proposed lead after another, stretching for as much drama as I thought the facts could sustain. Still, our series was a good deal less dramatic than the *Los Angeles Times*. The lead article Fanning finally approved ran under a question-mark headline: "Teamsters: How Much Power?" And it began this way: "Teamsters Union Local 959 is fashioning an empire in Alaska, stretching across an ever-widening slice of the life from the infant oil frontier to the heart of the state's major city."

Rather than breathlessly decrying generalized lawlessness and helplessness, the *News* reported on more concrete realities: How much money were the union's trust funds generating, and did the fact that they invested them with the state's richest bank give the union influence? (It did.) Did financial ties between the union's legendary lobbyist and various elected and appointed officials result in favorable decisions? (Sure enough.) Were there a surprising number of convicted felons on the roster at a Teamster-controlled warehouse supplying the trans-Alaska pipeline? (As a matter of fact, there were).

And while the hyperbole and "Outside agitator" status of the *Los Angeles Times* provoked outrage in the state, it was the steadier hometown reporting of Fanning's *Daily News* that brought results in the state. The final product was likewise an honest reflection of her steady judgment. Less flash. More substance. Ultimately, more impact.

Publishing the series required journalistic courage I couldn't appreciate at the time. On a personal level, I entertained predictable "boy reporter" fantasies when my old VW bug caught fire in my driveway one evening, and the *Los Angeles Times* later reported that its reporters worked in pairs in Alaska "partly as a matter of safety." But the genuine bravery involved was that of the beleaguered small-town publisher playing You Bet Your Newspaper on a daily basis. Though we didn't know it at the time, Kay was by this point only months away from the wrenching public acknowledgment that her paper was broke and close to folding. Still, instead of kissing up to the power structure in Anchorage, she gave us a flashlight and sent us looking in the shadows.

Anyway you sliced it, the odds were against us, a mismatch of Goliath-like proportions. The paper was at the time a distant number-two contender even in Anchorage, claiming a circulation of a little more than 13,000 to the 45,000 of the Anchorage Times. (Perhaps it was coincidence that the bigger paper, though staunchly Republican on most matters, delivered little substantive criticism of the union that was making big deposits to the bank owned by the publisher's brother-in-law.) Stacked up against the *Los Angeles Times*, the *Daily News'* odds looked incalculably longer; with a Sunday circulation then numbering 1.2 million and a staff of hundreds, the L. A. paper had already won eight Pulitzers, and its voice boomed where ours strained to whisper.

When contrasted with Local 959, the *Daily News* looked even more fragile. The union's dues-paying membership was more than double the paper's circulation and, as reporter Jim Babb detailed, its trust funds were growing by a million dollars a week. Where politicians jokingly asked the progressive *Daily News* editorial page to do them a favor and not endorse them, the Teamsters enjoyed a widespread reputation as kingmakers, and backed it up with campaign cash and the delivery of disciplined voters.

So what?

Kay Fanning never told me why she decided to investigate the Teamsters. I didn't ask, for the simple reason that I never wondered. I knew she did it because it was the right thing for the newspaper to do, a self-evident act of public service that many good newspapers elsewhere would have undertaken without a second thought.

The fact that tackling the project represented a rare act of independence and integrity says as much about the Anchorage power structure of the day as it does about Kay Fanning. The city's ruling elite was as cohesive as it was insulated in those days: the state's biggest union boss sat on the board of the state's biggest bank, whose owner was the brother-in-law of the publisher of the state's biggest newspaper. A lot of what went on in Anchorage then could be decided with no more advance work than booking a reservation for four at the Chart Room.

Kay Fanning stood outside that circle, partly by her choice and partly by theirs. What it cost her in dinner invitations and newspaper ads it repaid in independence, and she was splendidly unafraid to spend that capital.

Pulitzer jurors noticed. So did the American Society of Newspaper Editors, which later elected her its first woman president, and heard her say, "Profit is not the purpose of the press, as protected by [the] First Amendment; the free, unfettered flow of ideas is. In the end, ideas are more powerful than dollars."

A personal footnote: I was living in Juneau in 1976, the one-man legislative bureau of the *Daily News*. I was in Anchorage the day the Pulitzer was announced only because Kay, who knew about the victory beforehand, brought me to town under the pretense of planning for another Teamster installment. It was characteristically thoughtful, one of many classy, generous acts I'll always remember.

~

If winning the Pulitzer Prize was the zenith of Kay Fanning's experience at the Anchorage Daily News, *the sale of the* Daily News *by Kay to McClatchy Newspapers in 1978 forms the denouement to the story.* **Erwin Potts** *was vice president and chief operating officer for McClatchy Newspapers in 1978. In 1989 Potts became president and chief executive officer of McClatchy.*

I am browsing through a copy of *Editor & Publisher* magazine when my eye lands on a short story about a newspaper in Anchorage, Alaska. The town's second newspaper, the *Anchorage Daily News*, has sued its larger rival, the *Anchorage Times*, over management of the joint operating agency publishing both newspapers. The *News* has no staff save twelve news people and publisher Kay Fanning, under whom it once won a Pulitzer Prize for public service. It has no plant and no presses. Its circulation is in the 15,000 to 20,000 range. The *Times'* is about 50,000. Publisher Fanning vows to continue publishing.

"Good luck with that," I mutter to myself, wondering how anyone could be foolish enough to try such a thing. That was before I met Kay Fanning.

A month or so later I am sitting in my office at the *Sacramento Bee* when a call comes in from C. K. McClatchy a few doors down the hall. "I'm bringing somebody down to meet you," he said.

CK and Kay burst into my office like a small tornado. CK is as animated as I've seen him, talking about this wonderful opportunity in Anchorage to save a failing newspaper.

I make some feeble comments about how hopeless the task seems. But Kay, a woman with unmatched charm and presence, already has done a number on CK And as many others found over the years, resistance to Kay Fanning's persuasive charm and perseverance was itself a hopeless task.

So begins one of the longest and most spirited newspaper wars our industry has seen. It ends thirteen years later [in 1992] with the closing of the *Anchorage Times* and the emergence of the *Daily News* as the city's only surviving daily newspaper.

That day in Sacramento, CK and I agree to visit Anchorage with Kay and some of our senior executives to take a look at the situation.

Kay meets us at the airport bubbling with enthusiasm, a walking travelogue for Alaska. Her driving immediately terrifies CK and me. She sails over the icy roads from the airport with one hand on the steering wheel, another waving to various sights, and her head turned to talk to us in the back seat.

Somehow we make it to the Captain Cook Hotel. For the next few days we meet local people, talk to her editors to size up the competitive situation. But the most important meeting is with Bob Atwood, publisher of the *Anchorage Times*. Despite the bitterness of the joint operating agency breakup and lawsuit, Atwood is warm and welcoming in his well-appointed office.

"So you've come to save the *Anchorage Daily News*," he says as we are introduced.

"We're not sure," CK says. "We're just taking a look."

In that meeting we learn one important thing: Bob Atwood is convinced a morning newspaper (the *Times* was afternoon, the *News* morning) can never succeed in Anchorage.

"You can't get the paper delivered early in the morning here," he says. "It's too cold and dark."

CK and I glance at each other. We have just converted our three *Bee* newspapers from afternoon to morning in the face of opposition from what seemed to be everybody in the towns, including many on our own staffs. We have been given every imaginable reason why afternoon newspapers, which ours were at the time, could not succeed on the morning cycle. Yet our circulation growth has accelerated with each conversion.

Then we learn something else: circulation at the *Daily News* is not what Kay thinks it is. It is even worse. Atwood, who ran the JOA, tells us his circulation people couldn't give away the *News*. Since he controls the circulation, only his people know the true numbers. It is one of the issues in the lawsuit.

We leave feeling a little better. Atwood is complacent. Maybe this will work after all.

But there are major problems. We are in the midst of a newsprint shortage nationwide, and the *Times* has the newsprint allotment for Anchorage. We will have to supply newsprint from our California newspapers, which already have to buy at off-market premiums.

The *News* has no press, no office, no plant. In a final settlement of the lawsuit, Kay gets $750,000, two-thirds of which she gives to the Goss Company as down payment on a press. She says it's all she has. There is no more money to operate the *Daily News*, build a plant and hire a staff, unless McClatchy steps in.

CK and I confer. The only newspaper we have close in size to the *Anchorage Times* is the *Modesto Bee*. It is operating smoothly under a savvy new general manager, Robert Byerly. Perhaps Byerly and some of his people could visit Anchorage and help Kay get started.

So Byerly and his crew go to Anchorage [to offer assistance]. We are in for the duration.

We make a deal with Kay to buy the *News*, with Kay as publisher and a minority partner. We make a five-year plan. It calls for losses of as much as $500,000 in the first year, and then gradually declining losses, until by the end of the plan we are profitable. We lose $500,000 the first month.

We have gotten a plant and press in about three months and are up and running with temporary supervisors from Modesto. Kay likes Bob Byerly so much she wants him to come there permanently, but Bob can't wait to come in out of the cold.

We're looking for his replacement, a street fighter to complement the elegant Kay, a Smith College grad, who had danced with the Kennedys at the White House and is more at home in editorial offices than counting houses. All she knows about advertising is she doesn't have any in her newspaper.

We find her a partner in Gerald Grilly, a brash young upstart, graduate of Cleveland State, who's been publishing a group of shoppers in Florida owned by the *Chicago Tribune*. He knows how to run uphill. Kay and Gerry are an unlikely pairing, but they are a winning combination in newspaper combat: a sophisticated lady of unquestioned integrity and a scrappy brawler whose competitive juices seem to ooze from every pore even in ordinary conversation.

In the beginning, the losses mount and the gains come slowly. We bring in Steve Starr, a marketing guru with teaching credentials from Harvard Business School and the American Newspaper Publishers Association. Steve goes to Anchorage with CK, me, and other McClatchy executives from time to time to hold strategy sessions.

Kay and Gerry, editor Stan Abbott, and later his successor, Howard Weaver, have built a staff of young aggressive people who don't know they're trying to do something that can't be done. At each strategy session we lay out a list of objectives aimed at taking turf from the *Times*. We also estimate the costs. They are far beyond what we are anticipating putting into the *News*. We return to Sacramento shaking our heads, wondering what we've gotten into.

Always there is Kay, eternally optimistic, never doubting the outcome for a moment. I guess it is contagious.

A few months later we go back to Anchorage and find our young tigers chipping away at the *Times*, meeting their goals. They have some more goals. They need some more money. Already our losses each year are in the range of $5 to $6 million.

Maybe the most important strategy session comes when we are already several years into the battle. We ask Kay and Gerry and Howard to place the *Times* and the *News* on a table, side by side. Examine every feature, every section, every comic, all the news content, all the advertising content. Then tell us how we are going to match or beat what the *Times* has. And how much it is going to cost.

In my mind, that is the critical turning point. It takes several years for the Anchorage reading public to realize the *News'* superiority, but gradually it happens.

The battle is essentially over by the time Kay Fanning comes to Sacramento to tell CK and me she has taken a job as editor of the *Christian Science Monitor.*

~

Kay was always very interested in the ethics of journalism and quite frequently was asked for her views on how to handle ethical conundrums. Here, **Barry Flynn** *describes her approach to a journalistic dilemma he faced. Barry Flynn was a reporter on the* Anchorage Daily News. *He now lives and works in Florida.*

I've not met many people who more deserve to be remembered than Kay Fanning. She and Larry made a deep impression on me in the few years I was in Anchorage

But the incident that made the deepest impression on me was when I was still very young and working at the *Daily News*. It wasn't long after Larry died and Kay was publisher. Someone from a bank in Anchorage complained that I had quoted a bank officer in a story about a robbery at one of its offices. They said no officer had spoken to me. Kay very gently took me into her office and before anything else carefully explained that as a professional journalist, I did not have to disclose my sources. But, she said, she had promised the banker she would ask. "Now, can you tell me your source?"

I referred her to the story, in which we quoted an "official," not an officer. And by the way, following her lead, I said I couldn't give up my source. That was fine, she said, and it was the end of it. Except that for the rest of my career I carried a couple of good lessons on quoting anonymous sources and the risks of having to disclose them. And of course, a very warm memory of Kay Fanning.

~

Although Kay loved the idea of the Alaska wilderness, she was not totally at home in the wilds of Alaska. But she was well aware that the Great Outdoors, particularly hunting and fishing, was a fundamental component of the Alaska identity. Therefore, she wanted to experience the rigors of the outdoor life, especially if she could be guided by the savvy of an expert. Tom Gibboney's account of his fishing expedition with Kay gives a snapshot of her outside the newsroom. **Tom Gibboney** *was managing editor of the* Anchorage Daily News *in the mid-1970s, before leaving in 1977 to edit the* Homer News. *He now lives in Northern California, where he is publisher of two community newspapers.*

As managing editor of the Daily News in the mid-1970s, I spent virtually all my time in the newsroom. Today the job would be called city editor, but titles were nice and they didn't cost anything. One of the few perks tossed my way every year was a trip to the annual Associated Press meeting, which was usually held at a resort location that appealed to the state's editors, publishers, and the national AP brass who attended. In the Lower 48 states, that venue would undoubtedly include a golf course, but this was Alaska, and the closest equivalent macho activity often was fishing.

This presented a challenge for Kay, who was hardly a dedicated fisherperson, but was intensely interested in being accepted into the chummy world of the state's newspaper owners. As the only woman publisher, she worked hard to get to know all those who attended these mostly macho affairs at various places around the state.

One year in the mid-1970s, as I recall, it was my privilege to join Kay and executive editor Stan Abbott at the annual AP meeting at the Bell Island fishing resort, outside Ketchikan.

This picturesque place—accessible only by boat or floatplane—was well known as one of the premier fishing resorts in Southeast Alaska. And, much to Kay's delight, it was a year that *Anchorage Times* publisher Bob Atwood was attending, with his daughter Elaine. It was my observation that Kay relished every opportunity to meet on equal terms with the Atwoods, whose *Anchorage Times* led our fledgling *Daily News* by two to one or more in advertising lineage and circulation.

At the time, all of us, especially Kay, worked tirelessly to find a way to beat the *Times* to every story we could and to gain enough circulation and advertising to at least break even. That was a considerable challenge for the new-to-Alaska Fannings, who encountered Mr. Atwood's friends and business associates virtually everywhere they went.

Kay's agenda at Bell Island was to have some fun, but she was always working to promote the *Daily News* and even though trolling around a choppy cove wasn't her favorite way of relaxing, she honed her competitive instincts and decided I was to be her fishing partner.

She might have made that decision after seeing photos of me holding up a hefty silver salmon I caught on a party boat out of Seward a year or so earlier. Little did she know how I almost lost this monster and that I didn't even bait the hook. But when she challenged me to join her on this expedition, which was basically the only activity offered other than sipping cocktails around the pool, I cautiously accepted. Even the Atwoods, who were not known to be particularly athletic, had decided to try their luck.

"Gib, are you ready to go?"

I gulped and said "sure," and soon we were off to get outfitted at the dock.

Our tiny boat, about a twelve-foot skiff, was waiting, and although neither of us had experience, we were going to drive this small outboard motor boat around the cove. Kay decided she would fish and I would drive, so we headed out, and after a few zigzags, I managed to get in line with the other boats that were simply trolling around the perimeter of the cove. We got some lines baited up and sat back to see if anyone was having any luck.

Kay kept a close watch on all the other boats, and she noted that there were some fish being taken, but not many, even though they were jumping all around us.

Then all of sudden that changed. Bam! Kay's rod jumped, and after a few shrieks, we both calmed down enough to figure out how to drive the boat, play the salmon, and not fall overboard. Our technique eventually worked, and Kay landed a nice king, about 20 pounds or so.

I was next, and when mine hit we clumsily changed positions. And with Kay at the helm, we managed to bring another king aboard. Needless to say, we had plenty of bragging rights at dinner that night, an especially sweet experience for Kay in that all-male environment.

During cocktail hour we learned that the Atwoods came up empty that afternoon, giving Kay and the *Daily News* at least one opportunity to outfish the *Anchorage Times*.

~

If there was one word that describes Kay's approach to life and the impetus for her Alaskan experience, it would be "adventure." Kay liked to travel and enjoy news experiences, both in Alaska and beyond. The move to Alaska represented a great opportunkity to take advantage of the opportunities for adventure that her era in Alaska presented. Neal Menschel's account of a trip he took with Kay and Gail Miller, who became his wife, along the Alaska pipeline route, is the story of one such adventure. **Neal Menschel** *was a photographer for the* Anchorage Daily News *(1970–1974), and later for the* Christian Science Monitor *(1983–1995). He lives in North Groton, Massachusetts.*

Kay Fanning could carry on an intelligent discourse with anyone on any level about any subject with complete equanimity. Philosophers, pipefitters, fishermen, governors, welders, museum curators, paperboys, millionaires and the homeless were all pretty much the same to her—people. She treated them all equally, with dignity, and with as much fairness as possible.

Being the editor of a daily newspaper brings with it remarkable power. Kay understood the responsibility that came with that power. She was not without strong opinions, yet she was dedicated to upholding the integrity of fair-mindedness that came from being a member of the press.

Kay presided over an inherited staff of radical, gonzo journalists, spilling over with talent and hyperenthusiasm. Being a devout Christian Scientist, her views on drinking, smoking, and morality in general were very different from those of much of her staff. Yet she never criticized anyone for these differences, but rather appreciated the talent, individuality, and commitment to truth and justice each one exhibited. Kay respected them as individuals, and in the process she earned their respect.

I came to the *Anchorage Daily News* when it was located in a large pink metal warehouse on Post Road in an industrial section of Anchorage. The modest news offices and the presses and typesetting facilities were located in the same building, separated by thin paneled walls.

The pressroom could have passed for a museum on the history of printing. Linotype machines clattered continuously. The press itself was a dinosaur, even for its time. It looked like the warehouse it was, filled with a collection of complex, heavy machinery. Everything was covered with a fine layer of ink and dust. The newsroom was aesthetically grim: cement floors, cheap paneling, old used metal desks, high ceilings, fluorescents, and no windows. Kay's office was not that much better, but it had more paneling, lower ceilings, wooden furniture, and carpeting.

On holidays and occasional birthdays, someone would bring in a cake. Late in the afternoon there would be a break in the commotion of frantic deadlines, the cake would come out, someone would cut it, often with a pica pole (a special ruler for measuring type), punch and/or soft drinks would be served. Kay usually left the paper early evening.

At this point someone would produce a key to Kay's office (it was nicer), and then out would come the spirits. Not that the staff didn't sincerely celebrate while Kay was there, but at this point the activities would reach another level of mirth.

Still, the paper came out, on time, filled with meaningful and well-crafted stories. That was Kay's priority. Although nobody to my knowledge ever said anything to her, I have no doubt that she was aware of what was going on. I don't believe she ever said a word. Not that she didn't care, nor would she have approved, but she was patient, tolerant, and nurturing, and we were, after all, consistently cranking out good stuff.

Not too long after the completion of the Alaska pipeline, Kay decided to take a closer look at the project. The pipeline and accompanying haul road and their construction were very controversial. She wanted to experience them first-hand by driving the entire length of 800 miles. Arrangements were made and permissions granted with the Alyeska Pipeline Company, and we were on our way. Traveling with us were Gail Miller, a young reporter for the *Anchorage Daily News*, a friend of Kay's, and my future wife; Jeanne Abbott, an extraordinarily good and versatile writer/reporter for the *News*, and a close and respected colleague of Kay's; and myself, a photographer for the *News*.

We weren't just checking it out, we were collecting information that would later turn into several stories.

Throughout the length of the haul road, Kay was a study in curiosity and professionalism. It was fun but serious work to her. She was a seamless combination of tourist and private investigator. We stopped frequently, marveled at the scenery and wildlife, and talked to and/or interviewed everybody that we met. At one point we talked our way into getting a ride down the inside of part of the forty-eight inch pipeline on a tiny vehicle called a pig. It was used by pipe welders to weld and inspect the inside of the pipe. You had to sort of sit in the lap of a worker as he piloted the rig through this tiny, endless tunnel. It was fascinating, but dark and claustrophobic. Kay reveled in it. It was one of the highlights of the trip for her. I took a picture of her as she reemerged. She never enjoyed having her picture taken, especially in a formal situation, but this photo, of her sitting in the end of a chunk of the trans-Alaska pipeline dressed in blue jeans and mountain parka, became one of her favorites. I think she identified with it. She saw herself as an adventurer, and approached life in that manner.

Looking back on the trip, which took a little more then a week, what now seems odd to me was the choice of vehicle. For driving the miles of winding dirt road between Fairbanks and Prudhoe Bay (the arctic slope site where the pipeline began), a four-wheel-drive vehicle would have made sense. Instead we drove Kay's old Buick station wagon. A bit of a boat, really. By present standards it might have been referred to as a car. It was large, beige, with fake wood sides.

Kay insisted on driving the entire distance. For me it was a white-knuckle experience. The dusty gravel road often consisted of short straightaways linked by very sharp, sometimes banked curves. Kay's style was to punch the throttle coming out of the bends, gravel flying as the wagon fairly floated over bumps and potholes in a semicontrolled fashion. Approaching each corner, she would hit the brakes at the last possible minute, slowly round the curve, then repeat the process all over again. Each turn loomed ahead, and bit-by-bit the floorboards under my feet became a little more extruded. She never lost control.

We made it safely to Prudhoe Bay and back. This fact cannot be jokingly referred to as miraculous. Rather, it readily serves as a metaphor for this amazing woman's life.

Several years after I left the *Daily News*, by happenstance, both Kay and I found ourselves at the same time at the *Christian Science Monitor*. She was the executive editor, and I was a senior photographer. The *Monitor* used to sponsor Washington, D.C., media breakfasts with various important policymakers and politicians. A variety of press was always invited. About once a year, the president of the United States would be the featured guest. Since the *Monitor* sponsored the event, we would be well represented. It was Ronald Reagan's turn, and I was there to record the event. Thirty or so of the D.C. press corps were milling around one of the rooms of the White House waiting to be ushered into the room where breakfast would be served and President Reagan was waiting. People were discussing the news and making small talk. Kay and I were standing next to each other, waiting, when she turned to me and said, "Who would have thought, from that little paper in Alaska, to here."

∼

Gail Menschel knew Kay as a friend and mentor. Here she gives a glimpse of Kay Fanning as homemaker. **Gail Miller Menschel** *was a reporter for the*

Anchorage Daily News *from 1974 to 1975, and later worked for the Christian Science Publishing Society. She now lives in North Groton, Massachusetts.*

Kay Fanning was a model of graciousness and firmness. She was always there, a rock of right living, always animated about life, amused by its many characters, interested in world affairs, a steady church worker. She was the epitome of good posture, literally and figuratively. I always see her with her shoulders back and this big, honest smile on her face, looking you straight in the eyes. She was never judgmental, never had a sense of superiority, but seemed to delight in the various extremes of personalities that she worked with in the newsroom or in public life.

I was blessed to have been taken under her wing as a twenty-two-year-old seeking her first reporter job. She knew me only through my letter of introduction, as an earnest seeker of newspaper experience, a fellow Christian Scientist, trying to spread her wings from a copykid/clerk job at the *Christian Science Monitor.* But she unquestioningly took me in for a summer job, and even opened up her home to me as a place to live.

I still remember how I felt when this bright-faced woman strode up to me at the Anchorage airport and, with a firm handshake that almost made my hand hurt, looked me lovingly in the eyes and said, "I'm Kay." I felt instantly accepted, and suddenly totally worthy. All apprehension dropped away.

Life in the Fanning household with her two daughters—Kathy, home from college for the summer, and Barb, in high school—had a happy, systematic regularity. Cooking was not Kay's big interest, but somehow she always put a well-rounded, if not fancy, meal on the table at a scheduled time. They always ended with a salad, and then with ice cream.

Kay usually turned in fairly early. She always left for work in the morning right on time. She always wore tailored suits. She never missed Wednesday evening church. What I noticed about her lifestyle was that there wasn't any room in it for self-indulgence. The home was just a well-ticking clock, an organized launch pad for a busy life. At the same time, it was a welcoming haven with a rotating door for friends, extended family, and people she wanted to take in, enjoy, and boost along in their journey.

Kay was very kind and caring, but not emotional or sentimental.

Because of this, you knew she would always be there for you in need, ready to respond in a compassionate but level-headed way. Her office at the *Anchorage Daily News* was a homey place where anyone, including this novice reporter, could confide in her and feel comfortable. I remember once coming in and breaking down about some difficulty I was having covering stories. She smiled at me so affectionately, listened understandingly, yet was not drawn in; and somehow with a few right words about my ability, she restored my confidence and desire to move forward.

When the summer job was coming to an end, even though I was still proving myself as a reporter, she told me that a position covering the education beat had opened up and asked me if I would stay on full-time, and I did.

Having confidence in yourself, trusting your intuitions despite the doubts of others, was something that Kay herself consistently lived. I remember she once told me that a credo she followed was, Never apologize, never explain. Rather than arrogance, this approach was a humble confidence in prayer-driven direction and in what life was quietly unfolding to her.

Within the year, I had fallen in love with a long-bearded, motorcycle-riding, teacher-turned-photographer for the *Anchorage Daily News*, Neal Menschel, one of the unique individualities that Kay had brought aboard in her intuitive shepherding of talent. When Neal and I became engaged, she threw a party for us in her home. As she led a toast to our upcoming wedding, she cast a warm look around the room at this very assorted group and shared from her heart: This moment is very special to me, because the coming together of Neal and Gail brings together my two great loves—journalism and Christian Science.

In keeping with her loyal nature, Kay remained a staunch friend to us through the decades following as Neal and I raised a family. With all of us now living on the East Coast, I could count on a phone call from her at least once a year. "Gail, well, it's time we got together! So what are the children doing these days?" When I would get too busy to call, even though her life was ten times busier, she never forgot to care about us in this very tangible way.

Acknowledgments

All authors and editors owe thanks to many people. Unfortunately, Kay did not leave a list of the many people she wished to thank for making this book possible. Of course she would want to express appreciation to her husband, Mo Mathews, for his extraordinary support, both emotional and technical; Mo sorted out many computer glitches for Kay and provided invaluable advice. She would want to thank Lory Hahn, who provided editorial assistance, and many others mentioned in the book.

There were several people who were of great support to me, and I know they also encouraged Kay. Kay's dear friends, Jack Roderick, the former mayor of Anchorage, and his wife, Martha, would be at the head of that list. Jack also extended valuable encouragement to me along the way: he wrote a contribution for the book and also offered expertise about Alaska.

I would like to thank Kent Sturgis of Epicenter Press, for his enthusiasm for the project and his willingness to publish the book. I would also like to thank Ellen Wheat, who provided much wisdom in copyediting this book. The manuscript was unfinished and unpolished when Kay passed away, but we have nevertheless tried to publish it largely as written in order to preserve the authenticity of Kay's vision. I would also like to thank longtime Alaska journalist Dermot Cole of the *Fairbanks Daily News-Miner* for reading the manuscript for factual accuracy. And thanks to Sharon Palmisano, the librarian of the *Anchorage Daily News*, who answered my many inquiries about factual details with efficiency and goodwill.

I would like to thank my husband, Andrew Stephen, for his encouragement and counsel. And *Kay Fanning's Alaska Story* could probably not have been completed without the help of Howard Weaver, now vice president of news at McClatchy Newspapers. Howard took time from a business trip to Washington, D.C., to visit me and discuss the project in its early stages; he tirelessly answered my e-mail queries about Alaska, and he wrote two contributions for the book.

In addition, I wish to thank all the contributors who are published here. They have helped make Kay's book a reality.

Index

About the Authors

Kay Fanning had a life-long love of journalism. Her first reporting experience was on the *Anchorage Daily News* and she became editor and publisher in 1971. Under her leadership the *Anchorage Daily News* won the 1976 Pulitzer Prize for Public Service. In 1983 she became the first woman editor of the *Christian Science Monitor,* and later became the first woman president of the American Society of Newspaper Editors. She was working on the manuscript that forms the first half of this book when she passed away in 2000.

Katherine Field Stephen has worked as a journalist in Anchorage, London (England), and Washington, D.C., where she now lives with her husband and two children. She is the daughter of Kay Fanning.

Recommendations for readers wanting to learn
more about Alaska and its culture and history through biographies and
memoirs of notable Alaskans:

ACCIDENTAL ADVENTURER
Memoir of the First Woman
    to Climb Mt. McKinley
Barbara Washburn, paperback, $16.95

ARCTIC BUSH PILOT
From Navy Combat to
    Flying Alaska's Northern Wilderness
James "Andy" Anderson & Jim Rearden,
    paperback, $17.95

ART & ESKIMO POWER
The Life and Times of
    Alaskan Howard Rock
Lael Morgan, paperback, $16.95

FLYING COLD
The Adventures of Russ Merrill,
    Pioneer Alaska Aviator
Robert Merrill MacLean & Sean Rossiter,
    paperback, $19.95

GEORGE CARMACK
Man of Mystery Who Set Off
    the Klondike Gold Rush
James Albert Johnson, paperback, $14.95

NORTH TO WOLF COUNTRY
My Life among the Creatures of Alaska
James W. Brooks, paperback, $16.95

ON THE EDGE OF NOWHERE
Jim Huntington & Lawrence Elliott,
    paperback, $14.95

ONE SECOND TO GLORY
The Alaska Adventures of Iditarod
    Champion Dick Mackey
Lew Freedman, paperback, $16.95

RAISING OURSELVES
A Gwitch'in Coming of Age Story
    from the Yukon River
Velma Wallis, paperback, $14.95

SELLING ALASKA
A Pioneer Advertising Man's
    White Collar Adventures
Kay Guthrie, paperback, $14.95

SISTERS
Coming of Age & Living Dangerously
    in the Wild Copper River Valley
Samme Gallaher & Aileen Gallaher,
    paperback, $14.95

TALES OF ALASKA'S BUSH RAT
    GOVERNOR
The Extraordinary Autobiography
    of Jay Hammond,
Wilderness Guide and Reluctant Politician
Jay Hammond, paperback, $17.95

These titles can be found at or special-ordered from your local bookstore.
A wide assortment of Alaska books also can be ordered directly from the publisher's
website, www.EpicenterPress.com, or by calling 1-800-950-6663.

Epicenter Press   Alaska Book Adventures™   www.EpicenterPress.com